# KEEPING *the* SPARK ALIVE

*Preventing burnout in love and marriage*

# KEEPING *the* SPARK ALIVE

*Preventing
burnout in love
and marriage*

## DR. AYALA M. PINES

ST. MARTIN'S PRESS • NEW YORK

Note: Couples' names and some details about their lives have been changed,
to protect their privacy.

*Design by Maria Carella*

Library of Congress Cataloging-in-Publication Data

Pines, Ayala M.
  Keeping the spark alive: preventing burnout in love and marriage
  by Ayala Pines.
    p. cm.
  ISBN 0-312-01453-8
  1. Marriage.  2. Love.  3. Communication in marriage.
4. Interpersonal relations.  I. Title.
HQ734.P685  1988
646.7'8—dc19                                                    87-26109
                                                                      CIP

First Edition

10 9 8 7 6 5 4 3 2 1

*To Patrick, with love*

# CONTENTS

# Acknowledgments

One of the greatest pleasures in finishing a book is the writing of acknowledgments. It marks the end of a process, and enables a sentimental reflection on the whole of it. My work on the subject of marriage burnout, and this book, have benefited from the contribution of many people. I discussed every idea expressed in this book with Patrick Taffe, and gained greatly from his breadth of knowledge, intelligence, and love. My dearest friend, Lynn Freed, painstakingly read and reread successive drafts of the manuscript, very much improving it with her amazing talent for words. Lillian B. Rubin, who is a wonderful friend and role model, provided valuable criticism of many of the ideas expressed in the book.

Other close friends, in and out of psychology, have read earlier drafts of the book and made thoughtful comments that helped improve it both in content and in style. I would like to express my appreciation to Charles Alexander, Ruth Dieches, Dennis T. Jaffe, Barbara Jonas, Lynne Kaufman, Ellen Kirschman, Anya Lane, Rafi Malach, Uzi Nitsan, Cynthia D. Scott, and Lil Tulp. Linda Hermelin was helpful in editing the manuscript, and Linda Lee helped with the final style the book was to take.

While conducting the research on which the book is based I benefited from valuable discussions with several brilliant colleagues, whom I am also lucky to have as close friends; these include Elliot Aronson, Christina Maslach, Arie Kruglanski, Baruch Nevo, Ofra Nevo, Dalia Etzion, and Yuda Handelsman.

My agent, Judith Weber, of Sobel Weber Associates, deserves special thanks for her guidance and support. Nancy Coffey and Robin Desser of St. Martin's Press were an absolute delight to work with.

Most important, however, I would like to express my deep affection and gratitude to all the individuals and couples who took part in my research, who opened their hearts, minds, and lives to me, and on whose experience this book is based.

# TRAPPED IN AN IRON WOMB

**I:** How do you feel about your marriage?

JANE: I don't know how I actually feel about it as an entity. I see it in two ways. On the one hand, I see it like a piece of very fine china, a cup that is cracked and flawed, and held together simply because there is no movement in the air around it. So that if some slight wind came along, or somebody stepped too heavily on the floor, the whole thing would just fall apart. It is that fragile.

On the other hand, from the inside it seems like a . . . like a cell. It seems like a sealed-off cell, without windows. Inescapable. So solid and ironclad that nothing is ever going to allow me to break out of it. And these seem to be mutually exclusive ways of looking at it.

I often find myself, when walking on the street or sitting in a restaurant, looking at couples, or looking at married women, and feeling single. It's the oddest feeling, and I felt this way for years. I go on vacations and I look at married couples and I think, "It would be nice to be married." And I remind myself that I am actually married, too [laughs]. But I don't feel that I have a right to feel safe in this marriage. I've never felt safe . . .

**I:** How do you feel about your husband?

JANE: I find him physically aggravating. The sight of him . . . certain attitudes . . . irritate me. When he is overweight, the way he is at the moment, the sight of him revolts me. And certain physical gestures. When he scratches his genitals through his pants pockets, I find that extremely irritating. And it irritates me when he uses obscenities, which he does all the time, without any shame. He just uses scatological words ha ha . . . He irritates me almost without my being able to control myself when we are in company. He is either in an inappropriately enthusiastic mood, which I find extremely mortifying, or else he is belligerent, which I find equally irritating. In the private sphere, he tries to get between me and the children. This sort of thing is wildly infuriating to me because it is undercutting . . . I mean just about every aspect of marriage you can think of irritates me. The way he drives irritates me . . . various other things . . . On the other hand, there are some compensations I am aware of. He is an extremely good lawyer, but he never throws his weight around the way some of his corporate colleagues do. He is a marvelous

*(continued)*

lawyer. He cares about his clients. His main area of real competence is his work.

I: How is sex?

JANE: Once I get over the hump of my complete lack of interest at the thought of it, and even the onset of it, it's sort of efficient. He knows what to do in order to make me . . . to satisfy me. If anything it is an indication that sex is more than simply physical satisfaction . . . that one can go to bed with a man one finds very often physically revolting, and irritating in many other ways, and yet have an orgasm . . . then get up afterward and continue the fight . . . [laughs]. I have had lovers who were far less satisfying, and yet in so many many ways so much more satisfying.

I: What will you need to get out of the marriage?

JANE: Money. First of all money. I have absolutely no illusions about what it is like to be out there on one's own. I would also need the assurance that I would have the resources within myself to do without the caring, on a very mundane level, that one has in a long-standing relationship with a man who is not quite crazy. Who is not uncaring. I mean I would like to know that I could be happy living on my own without someone to call up if I am stranded somewhere with a broken-down car, or if I have a child with a broken leg . . . That sort of thing, I think can become extraordinarily burdensome. I don't know from the inside of this ironclad womb—which is the way I see this marriage, or mismarriage—whether I am actually even capable of that kind of independence. I just don't know. I have a feeling that when things start breaking down, inevitably, one stops worrying so much about these things in the abstract. Because you have far more concrete things to object to . . . I don't know.

# CHAPTER 1

# Burnout: The Failure of Romantic Love

. . . how we loved in the fashion of all lovers, and strove not to let the little things of existence destroy us. How they did, and how we forgot. Just like everyone else.

Han Suyin,
*A Many Splendoured Thing*

## BURNOUT AND LOVE

Love at first sight? Made for each other? Happily ever after? For most of us growing up in this culture, the expectations from love and marriage are extremely high. These expectations set the stage for burnout. Even if we should know better, when we fall in love we hope that our love will last forever. This hope has the power to blot out awareness of faults, reduce common sense, and obliterate foresight. Burnout occurs when, maintaining these idealistic notions about love, we run into the stark reality of everyday living. It is the psychological price many of us pay for having expected too much from our relationships, for having poured in more than we have gotten back. Or believing we have done so.

Burnout is caused by too great a discrepancy between expectations and reality. At times the expectations are so high that no one person can fulfill them. At times the reality is so stark that it defeats the expectations even if they are not too high. In both cases, when the discrepancy between expectations and reality is chronic, the result can be devastating. With the accumulation of disappointments, with the stress of daily living, comes a gradual erosion of spirit and eventually—burnout.*

Dona is a tall, striking woman and a successful architect in her

---

*Those among the readers who are interested in finding out their own level of marriage burnout are invited to take the Burnout Test at the end of the book.

3

early forties. After fourteen stormy years of marriage, Dona is totally burned out:

> I feel hollow in this relationship. There is nothing between us: no bond, no communication, no sharing, no contact, no feelings, nothing. We have no plans together, no interests together. The tensions are making me tired and sad. There is no hope for us. There is nothing that he does that enhances my life in any way—emotionally, intellectually, physically. I don't feel like a couple; I feel emotionally deprived. I feel resentful and irritated. I have to close myself off emotionally to stop feeling that way. I can't give myself sexually or emotionally any more. I don't believe life has anything to give me. I would do anything to be free of him. I have no feelings for him except irritation and sometimes pity. When I come home and he is there I get all uptight. I wouldn't stay with him for anything.

Dona's husband, Andrew, a dark, good-looking man in his mid-forties, is an accountant. Describing life in a burned-out marriage he says:

> It's awful. I mean, it really is almost like living with a stranger. That's how bad it gets. Once there's no more interaction it's just—poof, it's gone. I'm really living a life of quiet desperation. . . .

You will hear about Andrew and Dona throughout this book. Their feelings of emotional depletion, hopelessness about the future, and helplessness to make things better are the hallmark symptoms of burnout—a painful denouement for many marriages.

While marital problems are as old as the institution of marriage, burnout is a modern phenomenon. It has to do with the importance of romantic love to our generation, and the fact that love has become a highly valued foundation for marriage.

There are few adults who do not know what "romantic love" is and who have not experienced it at one time or another in their lives. Modern scholars define romantic love as "a state of intense absorption in another," and of "intense physiological arousal." At times it involves only "longing for complete fulfillment." For the lucky it involves "ecstasy in finally attaining the partner's love."[1]

While romantic love has reigned supreme among other forms

of love since time immemorial, only in recent years has it been promoted as the basis for the selection of a mate. This promotion has been so influential that some people have to convince themselves that they are in love before they can decide to get married. There is a universally shared desire to believe that the emotional bond of love is enough to sustain a marriage. The voice of reason, which would be welcomed in any other human endeavor, is scorned when applied to the selection of a mate. Consider, for example, a scathing description of today's young urban professionls that appeared in a 1987 *New York Times* article. Bruce Weber, the author of the article, dubbed the Yuppies "unromantics." The reason: They are considering each other's assets (country house, income potential, schooling, family) before they are deciding that they could make suitable marriage partners. The Yuppie approach to marriage fits the description of a famous sociologist, Erving Goffman:

> A proposal of marriage in our society tends to be a way in which a man sums up his social attributes and suggests to a woman that hers are not so much better as to preclude a merger or partnership.[2]

To a romantic society such as ours, this kind of a steely-eyed materialism about marriage seems cold and cynical, if not entirely inaccurate. We do not want to perceive marriage as a business proposition. (It is well we don't. Very few businesspeople get into a lifelong partnership with the scant information most couples have about each other.) Love and marriage, for us, are affairs of the heart. Love defies reason. It is meant to defy reason.

Romantic love appeals to us on several scores. It carries individualism to its furthest extreme. The beloved is unique and irreplaceable. Love is seen as an act of freedom and self-determination. In a country that considers the pursuit of happiness a birthright, it is a pure expression of this pursuit, pulling with it intimacy, family, and hopes for the future. It is even an expression of equality—differences in background do not matter to lovers. Since they are glorified in each other's eyes, there is a sort of star-crossed equality between them.

All this is part of the ideology of romantic love. In fact, the ideology does not always match the way we actually pick our mates.

In reality, class, ethnic, and racial differences do matter, but there is a belief on the part of the lovers (a belief shared and reinforced by society at large) that love will conquer these differences. We want to believe that love can conquer all—and why not? What else do we have left that *can* conquer all?

While we are exposed to information about the failure of love, and some of us have a firsthand experience with its fragility as the foundation of marriage, we still want to continue believing in it— probably because we see no immediate or better alternative. The high divorce rates do not deter; most divorced people cannot wait to remarry and give love another chance. In fact, more people are marrying and cohabiting today than ever before in history.[3] As Ingrid Bengis concluded: "The only permanent thing about love is the persistence with which we seek it."[4]

Love. Why are so many people today so obsessed with love? The answer, I will argue, has to do with our need to give meaning to our lives. Romantic love is an interpersonal experience in which we make a connection with something larger than ourselves. For those of us who are not religious and who do not have another ideology we strongly believe in, love can be the only such enlarging experience. As Otto Rank so aptly noted, people are looking for romantic love to serve the same function that religion served for their predecessors—giving life a sense of meaning and purpose.[5]

The ultimate existential concerns about the meaning of life are universal. They include the terror of the inevitability of death, the dread of groundlessness in the vast universe surrounding us, the total isolation with which we enter life and with which we depart from it, and the meaninglessness of our own self-created mortal life.[6]

The tremendous sense of isolation and fright attached to these concerns results from the unique duality of human beings, which Kierkegaard described almost 150 years ago as a "synthesis of the soulish and the bodily,"[7] the paradox of the spiritual self that can transcend life, imprisoned in a mortal body that cannot escape death.

From time immemorial people have attempted to deal with their feelings of existential isolation and fright by giving meaning to their lives. Religion has been one such attempt. This can account in part for the importance of romantic love to Americans. Ever since its founding by people escaping religious persecution, America has struggled to remain secular. Since a secular society does not provide answers to the existential dilemma, "love," as Erich Fromm put it, becomes "the answer to the problem of human existence."[8]

In his Pulitzer prize–winning *The Denial of Death,* Ernest Becker expanded on this idea. He talks about the universal need to feel "heroic," to know that one's life matters in the larger "cosmic" scheme of things, to merge with something higher than oneself and totally self-absorbing. For modern man, who rejects the religious solution to his existential dilemma, one of the first alternatives has been "the romantic solution." His "urge to cosmic heroism" is fixed on the lover, who becomes the divine ideal within which life can be fulfilled, the one person in whom all spiritual needs become focused.[9]

Even people who believe in love may have difficulty admitting that through it they are seeking a solution to the existential dilemma. First, this admission would imply that they need other human beings to make their lives matter—something that can be construed as weakness of character. Second, to admit that a love relationship is the vehicle for finding ultimate meaning in life is to agree that the quest for love is essentially a religious quest. This would probably be unacceptable to most people, since the substitution of romantic love for God would seem positively sacrilegious to the faithful, and unseemly to the rest. Nevertheless, that is what it seems to be for people who do not feel a personal connection with God, and who seek a connection with something larger than themselves in love. Love promises to fill the void in their lives, to eliminate loneliness, to justify their existence, to provide security and everlasting happiness.

The promises of love do not remain abstract or philosophical. Consciously or unconsciously there is a concrete image of a person and a relationship attached to them. When we meet a person who fits that romantic image and we fall in love, we expect the relationship to make all the promises of love come true. When the person or the relationship fails us, we burn out.

Our society would have us believe, then, that love can answer the question of human existence, provide the best basis for marriage, and in addition celebrate democracy, equality, freedom of choice, and the pursuit of happiness.

These expectations are transmitted via popular songs, books, television, and the movies, which preach continually that love is the most important thing in life. Love, we are told, is what "makes the world go 'round." We are also told that true love lasts forever. A couple can live "happily ever after," "till death do us part."

These romantic ideals have a powerful effect on all stages of a love relationship. Since we all internalize them to a certain degree, they determine our expectations and affect the understanding we bring to bear on our relationships (even if we use more practical considerations in choosing a mate). People who internalize such romantic ideals uncritically enter relationships with expectations not only that they will find someone they can comfortably live with, but that that person will solve all their problems, never have any problems of his or her own (except cute ones, little foibles like not being able to find the sugar), and give meaning to their existence. When these expectations are not fulfilled (and how could they be?) such romantics are not only disappointed in their mates and in themselves; they feel the whole world has lost its meaning.

In fact, some romantic expectations *can* be achieved in marriage. If it is your expectation that you receive flowers on your birthday, that once a week the two of you sit down for a quiet glass of wine and listen to soft music, chances are good that you will get it. Other expectations take more effort—such as deep conversations, intimacy, and emotional support.

Some romantic expectations are totally unrealistic. If you want life to be lived on a dream cloud of love, constant intimacy, and magic—if you expect the simple act of marriage to give focus and meaning to your life, to answer all of life's basic questions—you are going to be disappointed. Hanging on to those notions guarantees burnout. Yet, as we have seen, we are actually socialized to believe in them.

Culturally shared expectations are often expressed in truisms and proverbs. In one of my studies of marriage burnout I asked a hundred married couples to what extent they believed in ten romantic truisms such as "love at first sight" and "a match made in heaven." (All ten are presented in the box on page 9). I discovered that belief in such romantic truisms was related to marriage burnout.[10] This can mean that the level of marriage burnout (which reflects people's actual experiences) influences their belief in certain truisms. Alternatively, it can mean that the belief in those truisms (by creating unrealistic expectations) influences their level of burnout.

Because we have, as a society, continually raised our expectations as to what constitutes a romantic success story, today we are more ready than ever to abandon a relationship if it fails to fulfill our expectations. The high divorce rates (highest in the world) are one testimony to that.[11] There is no longer a requirement to prove moral incertitude or "breach of contract" to end a marriage. Incompatibility—the failure of love to meet our expectations—is grounds enough for giving up.

---

To what extent do you believe the following ten truisms, using the scale:

| 1 | 2 | 3 | 4 | 5 | 6 | 7 |
|---|---|---|---|---|---|---|
| do not believe at all | | | believe to certain extent | | | believe totally |

____ "love at first sight"
____ "a match made in heaven"
____ "they lived happily ever after"
____ "marriage kills love"
____ "true love is possible only after the infatuation is over"
____ "love, like a good wine, can get better with time"
____ "one should not marry for love"
____ "people who wait for the perfect mate remain single"
____ "using a matchmaker is the best way to ensure a happy marriage"
____ "true love is forever"

It might be interesting for both you and your mate to examine your belief in the ten truisms, guess each other's answers, and then compare notes. Are your answers related to the way each one of you feels about your marriage?

---

The expectations we have today of love are not built into human nature. As Nathaniel Branden noted in his book *The Psychology of Romantic Love,* throughout most of human history this notion about love and marriage was unknown:

> Young people growing up in twentieth-century North America take for granted certain assumptions . . . that are by no means shared by every other culture. These include that the two people who will share their lives will choose each other, freely and voluntarily, and that no one, neither family nor friends, church or state, can or should make that choice for them; that they will choose on the basis of love, rather than on the basis of social, family, or financial considerations; that it very much matters which human being they choose and, in this connection, that the differences between one human being and another are immensely important; that they can hope and expect to derive happiness from the relationship with the person of their choice and that the pursuit of such happiness is entirely normal, indeed is a human birthright; and that the person they choose to share their life with and the person they hope and expect to find sexual fulfillment with are one and the same. Throughout most of human history, all of these views would have been regarded as extraordinary, even incredible.[12]

Denis de Rougemont made in 1940 similar observations about the unparalleled importance given to love in modern times:

> No other civilization, in the 7,000 years that one civilization has been succeeding another, has bestowed on love known as *romance* anything like the same amount of daily publicity. . . . No other civilization has embarked with anything like the same ingenious assurance upon the perilous enterprise of making marriage coincide with love thus understood, and of making the first depend on the second.[13]

Ironically, the celebration of love, the "daily publicity" bestowed on it, and the importance and glory attributed to it have produced an apparent scarcity rather than an abundance. Never before in history have so many people been disppointed in the promise of love.

Could the importance attributed to love make people more susceptible to burnout, or is this insidious process of love's erosion indigenous to all long-term intimate relationships? My interest in these questions was the original impetus for studying marriage burnout.

As part of this research, I analyzed answers to several thousand questionnaires (all of them included the Burnout Test, which you can find on p. 257 and fill out to discover your own level of burnout). I interviewed, in depth, hundreds of individuals and couples—both those who were burned out, and those who were happily married. I interviewed couples in traditional marriages, companionship marriages, and unconventional marriages. I interviewed straight and homosexual couples. (Quotations from these interviews are interspersed throughout the book.) I conducted burnout workshops, both in this country and abroad. In addition, I worked with burned-out individuals and couples as a therapist in my private practice. My goal was to understand what burnout is, what causes it, what are its consequences, and how best to cope with it.

Understanding the process of burnout is the first step in learning to cope with it. Again and again I saw in my work with couples that merely identifying burnout for what it is can have a healing effect. A typical reaction was: "So it's burnout! And I thought it was *us*! I thought there was something seriously wrong with us!" Guilt and blame were replaced by renewed energy for coping simply by labeling the problem "burnout."

## WHAT IS MARRIAGE BURNOUT?

Burnout, as we have seen, is a painful state that afflicts people who expect romantic love to give meaning to their lives. It occurs when they finally realize that, in spite of all their efforts, their relationship does not and will not do that. Marriages can be disappointing and unhappy without being burned out. When a mate is sloppy or inconsiderate, one can decide to live and let live, but when one looks for marriage to give meaning to one's life, these annoyances can be unbearable. Burnout is caused by a combination of unrealistic expectations and the vicissitudes of life. It is not caused, like some other marital problems, by the pathology of one mate (chronic depression, alcoholism), both mates, or the relationship.

The burnout of love is a gradual process. Its onset is rarely sudden. Instead, there is a slow fading of love accompanied by a general malaise. In its extreme form burnout marks the breaking point of a relationship, a point beyond which endurance, communication, and all attempts at positive coping are severely hampered. The burned-out person is saying: "This is it! I've had it with this marriage. I can't take this anymore."

Burnout is formally defined (and subjectively experienced) as a state of physical, emotional, and mental exhaustion. It is caused by long-term involvement in situations that are emotionally demanding—situations in which there is a discrepancy between expectations and reality. Let me describe each component of this lengthy definition in some detail.

## PHYSICAL EXHAUSTION

The physical exhaustion of burnout, unlike that caused by running a marathon or spending the day raking leaves, appears as chronic fatigue that is unrelieved by sleep. On Monday morning, after you spent a whole weekend in bed, you wake up exhausted. You drag your feet all day, longing to get back to bed. When night finally arrives, you are so annoyed with your mate that you cannot fall asleep. Your stomach churns as you remember every unkind word, every inconsiderate act: the way he drove back from your mother's house, the way she fought with the neighbors. Each "crime" becomes magnified in the twilight of sleep. You are furious. You toss and turn. When you finally manage to fall asleep, you are haunted by nightmares: a volcano erupting; your home struck by an earthquake, caving in, sliding down the hill, surrounded by flood waters. When you awake in the middle of the night, you grab a bottle of sleeping pills or a decanter of brandy on the bedside table. With that you calm down enough to fall asleep again, but the next morning you awake fatigued, groggy, and with a splitting headache.

You feel more and more weary. Sometimes it seems as though your whole body hurts. Occasionally you have headaches, stomachaches, or back pains. You become susceptible to illness, catching every cold or flu around. Because you are upset, you don't feel like eating ("I feel like I have a gigantic lump in my throat, so that I can't swallow a thing"). Or else you may be eating compulsively

("At least I can get this enjoyment out of life"). When you look at the scale, you hate yourself.

## EMOTIONAL EXHAUSTION

You feel emotionally drained. You can remember once having passionate feelings: seeing for the first time the depth of her blue eyes, the glow of his sunburned skin. You remember thinking to yourself "I'm going to marry him," before you were even introduced. Now nothing seems to be left of those wonderful feelings, except memories. You feel disillusioned and resentful. You don't feel like explaining anything, and you don't want to work through problems even if they seem very simple. You are convinced that there is no hope for the two of you, and not much hope that you will ever find someone else you could love. "Besides," you reason, "what's the point anyway, if this is the way it always ends?"

You grow increasingly unhappy. Every day seems worse than the last. Your whole life feels empty and meaningless. Nothing seems to matter anymore. You are frequently depressed, the joy of life drained out of you. You need what little energy you have left in you for the children and your work. Worst of all, you see no light at the end of the tunnel. As bad as things are, and as much as you would like them to be different, you feel helpless to bring about change. You have given up by now on the idea that you can change your spouse, and you don't have the energy or the inclination to try to change yourself. Since you see no hope for change, you feel trapped. In extreme cases, the feelings of futility and despair can lead to an emotional breakdown or to serious thoughts of suicide.[14]

## MENTAL EXHAUSTION

The mental exhaustion of burnout manifests itself most clearly in a lowered self-concept and in a negative attitude toward everything about your relationship, particularly your mate. When you were first in love you not only adored your mate, you also felt pretty good about yourself. This, in turn, made you feel good about the rest of your life. It was as if the magic of love touched everything. Through the rose-colored glasses of love both of you looked handsome, charming, and sexy. Life made sense and was all promise.

Now things are not so wonderful. You are painfully aware of all those little (or not so little) things that your mate does that make you want to jump out of your skin ("the way he coughs," "the way she drives," "the sight of his back," "her unshaved legs"). The feelings of disenchantment are not limited to your mate. You have a terrible feeling of personal failure: You have failed in the most important relationship in your life (even if it was not your fault and even if you did everything in your power to prevent it from happening). Looking at yourself in the mirror, you see a person you don't like. You are no longer the warm, loving person you once thought you were. You discover some nasty streaks in yourself you never even knew existed. Sometimes you catch yourself being bitchy and you think, "Who *said* that?" The sense of disappointment, like the love before it, transcends the two of you. It affects the way you feel about other people, your life, the future, and your ability to love.

## EMOTIONALLY DEMANDING SITUATIONS

Living with another person is always demanding. It requires adaptation and compromise, because, by definition, people are different, see things differently, and have different values, needs, and expectations. One has to accommodate the other person in one's emotional, as well as in one's physical, space. That accommodation is never easy. It is especially hard to accomplish when one cares deeply about the other person. In the same way, a long visit by a close family member can be much more stressful than a long visit by a casual acquaintance.

What makes the accommodation to a mate so hard is the realization that it is supposed to go on forever. Forever can seem like a very long time, especially if you think that when he throws his socks on the floor it's a direct comment on your role as a "picker upper." Especially if the sight of her picking her nose makes you wonder "How did I end up with a woman like this?"

It is one thing to have a wild affair on a cruise ship, knowing it will be over when the ship reaches shore. In such a situation it is relatively easy to overlook or disregard annoying habits, even irreconcilable differences. It is far more difficult to look the other way when your husband throws a wet towel on the bed for the hundredth time, when your wife chews with her mouth open (again!), and you know this is going to go on for a lifetime.

The stresses inherent in living with another person "until death do us part" are amplified by the very romantic notions that often lead to marriage. If you believe that love conquers all—even socks on the floor, even chewing with the mouth open—and find yourself blowing up at your mate over socks and tonsils, you either have to conclude that love doesn't conquer all, or else that love does conquer all but you don't love your mate enough.

If you were in an arranged marriage, and your mate did not turn out to be a paragon of virtue, you would no doubt be disappointed. If you married for love, you would probably burn out. Burnout is most likely to afflict people who enter marriage "starry-eyed" and infatuated, who idealize their mates and think they found their prince/princess charming. The stresses that they find most unbearable are the daily drudgery, the hassles and pressures so typical of everyday life, and yet so terribly unromantic. Burnout is far less likely to afflict those who enter marriage feeling practical, even cynical, and who view marriage as a business arrangement. In short, *in order to burn out one must, by definition, have once been "on fire."*

Although being "on fire" involves the danger of burnout, being too cautious about an emotional commitment carries its own dangers. A marriage that starts as a practical arrangement is not necessarily going to succeed—quite the contrary. Planning for the end of a marriage seems to be one of the surest ways to end it. A well-known palimony lawyer says that most marriage contracts with a divorce clause end up being challenged in court.

## THE ONSET AND AFTERLIFE OF BURNOUT

Romantic love is not an eternal flame. If fuel is not added to it, sooner or later the flame is going to burn out. The onset of burnout is rarely sudden. It is insidious. It seldom results from a single traumatic event or even several traumas. It starts, rather, with a growing awareness that things are not quite as good as they used to be, that your mate is not quite as exciting and wonderful as he or she used to be. Both are reminders of the reality so effortlessly denied during infatuation. You have the irritating conviction that your mate is not giving to the relationship as much as you are, that your most important needs are not being met. If nothing is done at this stage to stop the process, things are bound to go from bad to worse. The infrequent periods of discontent become more and more frequent. The mild feelings of dissatisfaction grow into a smoldering fury. After reaching a crisis point, when you have given up, you have a choice between staying in a dead, listless marriage, and leaving.

When we hear about a friend or neighbor divorcing, and try to figure out what led to the schism, it is tempting to seize on concrete traumatic and dramatic events: The husband is seeing other women. He gets drunk, beats his wife, and screams at the children. The wife has a lover. She insults her husband's integrity and manhood in front of his friends and colleagues. These things occasionally *do* cause the breakup of a marriage, and occasionally they are the *signs* of burnout, but these are not the *causes* of burnout.

I hope I have managed to convince the reader by now that burnout results from disappointment in marriage as an answer to the existential dilemma. It is aided by an accumulation of stresses that erode love, a gradual increase in boredom, and a buildup of petty annoyances and minor dissatisfactions. It is virtually impossible to single out one precipitating factor. Like the camel's back, love is squashed by the accumulated weight of trivial "straws": "He would squeeze the toothpaste in the middle." "She would take things from my desk and not bring them back. I could never find anything I was looking for." "He never put the toilet seat down." "She spent money on stupid things." Let's listen to Dona describe the "causes" of her burnout:

> There were many incidents. Every morning something would happen. Like he'd bang a door shut that I hadn't shut. I often leave doors open. Instead of thinking, "What a charming thing—here's a person with an open personality" (I think it's very symbolic)—he'd bang this thing shut. And it immediately caused tension. And my immediate thought was: another nail in your coffin. That's what I kept thinking every time he'd do something. Every day cemented my feelings. . . .
>
> I like to have things around and Andrew doesn't like things. He was always clearing things out and putting them in the garage. He wouldn't even ask me. Like he'd take all of our daughter's mugs—leave her only one—and put the rest in the garage. It would just infuriate me. . . . His smoking cigars drove me up the wall, too. Every night he would smoke one cigar. I just hated the smell and the sort of staleness of it. . . .

Andrew used to clear things out and smoke cigars even when he and Dona first met, but Dona was in love with him then. Now there is no love to balance out the negatives, so the irritation accumulates.

Is it possible to turn a burned-out marriage into an exciting one? Yes. Mind you, I'm not saying that all burned-out marriages can or should be saved, that the spark should be rekindled no matter how small and at what cost. I have worked with couples whose love for each other is long gone, couples who nevertheless cling to the marriage. On the other hand, I have worked with couples who gave up too quickly. As soon as the first blush of love is gone, as soon as they experience a few problems, they split up—even though there is a great deal of affection and caring between them.

The decision as to whether a relationship is dead or still has a spark that can be rekindled should be made only by the two people involved, and made jointly. It is not enough for one person in a couple to want to rekindle the spark. Where the spark is gone completely, often it is better to part amicably, and give each other a chance to start a new life with another person. Burnout can be a positive turning point not only when conquered, but also when it is the signal to leave a dead marriage behind and move on to a new, perhaps quite different relationship.

In saying that burnout can be a positive experience, I of course do not mean to imply that it is a prerequisite to having a good relationship. There are couples who figure out on their own, from the start, what is necessary in order to keep the spark alive, and they do it. Unfortunately, they are the rare exception.

Studying the things that happily married couples do that are different from what burned-out couples do (who have been married the same length of time, have the same number of children, etc.) was one of the most rewarding parts of my research on marriage burnout. It is also one of the most important aspects of this book.

For a relationship to be truly alive, the romantic flame does not have to be raging in full force all the time. Sometimes the flame dies down. Other times it flickers. In a healthy relationship neither event is perceived as a major disaster or a serious threat. Actually, a typical characteristic of relationships that are exciting and alive is that the mates are not too worried about the spark. "One of the best things about my relationship with Colleen is that we can let things die down once in a while," says George, who has been living with Colleen eleven years. "We even go as far as talk about breaking up, and about me moving out of the house. Then, when we calm ourselves with the knowledge that we could live alone if we wanted to, we enjoy starting the romance again." Romantic ideals notwithstanding, it is hard to imagine actually living in a relationship in which the romantic flame is at its maximum intensity all the time. It would be too exhausting and too all-consuming. Notwithstanding fairy tales, in real life boy and girl do not "live happily ever after"—unless they take steps to protect the romantic spark. If these steps are not taken, burnout is inevitable.

## BURNOUT AS A HALLMARK OF OUR TIMES

While burnout has been a "dictionary word" for many years, its introduction as a psychological concept is fairly recent. It was only in the mid-seventies that the first articles dealing with job burnout appeared in scientific journals. Soon there were books, magazine articles, and television talk shows dedicated to the problem. Scholars started doing research on burnout and developing theories to predict when it would happen and why. It is interesting that despite its obvious relevance to areas outside the work sphere, to the best of my knowledge, heretofore nothing has been written on the subject of burnout in marriage.

As one of the pioneers in the research on burnout, I witnessed firsthand people's excitement and relief when introduced to it. Even then, and more so now, I have had the sense that, while burnout was not a new phenomenon, its ubiquity was new and was a statement about our times. It had little to do with the personalities of the people involved, and a lot to do with existential concerns and our culture's answer to them.

Because it is the culture in which we live that makes all of us more likely to burn out, in order fully to understand the concept, we need to expand from a focus on the individual (who experiences it) to a focus on our culture. Several cultural trends that took place over the past century have radically changed the institution of marriage. These cultural trends increased the stress on modern marriages, and thus contributed to burnout.

One such cultural trend has been the breakup of the extended family and the loss of many family functions to formal institutions and agencies. (Care for children, for example, is often transferred to child-care centers, care for the elderly to homes for the aged.) This removed some of the traditional reasons for keeping marriage intact.

In the past, marriage involved two extended families and was forever, regardless of how the couple felt about each other. Mothers told their daughters, "You're not just marrying him, you're marrying his whole family," and they meant it. Two families joined by marriage had a vested interest in keeping couples together. When a problem arose, it was treated as natural and normal. ("I had the same trouble with your father. That's just the way men are.") Unhappiness alone was rarely seen as a justification for breaking the marital bond. ("He doesn't drink, he doesn't beat you up, and he brings home all the money he makes. What else could you want?") Many modern couples, on the other hand (especially what the British call DINKs—Double Income, No Kids) consider happiness as the sine qua non of matrimony. When happiness vanishes, so does the reason for staying married.[15]

Today extended families are rare. Young couples often move away from home and sever ties with relatives and childhood friends. When their work demands it, they move again. The absence of close friends and family makes modern couples need, expect, and demand more from each other.

Being without an extended family is not *all* bad. According to the authors of *Habits of the Heart,* it gives mates the advantage of greater personal freedom to define their roles, their expectations, and the nature of their relationship.[16] Modern couples have greater individual freedom to create the kind of life they want for themselves. This freedom, combined with the greater demands couples make on each other, is manifested in yet another cultural trend that has influenced modern marriage—the high rate of divorce.

Burned-out marriages bring out the worst in people. "Husbands and wives are capable of creating a whole range of miseries for each other, ranging from loneliness in marriage, bitter frustration, cruelty, degrading conflicts . . . or waiting for each other to die," wrote the renowned family therapist James L. Framo.[17] For people who base their marriage on love, living in a loveless marriage is, obviously, unacceptable. The alternative they often opt for is divorce.

There has been, in recent years, a growing acceptance of the principle that divorce is a reasonable alternative to an unhappy marriage. It wasn't long ago that couples would stay in miserable marriages because they could not face the social stigma associated with being a "divorcee" or having a "broken home." Now even the law recognizes incompatibility as grounds for divorce. In the eyes of the law it is possible for two people to discover, after many years of living together, that they were simply not made for each other.

Breaking up isn't so hard to do anymore. In the 1970s, most states expanded the grounds for divorce to include some form of no-fault divorce, with the result that it has become much easier to end a marriage. In addition, the consequences of obtaining a divorce aren't as harsh as they used to be.[18] In 1980 and again in 1984 the people of the United States elected Ronald Reagan, a divorced and remarried man, president. At no time did Reagan lose his position as representative of traditional and conservative values.

Changing roles of men and women are yet another cultural trend that has put a stress on marriage. According to one view, the changing role of women is most often the cause of marital problems. Marriage therapists James and Janice Prochaska report, for example, that "the most common reason for couples coming into marital therapy is that the marriage is being shaken by the wife's struggle for equality."[19] Similarly, Philip Blumstein and Pepper Schwartz, in their survey involving over twelve thousand American couples, reported that "women who can support themselves can afford to have higher expectations for their marriages beyond financial security, and because they are more self-sufficient, they can leave if these are not met."[20]

According to another view, it is the changing role of men that most often precipitates marital problems. Barbara Ehrenreich, for instance, in her book *The Hearts of Men,* says that the collapse of traditional marriage was caused by "men's revolt" against their breadwinner role. The men's revolt preceded the women's liberation movement and in large part caused it.[21]

## OUR FALLACY OF UNIQUENESS

Most of us are aware of the changing social norms regarding love, marriage, divorce, and the roles of men and women. It is easy for us to talk about trends and demographics, "most" and "some." We can discuss them in the abstract with great articulation, yet (consciously or unconsciously) we believe that we ourselves are immune to—and above—such generalizations. Social psychologists call this our "fallacy of uniqueness." One of the best literary descriptions of this fallacy can be found in the preface to Han Suyin's *A Many Splendoured Thing:*

> "Do you really think, then, that other people get as much pleasure and happiness out of their bodies as we do? Do you really think this love will not last for ever? I do not believe it." And he looked round him for confirmation. But there was only myrtle and long grass and bracken, hill slope and sea, and ourselves all golden with lying in the sun.
>
> "Dear love, even the paunchy, ugly people of this world believe they love as much as we do and forever. It is the illusion for all lovers to think themselves unique and their words immortal."[22]

When we fall in love we are sure that no one has ever loved as we do. When we are in pain we are convinced that no one has ever suffered as much as we have. And when we burn out we rarely place the blame where it belongs. We seldom think, for example, how cultural forces have shaped our unrealistic expectations. Instead, we blame our mates. We think about all the things our mates do that are so aggravating. "He is a narcissist." "She is controlling, aggressive, manipulative."

We not only deny that we have fallen for the romantic ideals promoted by our culture hook, line, and sinker. What is even more surprising is that we do not acknowledge the effect on our marriages of outside stresses that are far more concrete and evident—financial difficulties, problems with in-laws, having young children at home, illness or injury, unemployment, chronic job stress. The struggle to make it to the top of a career ladder can be draining. So is the tedium of caring for young children day in and day out. Pressures and stresses like these are part and parcel of life. It's hard to be romantic when you are exhausted from office work, physical labor, tending children; it's hard to feel butterflies of love in your stomach when your stomach is churning with anxiety over money. Stresses such as these, which have nothing to do with a couple's love for each other, can erode a marriage as much as a woman's aggression or a man's narcissisism.

While we may understand (in our heads) that such stresses affect marriage, in our hearts we still blame our mates for not making it right. Or else we blame ourselves for things beyond our control (such as unemployment), which is just as bad. Both kinds of blame are part of the price we pay for believing in our own uniqueness. Rather than say, "The expectation of living happily ever after with a person I met at a young age, whom I expect to fulfill all my needs and give meaning to my life, is unrealistic," or "Sex has gone bust because we're exhausted when we get to bed," we ask, "What's wrong with us?" Worse yet, we ask, "What's wrong with my mate?"

## WHY DO WE NEED TO KNOW ABOUT BURNOUT?

In working on the problem of burnout, my focus has been on the shared expectations and shared stresses common to love relationships, and the shared cultural values contributing to these stresses. My assumption has been that it is fiendishly difficult for couples to stay together in a society in which love is exalted yet where breaking up is the norm. In such a society, the informing wisdom is "get the most out of life," "look out for number one," and "do your own thing"; there is no extended family to help a couple stay together when there is trouble and to remind them how much they meant to each other.

The pressures and stresses built into sharing a life together are enormous. It is almost inevitable that these stresses will become intense and at times unbearable. With all the erosive tendencies indigenous to love relationships, instead of being surprised by the high levels of burnout we should marvel at the fact that some marriages, even after many years, are still exciting and mutually supportive, that the romantic spark in them is still alive. Identifying the effect of unrealistic expectations and of outside stresses on the erosion of love is essential for combating burnout. Knowing that these kinds of stresses can lead to burnout in any relationship helps break us from the fallacy of our uniqueness. Realizing that burnout is a common response of romantic people to stressful situations can free us to direct our efforts toward changing those situations, rather than trying in vain to change each other.

*While burnout can be an extraordinarily painful experience, it can be conquered.* As with most difficult emotional experiences, burnout, if properly dealt with, can be a chance for a couple to reevaluate their relationship and thus provide an important trigger for growth. Couples who burn out, and who learn to cope with it effectively, often emerge with better, fuller, more exciting relationships.

# CHAPTER 2

# Falling In and Out of Love

For love is strong as death, passion deep as the grave; it blazes up like blazing fire, fiercer than any flame. Many waters can not quench love, no flood can sweep it away.

*Song of Songs*

## FALLING IN LOVE

All romantic relationships start the same way—with falling in love. If you don't initially have passion, obviously you can't lose it later. Thus, those people who do not believe in love—or who are forever seeking but never able to find the "right" person—cannot burn out in a love relationship.

Falling in love, whether it is love at first sight or a slowly developing obsession, is the ideal stage against which the rest of the relationship is judged—most often unfavorably. This is the stage that lovers want to preserve or go back to. A woman in her late thirties describes it:

> The night we met (we were both invited to a dinner party at a mutual friend's house) I was so excited I couldn't sleep. I kept going over every word he said, wondering whether he was experiencing some of the excitement I was feeling. After we became lovers I was happier than I had ever been before in my life. I felt I was floating on air. I was so excited I couldn't eat. He occupied my mind every single moment. I thought he was the smartest, most handsome, most sexy man I had ever met. Life had an incredible intensity. Everything was painted in bright colors. Sex was fantastic! I felt alive.
>
> Now I notice all those little obnoxious things I was totally unaware of before, like the way he eats, the way he talks, how infantile he can be. He doesn't seem so good-looking to me any

more. I realize now that sex at the beginning had more to do with my own infatuation than with his skill as a lover.

But oh, how I miss the excitement and the romance. I would happily exchange all of my grown-up insights for the blindness and passion I had before.

Infatuation, blindness, passion. We want to believe that our love is unique, magical, something best left to poets. We want to believe that the attraction between lovers is a mystical coming together of souls, what Victor Herbert described as "the sweet mystery of life." Psychologists, however, are not willing to leave love to poets, romantic dreamers, and lovers. They want to find out what attracts two lovers to each other, to explain how someone falls in love with a particular person and why.

If I were to ask you why you fell in love with your mate, if you are like most people, your answer would no doubt include a list of attractive attributes describing your mate: looks, personality, achievements, and attitudes (similar to yours, and hence the "right" attitudes). You, most likely, would not list the ways in which your beloved satisfied our culture's norms. ("She's from a good family, with the proper schooling; she grew up in the right neighborhood.") Nor would you mention the totally unrelated emotional state in which you were when you fell in love. ("I had just finished running my first marathon. I was elated, and there he was, standing at the finish line.") When we fall in love we tend to assume that the magic was created exclusively by the endearing attributes of our beloved. Somehow we feel that if we were to admit how much outside forces affected us, it would diminish the magic of love (or the magic of the loved one). We prefer to think that we are independent, different, that our love is capable of breaking formulas. But psychologists have discovered that the circumstances under which we meet someone are almost as important as whom we meet.

## EMOTIONAL AROUSAL

When we are frightened we are much more likely to fall in love—also when we are angry, jealous, feeling rejected or euphoric. Anyone, in fact, who experiences the physical arousal that goes along with strong emotions is potentially a romantic person. If a man should meet an unusually desirable woman while he is agitated, he is more likely to be intensely drawn to her than he would be under normal circumstances. So concluded social psychologists Elaine Walster and Ellen Berscheid, writing about their two-factor theory of love:

> To love passionately, a person must first be physically aroused, a condition manifested by palpitations of the heart, nervous tremor, flushing, and accelerated breathing. Once he is so aroused, all that remains is for him to identify this complex of feelings as passionate love, and he will have experienced authentic love. Even if the initial physical arousal is the result of an irrelevant experience . . . once he has met the person, been drawn to the person, and identified the experience as love, it is love.[1]

This sort of explains all those couples who met jogging, doesn't it? According to Walster and Berscheid, it takes two things to fall in love: arousal and romantic interpretation. You do not need to go jogging to become aroused, however. A man suffering from the pain of rejection is ripe for a rebound love affair. Wartime lovers find passion in the shadow of death. A woman who is recovering from the loss of her father is ripe for falling in love, and so are people who are about to leave a place forever. Happy occasions, too, lead to love. Think of couples who meet at weddings, on vacation, at parties, and on the first warm day of spring.

Anthony says:

> There was something in the air. It was early spring, bright and crisp; I was exhilarated. I just knew something exciting was going to happen to me that day. It turned out to be Gail.

Researchers have tested the theory that arousal makes people fall in love by telling subjects that they were going to get a "pretty stiff" electric shock, by making them walk across a very deep river on a shaky rope bridge, by having them be rejected by a young woman who was previously warm and accepting, and by actually giving them an injection of adrenaline. In all cases the aroused subjects, when presented with an attractive person of the opposite sex, were more likely to interpret their arousal as a romantic attraction than were unaroused subjects. All this research lends support to Walster and Berscheid's tongue-in-cheek conclusion that "adrenaline makes the heart grow fonder."[2]

The effects of emotional arousal are most noticeable during infatuation, but, as the next example shows, they continue influencing couples' love throughout the relationship. Steve and Susan have been married seven years. During that time their romantic feelings toward each other have gone through major changes. Susan describes their first meeting:

> We met a week before Steve was supposed to leave the Bay Area and move to New York. The attraction between us, from the very first moment, was very strong. I was dating several guys at the time, but suddenly I didn't want to see them. I wanted to be with Steve every moment of the day and the night. During the first week we hardly slept at all. We made love for hours. We couldn't bear the thought of going to sleep and missing time that we could have spent together. Nothing else mattered—my work, my friends, my family. It was only the two of us and the incredible magic between us.

A week later Steve decided not to move to New York. He describes how he felt:

> The relationship was so intense, and there was a quality about it that was absolutely the most perfect romantic love affair that you would ever know. I wanted to make sure that I gave it everything I had and didn't waste a single moment.

After seven years Steve and Susan still described themselves as loving each other, but the intensity of the first week is gone. Susan says:

> Both of us are very involved in highly demanding careers. By the time we get together at night, we are both so exhausted often we don't have the energy to make love. When we do it is still an incredible experience. The difference is that at the beginning it was the most important thing for both of us. Now there are other things competing for our attention.

Jealousy is a powerful trigger of emotional arousal. As is often the case, the love between Susan and Steve returned to center stage when Susan became attracted to another man whom Steve considered a "real threat." Steve says:

> I was so threatened by this man I was panic-stricken. I was convinced the relationship was over. I wanted to take advantage of every last moment we had. Our lovemaking returned to the intensity it had when we thought we had only one week to be together.

Jealousy can put the oomph back in a marriage, but jealousy is not the only energizing experience possible for a sagging marriage. Good experiences and personal triumphs that are emotionally arousing work too. Professional success can energize a relationship from without; mutual happiness can energize it from within. Mates who love each other after many years often describe being overwhelmed by warmth and fulfillment when they realize their marriage is everything they dreamed of. While the emotional arousal of infatuation represents the promise of a love relationship, the happiness in a marriage that maintains the romantic spark represents the fulfillment of that promise.

An important part of the emotional arousal of infatuation comes from the challenge and risks involved in falling in love. While to most of us falling in love is wonderful, it is also dangerous and risky. It means we will be vulnerable. It means we may get hurt. It means we may be disappointed. Just as rock climbing is more exciting than hill climbing—because it involves greater risks—falling in love is more exciting than falling in like. This kind of emotional arousal is recreated whenever the relationship is threatened, as the example of jealousy shows.

The happiness produced in a good marriage does not involve risks. Its power to energize derives from the realization that you have managed to achieve in the marriage something of great value that you wanted very much. In order to energize a marriage you don't need to *recreate* the magic of infatuation (as suggested by a popular misconception). You need, instead, to *create* the new magic of a truly intimate and loving long-term relationship.

Physical and emotional arousal alone are not, however, enough for you to fall in love. The next prerequisite is meeting someone who fits your romantic image.

## ROMANTIC IMAGES

Romantic images develop very early in life and are particularly powerful because they are based on memory of experiences that occurred before the development of language. Parents pass on romantic images to their children in two ways: by the way they express love toward the child and by the way they express, or do not express, love for each other. Since their parents' relationship is, for most people, the relationship they observe first, most closely, and over the longest period of time, it has the strongest influence on their image of love. People who grew up in families filled with tension and conflict develop concepts of love and marriage different from those of people who grew up in warm and affectionate families.

Romantic images are then strongly influenced by our first *personal* experiences of love. We internalize the image of the person who taught us the meaning of love by satisfying our physical and emotional needs during the first days of life. As adults we look for a lover who will fit that internalized image. Sometimes we look for a physical fit (a woman is attracted to men who, like her father, are short, dark, and tough-but-good-looking). Sometimes we yearn for an emotional fit (a man is attracted to women who are like his mother: bright, articulate, and vivacious). Sometimes we look for the exact opposite of our parents (a man whose mother was intrusive, emotional, heavy-set, and dark-haired is irresistibly attracted to aloof, emotionally reserved, skinny blonds).

When we are emotionally aroused and meet a person who fits this internalized image in some important way, we project the whole image onto him or her. This is why when we fall in love we often say "I feel as if I've known him all my life." This is also why we are so often surprised and disappointed to discover, when the infatuation is over, that our beloved has some nasty personal characteristics we had overlooked, and does not possess all of the wonderful qualities our love-struck eyes first beheld. It is as if we couldn't see the actual person, but only the projection of our internalized image.

Marilyn French describes the disappointing discovery of the person behind our projected image in her book *The Women's Room:*

Then one day, the unthinkable happens. You are sitting together at the breakfast table and you're a little hung over, and you look across at beloved, beautiful golden beloved, and beloved opens his lovely rosebud mouth showing his glistening white teeth, and beloved says something stupid. Your whole body stops mid-stream: your temperature drops. Beloved has never said anything stupid before. You turn and you look at him; you're sure you misheard. You ask him to repeat. And he does. He says, "It's raining out." And you look outside and it is perfectly clear. And you say, "No, it isn't raining out. Perhaps you'd better get your eyes checked. Or your ears." You begin to doubt all his senses. It could only be a flaw in his sensory equipment that would make him say a thing like that. But even that flaw isn't important. Love can't be stopped by locksmiths, contact lenses, or hearing aids. It was just that you were hung over.

But that's only the start. Because he keeps on, after that, saying stupid things. And you keep turning around and looking at him strangely, and my God, do you know what, you suddenly see that he's skinny! Or flabby! Or fat! His teeth are crooked, and his toenails are dirty. You suddenly realize he farts in bed. He doesn't, he really doesn't understand Henry James! All this while, he's been saying he doesn't understand Henry James, and you've thought his odd, cast-off remarks about James showed brilliant perception, but suddenly you realize he missed the point entirely.[3]

It has been said that some people marry their worst nightmare: People who fear rejection and abandonment, for example, marry people who fear intrusion and engulfment. As one mate seeks closeness, the other mate seeks distance. While the marriage may appear like a living hell, it actually offers both mates an opportunity to master their fears.

Some people choose to marry a person who represents a part of themselves they do not like, or can't admit even to themselves. Instead they confront this "split-off" part in their mate. For example, a woman who as a child was punished for being aggressive learns to suppress her hostility and aggression. She suppresses them so well she is not even consciously aware of her hostile and angry feelings. Yet she is irresistibly attracted, without knowing why, to very aggressive, even violent men. She eventually falls in love and marries one of them, which strikes her friends as crazy since she appears so mild-mannered and gentle. Through her interactions with her husband (in which she plays the role of the sweet and gentle woman forced to deal with an aggressive and hostile man) she is able to confront her own hostility without needing to admit to it in herself.

At times internalized images can be very negative. When the first love-models a baby experiences are withdrawn, cold, and punitive, these will be the internalized romantic images that child will carry as an adult. Such adults tend to repeatedly fall in love with people who are cold and punitive, who are sure not to return their affection.

In extreme cases, romantic images can be self-destructive, compelling the individual to repeat a childhood trauma of abuse. A woman who was beaten and sexually abused by her father as a young girl was married three times—each time to a violent man who beat and raped her regularly. After she managed to escape from the third husband and was recuperating at a shelter for abused women, she met a sweet man who was warm and loving to her and who offered to take care of her. She refused his advances because, she says, he was "boring," and "there was no spark in the relationship." It was as if the woman were saying that the only way there could be a spark for her was if the man was a potential abuser, like her father. For a woman like this it is extremely important to deal with the unresolved childhood trauma that created her destructive romantic images through long-term psychotherapy. Otherwise she is guaranteed to continue repeating the trauma by getting involved with abusive men. Romantic images are so powerful, however, that even after she realizes how destructive her attraction to these men is, the woman is still likely to feel it. The insights she gains will only help her resist getting involved with them.

This doesn't seem at all similar to falling in love with someone who reminds you of your wonderful father, but there is a great similarity. When we are attracted to someone, it is because of an image we carry in our heads and hearts independent of that person. Our personal vision of love often provides a script for marriage. Problems come when husband and wife follow contradictory scripts.

Dona (the architect who burned out after fourteen years of marriage) came from a broken home where she never had a chance to observe love between her mother and father. Dona thought a great deal about her romantic image:

My image has always been of total sharing. To me the idea of perfect love is an incestuous brother-sister who love each other, look alike, and who have similar interests, similar backgrounds, who are like the male and female of the same person—it's total sharing.

This image, which created very high expectations on her part, had a profoundly negative impact on Dona's marriage:

All your images are locked up in what you think, and Andrew does not match my images. There is no bonding between us. And that word *bonding* has become very important to me. I really want a friend in a man. I want someone I can share everything with. I have a lot of friends and know how to share with friends. But Andrew doesn't. He doesn't have a lot of friends, and he doesn't know how to share with anybody.

It is surprising how few couples discuss their romantic images openly, even at the beginning of a relationship. Dona and Andrew were clearly not among those few. Andrew came from a very close-knit family (a family he perceived as "too close" and engulfing). The main features of his romantic image were freedom and independence:

The fact is that I sort of like things to be unstructured. I like the freedom it gives me. Freedom to do my own thing, I guess. . . . We all need emotional relationships. That's for sure. Or at least I do. And I can't get emotionally involved with someone unless I have some respect for them on a professional level. It is important to me that the woman I am with have some self-sufficiency. What absolutely turns me off is a dependent woman. I like to get some response from the other person, some feedback . . . I hate being manipulated. I like to live and let live.

Andrew's romantic image, almost the antithesis of Dona's image of total sharing, was also a source of problems:

Dona was trying too much to make me do what she wanted me to do. She was too pushy, too manipulative. . . . A pretty good definition of tyranny is when one party says to the other, "Look, you gotta do this, and I don't care whether you get anything out of it or not, because that's what I want. . . ." She always wanted security, security, security. It became oppressive.

Dona's and Andrew's romantic images generated two different scripts, two different sets of expectations, which was guaranteed to frustrate at least one of them. Hence, couples who do not share romantic images have a higher probability of burning out, and vice versa. Take for example a happily married couple, Ellen and Anthony. This is a second marriage for both of them, and it has lasted over thirteen years. Ellen describes them as very clear about their own and each other's romantic images:

> When I was still married to my former husband, during the time our marriage was going sour, I used to have a recurrent daydream in which I saw myself in bed with a man I love. His face wasn't clear. What was clear, however, was that it was morning. (My husband and I would never make love in the morning, so that became an important part of my fantasy.) But what was even more important in my fantasy was the knowledge that this man was someone who loved me, who loved touching me (something my husband rarely did), and with whom I could talk about everything. Someone with whom I could be totally honest. That's what was most important to me: good talk and good sex. My relationship with Anthony is the realization of these fantasies. I am quite sure the same is true for him.

Anthony's romantic ideal seems very compatible with Ellen's:

> I always had an aversion to concretizing romantic ideals or images, in part because I felt that an important part of the magic of love is that it is not specified in advance. So, on the one hand, all my life I had the desire to keep my options open to all exotic possibilities, and on the other hand, my personal experience has shown me that the odds are very small of a relationship lasting any length of time without a similarity in background, culture, and world view. As I am saying that I am realizing that in my relationship with Ellen I was able to have my cake and eat it too. Because there is something very exotic about the fact that she spent her childhood in the Far East, and yet our world views and romantic ideals are very similar. I want the person I am with to be able to defend themselves verbally and talk openly about feelings. That sex has to be good is obvious.

What attracted you to your mate and your mate to you when you first met? What is your ideal relationship? What is your mate's ideal relationship? Think about your childhood memories. How did your parents treat you? How did they treat each other? Is there any similarity between your mother and your mate? Between your father and your mate? Is your mate the complete opposite of your parents? You can discover your and your mate's romantic images through an honest exploration of these questions.

Often, such clarification alone is enough to unearth differences in romantic imagery that were at the source of many repeated conflicts. A humorous example is a cartoon showing a bride and groom exchanging vows with balloons over their heads to show what each is thinking. In the balloon over the groom's head there is a vision of the bride serving him breakfast in bed. In the bride's balloon there is an image of the groom serving *her* breakfast in bed.

Romantic images are internal pictures of the happiness love can provide, the kind of happiness that makes life worth living. We feel that if we can find a person who fits this image we are going to find total bliss and contentment; all our questions and doubts about ourselves and about life will be answered. That is why we fall in love with the parts of our beloved that most closely match our romantic image. That is also why when love fails us, these very same characteristics become a major source of stress.

For a woman like Dona, who came from a broken home and never experienced the warmth and security of a loving family, the image of "perfect love" was associated, as she herself says, with "total sharing." She longed for a man who was similar in looks to her adored father (who abandoned the family when she was a young girl), someone "very romantic . . . very handsome . . . the strong silent type." She felt that total sharing with a man like that could compensate her for all her childhood pains, alleviate all her fears, and provide an answer to all her dreams. When it became clear that Andrew could not, or would not (as Dona perceived it), share her romantic image, she felt disappointed not only in him, but in her whole life.

If romantic images are so important, why don't couples share them more openly? One reason is that sometimes it is hard for people to say what is *really* important to them. Another is that people tend to think they share romantic images (and identical expectations) with their lovers. Only later do they discover that the two of them view things very differently. A colleague of mine, who is a brilliant couples' therapist, told me that only after seventeen years of marriage did it dawn on him that his wife *really* meant it when she said that gifts of expensive jewelry were to her a sign of love. Other relationships don't survive seventeen years.

Sonya's father died when she was five, and her romantic image of a mate was a daddy substitute. Gary grew up in a Mideastern family in which his father was "the ruler of the roost" and his mother was a weak yet a very warm and nurturing woman.

When they first met at work, both Gary and Sonya were in a period of transition. Sonya had moved from the West Coast, where she had lived all her life; Gary had just taken a new job after working for the same company for many years. In addition to being emotionally aroused because of these changes, Gary's and Sonya's looks matched each other's romantic image: Like their opposite-sex parents they were both tall, dark, and very attractive; they both took care to enhance their appearance with fashionable clothes. Since they worked at the same place and interacted with each other daily, it did not take long before they fell in love. Gary loved the way Sonya looked up to him, yielding and demure. Being in control made him feel "like a man." Sonya loved the fact that Gary was taking care of her and acting like a "real man and a gentleman." In short, both found in each other the materialization of their romantic images.

Yet their courtship did not turn out to be the blissful relationship they had both hoped for. For one thing, Sonya had temper tantrums whenever she wanted something from Gary and didn't get it. For her, those tantrums were just another expression of her childlike feelings toward a father substitute. For him, the tantrums expressed disrespect and made him feel less like a man.

What this example shows is that even when two people are emotionally aroused, and their romantic images match, further screening is necessary before they can decide to share their lives together.

LOVE FILTERS

Love filters help people screen out "unsuitables" and establish among potential candidates the one with whom they can "let themselves" fall in love, the one to whom marriage seems plausible. Say a conventional woman notices a man at a very dramatic moment—during a bank holdup. He is dark and handsome, just like her father, and seems in command of himself. She is quite clearly emotionally aroused, because of the danger. This man fulfills her romantic image. Will she fall in love with him? It is not likely if he is the bank robber. Her love filters tell her he is not a suitable candidate for a happy marriage.

You can discover your own love filters with the help of a simple exercise. Think back on your entire life, and choose from all the people you have ever known the two with whom you were most passionately in love. Try to recall as many details about these two people as you can: their personality, behavior, looks, attitudes, background, and anything else you can think of. Now consider everything and anything they have in common. Are they both warm? Cold? Good in bed? Good to you? Were you attracted to their strength? Their intelligence? Their ability to get close? The size of their family? Their religious commitment? Was it their education, height, age, athletic build, or exotic look? Whatever the people you have loved most passionately have in common represents something in you—your own personal filters for selecting an appropriate lover and mate.

Psychologists have focused a great deal of research effort on studying love filters (who falls in love with whom). The two filters that have received the greatest attention (probably because they were the easiest to study) were proximity and similarity.

Several studies have shown that people do, at least figuratively, marry the person next door. In one study, in which 5,000 marriage licenses were examined, 33 percent of the couples lived within five blocks of each other. The percentage of marriages decreased steadily and markedly as the distance between the couples' residences increased. Apparently, two people must not only have a chance to meet before they can fall in love, but they have a higher probability of falling in love if they see each other frequently.[4]

A salesman from Connecticut just closed the biggest deal of his life in California's Silicon Valley. He worked on this deal for over two years and was feeling ecstatic. In this state of intense emotional arousal, he noticed that one of the managers with whom he was interacting was exactly his type, a petite red-haired beauty. He started flirting with her, and she seemed friendly and responsive. He felt his heart pounding with excitement. This could be the woman of his dreams. However, since he had appointments for the rest of the day and then was supposed to leave on the night flight, he could not pursue his feelings. After returning home he was so busy with work that he forgot about her.

Similarity is another filter that operates at the beginning stages of falling in love. A single woman has just ended a long-term passionate love affair with a married man who was a computer programmer like herself. At a crowded party she notices an attractive stranger across the room. She is immediately drawn to his masculine energy and his warm and animated conversational style. She manages to push her way close enough to listen and hears him mention the fact that he is a truck driver. She withdraws disappointed, the spark that flashed gone. What in the world can she possibly talk about with a truck driver?

In a study of engaged couples, similarities were found in family background, education, income and social status of parents, religious affiliation, types of family relationship (happiness of parents' marriage, attitude toward parents, and sex of siblings), sociability (being a "lone wolf" or socially gregarious), leisure-time preference ("stay at home" vs. "on the go"), drinking and smoking habits, number of same-sex and opposite-sex friends, courtship behavior—including number of previous engagements and steady dates, and attitudes toward marriage.[5] Other studies discovered, in addition, similarity in such things as intelligence, physical attributes and attractiveness, mental health, psychological maturity, and even developmental failures. The bulk of the research, however, focused on similarities in attitudes and personality. The conclusion was that happy couples are more alike than unhappy couples.[6]

This research documents what folk wisdom has known all along, that "birds of a feather flock together." However, there is clearly more to falling in love than simply finding the person who is most like us in every way possible. (Would you really fall in love with an exact replica of yourself?) As is often the case, folk wisdom has a contradictory law: "Opposites attract." Which "law" should we trust? The answer, as one would guess, is that both laws operate, but at different times. Only after our beloved has passed the initial screening in which similarity ("birds of a feather") is the key filter does complementarity ("opposites attract") come into play. When two people have similar needs for closeness and intimacy, similarity is an advantage. When one person needs to be in charge or make decisions and another needs to be taken care of or protected, complementarity is an advantage.

Theodor Reik observed in *The Need to Be Loved* that people fall in love for selfish reasons. They sense something lacking in themselves and seek the missing quality (or qualities) in a mate.[7] Thus, a compulsively logical man will be attracted to an excessively emotional woman. Each supplies part of the qualities needed for a complete joint personality, and each benefits from the part provided by the other. According to Robert Winch's theory of complementary needs, love is the experience of two people jointly deriving maximum gratification for important psychological needs, yet doing so with the minimum of pain.[8]

Carol, an attractive woman in her mid-twenties, married to a wealthy man much older than herself, explains:

> My father left my mother and the four children when I was just a baby. My mother had great difficulty making ends meet, and I grew up feeling very insecure about money. I used to dream that my father returned and made everything all right. My husband gives me the fathering and economic security I so much longed for.

More recently, Bernard Murstein proposed an elaboration on the theory of complementarity in *Who Will Marry Whom?:* the exchange theory.[9] Murstein believes that attraction depends on the fairest exchange value of the personal assets and liabilities that each partner brings. He sees people as rational beings who screen potential lovers and form relationships that are likely to provide them with maximum potential gratification at the lowest cost. Like any good business executive, he says, people choose to marry the person who provides them with the best all-round package deal.

A forty-two-year-old man I interviewed explains his decision to marry his wife by saying:

> Maybe she wasn't the hottest romance of my life, but she was a beautiful woman, warm, kind, and sensitive, and she said she loved me. Even then I knew she was going to be a wonderful mother. I was sure we could build a home together, and that was the most important thing to me. It was certainly more important than the intensity of sexual infatuation, which I knew never lasts anyway.

Love, according to Murstein's theory, is the mutual satisfaction two partners derive from knowing they got the best "exchange value" for their relationship; in other words, when both partners feel they made the best possible deal.

The funnel of screens people use when selecting a lover and a mate is described best by the filter theory. The theory focuses on the process that starts with falling in love and ends with marriage. Social background, values, interests, and complementary personality needs all come into play, but at different stages of a romantic relationship. Different filters operate during infatuation, courtship, and marriage.

When people are getting acquainted, background and residence usually limit the field of eligibles. Only after passing this initial stage can couples discover that they have shared values and interests. A disagreement on important values makes further development of the relationship unlikely. Only a deepening of the involvement can establish the intimacy necessary for discovering whether a couple has complementary psychological needs. Most people need to feel a certain degree of security in a relationship before they let their guard down and admit which emotional needs they want fulfilled. For some men that means admitting a need to be "mothered." Similarly, for some women that may mean admitting a need to be "fathered." If such a man and a woman enter a relationship, even if they pass all the other filters, they are bound to have problems because their needs are not compatible—both want to be childlike and to be taken care of. A far more compatible marriage is between a man who likes to be mothered and a woman who enjoys mothering; between a woman who wants to be fathered and a man who enjoys being paternalistic.[10]

Family therapist Steven Yellan and his collaborator Gerald Kaplan emphasize a more primitive, animalistic prerequisite for romantic attraction: smell, touch, and taste.[11] A woman who finds a man's breath offensive is not likely to agree to go on a date with him, even if he fulfills all her other selection criteria. Similarly, a man is not going to pursue a relationship with a woman whose touch he finds sweaty and unpleasant.

On the other hand, if two people touch hands, or lips, and "electricity" passes between them, they are likely to be drawn toward each other in spite of differences in background and in spite of social objections. The best literary example is, of course, Romeo and Juliet. After being attracted to each other's looks across the dance hall, after their first words, the first touch, the first kiss, not even the long-standing feud between their families could stop them from falling in love.

The sensual responses of sight, smell, touch, and taste are not only filters during the selection process. They continue to play an important part throughout a relationship. A woman, married ten years, describes how her senses told her it was over:

> As I looked at his pimpled back, I felt a wave of nausea. I couldn't bear the thought of him touching me. At that moment I knew I had to get out of the marriage, and fast.

Even couples in love, who have a similar background, who share values, have complementary needs, and are attracted to each other's sight, touch, and smell, are never matched in *all* areas. Early in the relationship there is a tendency to downplay differences. There is a tendency to think that love can overcome these differences when, in fact, experience has shown that time tends to exacerbate them. For example, let's look at a couple in which the husband is a two-pack-a-day smoker, and the wife a nonsmoker. During courtship the woman dismisses smoking as an issue. She says that smoke doesn't bother her—but then again, she has never lived with a smoker. No one in her family smokes, neither her parents nor her siblings nor her ex-husband. After two years of living with foul-smelling ashtrays around the house, a stale-smelling bedroom, and cigarette smoke trailing through the bathroom and kitchen first thing in the morning, it begins to grate on her. She starts nagging him to quit. She claims she can't breathe when he smokes in the same room. She demands that he open the windows, even if it is freezing outside. He is resentful of her change in attitude. ("You knew I smoked. You never complained about it *before.*")

For the two of them the issue of smoking becomes like the proverbial cap left off the toothpaste tube—a cause for perpetual arguments and fights. This couple's marriage has not broken up over the issue of smoking, but it remains a sore point between them, especially when the wife points out the health risks involved, both to her husband and to herself. The wife now insists that if she had to do it all over again, she would be sure to marry a nonsmoker. The husband, likewise, says he wishes he had chosen a smoker. This may sound trivial, even funny. But these kinds of trivial issues— windows open at night, windows closed, pets on the bed, pets off the bed, TV on during dinner, TV off during dinner—slowly scrape away at goodwill and intimacy between lovers.

Of course, the filters I've mentioned are not the only ones people use. Some women would not marry a man who was not successful in his chosen line of work, for instance, and some men would not marry a woman unless she was willing to have a big family. All filters operate in different degrees for different people and during different stages of falling in love.

Love filters, romantic images, and emotional arousal work together. Love filters help an emotionally aroused individual select—from all potential lovers that match his or her romantic image—the one to fall in love with. There is a major difference between love filters or romantic images, on the one hand, and emotional arousal on the other. Our standards for background, attitudes, and personality are rather stable. Our romantic models and images are engraved on us at a very early stage and are thus resistant to change. Emotional arousal, on the other hand, is by its very nature temporary.

After twenty-five years of marriage, it is unlikely that your standards for your mate's background and personality have changed too much. But after twenty-five years of marriage the emotional arousal of infatuation is gone. It was based on the promise of the relationship, a promise that was either fulfilled or frustrated during your years together.

## THE EFFECT OF THE ENVIRONMENT

When two people fall in love they are emotionally aroused; they share a world view and feel compatible both in personality needs and in romantic images. They want nothing more than to continue being in love forever. However, fortunately for some and unfortunately for others, they do not live in a vacuum, and the interaction with the environment determines to a large extent what happens to all relationships.

Lucky lovers end up in a supportive environment where challenge, encouragement, rewards, and opportunities for growth are abundant. Unlucky lovers land in an environment dominated by pressures and stresses. Because environments are different, some supportive and growth-producing and some stressful and demanding, the passage of time has a different impact on different relationships—enhancing some and eroding others. Thus time, in and of itself, does not cause burnout (this is an important point, to which I will return later).

By emphasizing the role of the environment I do not mean to disregard the importance of personality. Obviously, mates' personalities play a significant role in all intimate relationships. This is especially true in the initial stage of mutual selection when they are falling in love. Even if certain personality characteristics eventually come to cause stress in a relationship, they were not enough of a hindrance during the infatuation stage and could even have been an attraction.

Much as they would like to remain immersed in the magic of their love, sooner or later all couples—no matter what their personalities, no matter what their expectations, no matter how compatible or incompatible, and no matter how many or how few unconscious, unresolved conflicts they bring with them into the relationship—have to deal with the environmental reality. It is no longer "just you and me and the magic of our love," but rather "you, me, and the world around us"—in fact, sometimes "you and me *against* the world."

People interact with their environment in individual ways. Some people have robust physiques, some are frail. Some people are bold and aggressive, others are shy. Some people can handle anything and others fall apart at the slightest provocation. These characteristics seem to hold true even in different situations, though people can and do change. People can modify their way of relating to the world when conditions demand it, but only to a certain extent. In fact, it is usually easier to change the environment than it is to change people's personalities. Since the environment affects marriage so strongly, it is important for couples interested in preventing burnout to know what in the environment causes burnout, and what prevents it. Finding that out was one of the goals in my research on marriage burnout.[12]

I will discuss three features in the environment that were found to most enhance burnout and three features that were found to best buffer against it.

## WHAT IN THE ENVIRONMENT
## ENHANCES BURNOUT?

*Overload.* How often do you experience overload in your marriage, which is to say, a feeling that you have gone beyond the point of endurance, because the tasks imposed on you are either too many or too hard?

Results show that the higher the frequency of overload, the higher the level of burnout.[13] This was true with regard to the two kinds of overload addressed in the question—quantitative and qualitative. Quantitative overload happens when you feel that you have more tasks than you can perform well, or too many tasks to perform in the time alloted. It can happen when a devoted mother, who also works, doesn't have enough time to bake a cake for her child's birthday. It can happen when a husband feels torn between his job obligations and his obligations to his family. It can happen when a couple decides to fix up an old house and then spends every minute plastering, wiring, plumbing, and painting. Qualitative overload— a feeling that the required jobs are simply beyond your capabilities—can happen when a wife who never learned how to cook is expected to fix fancy meals for her husband's distinguished colleagues. A husband can feel the job is simply beyond him when he has to singlehandedly discipline unruly teenagers or keep the entire family afloat financially.

Over time, such problems can eat away at a good marriage. Steve describes it:

> I spend too many hours at work, and the work is too intense and too high pressured. The sheer number of hours I am working with people there is creating an intensity that diminishes the intensity of my relationship with Susan. I don't have enough emotional resources to come home and be anything more than perfunctory. It is perfectly obvious to me that I have to change the way I am working. But, on the other hand, if I really want to succeed in this business I can't afford to pull back in any area that I can think of. So I am in a classic Catch-22 situation.

*Conflicting demands.* "How often do you feel caught by conflicting demands caused, at least in part, by your spouse?" Research findings indicate that the more frequent such conflict, the higher the burnout.[14]

The wife feels caught in a conflict between the demands for time, attention, and nurturing of her children and those of her husband; the husband feels caught in a conflict between the demands of his wife for financial security and her demands for his time and attention. They experience a similar conflict. Such demands, whether legitimate or not, whether real or imagined, can be impossible to satisfy altogether, or impossible to satisfy at the same time, and thus be extremely stressful. Susan says:

> I feel torn between all the people in my life who, as dear to me as they are, seem to just want, want, want. If I respond to all those demands they could fill my days completely leaving no time for my work or anything else. And it's not the preparing meals or driving the children around that wears me down, but all those "little" errands. So little that I feel embarrassed to object or refuse, but so many that they drown me. They all feel they have the right to ask me for those "little" favors, because they love me, or because they are family, or because they are friends. The worst part is, I agree with them. I feel they *do* have a right to ask me. So I do it. But at the end of a day during which, in addition to my work, I had to run around doing favors for everyone, I am not only exhausted, I am also furious. I am especially furious at Steve, who is never home to help out but is always the first to ask me to run this or that errand for him. I can feel it is slowly but surely eroding my love for him.

*Family commitments.*  How often do you feel pressured by family commitments? The more frequent such a pressure is, the higher the burnout.[15] Overload, conflicting demands, and family commitments have an important thing in common: All three reflect a failure to perform according to some expectations, standards, or "shoulds." These expectations can be imposed by some external force, by one's own standards of excellence, or by one's romantic ideals. The failure, or the fear of failure, causes the overload, the pressure, and the conflict.

Another similarity is that all three drain energy. When we feel overloaded we feel that the things expected of us are more than we can bear. Conflicting demands make us feel that no matter what we do we cannot satisfy everyone. Family commitments (even those we saddled *ourselves* with) make us feel we are beyond our emotional or physical depth. In all three cases the overwhelming feeling is exhaustion. The feelings of failure deplete the emotional arousal that was present during the "falling in love" stage, and with it comes the depletion of the couple's love.

Since the source of stress is perceived as coming from the outside, it is not surprising that people tend to focus their blame for the erosion of love outward. The problem is that all too often that outward focus of blame is not directed at the stressful environment, but instead it is directed (unfairly) at the mate. Gus and Lana are an example of such misattribution of blame.

Gus and Lana always came to my office late in the evening. That was the only time both of them could get away from their respective jobs—he as an organizational consultant, she the mother of five young children. Both described themselves as physically, emotionally, and mentally exhausted, and they looked the way they felt. They described their problem as burnout. Their sex life was practically nonexistent. Their communication was limited to the details involved in sharing a household, such as who would pick up two quarts of milk from the supermarket and who would drive the eldest child to a piano lesson.

Gus and Lana both had demanding work schedules. After many years with a large corporation, Gus had decided to start his own consulting firm. While his former job had been very well paid and secure, his new job was neither. He spent a lot of time convincing companies to give him contracts. In addition to the actual work those contracts demanded, he had to take care of all the administrative details. The financial pressures had been wearing him down. Lana's work was stressful in a different way. With five children in the house (two still in diapers), she could not remember when she had last slept an entire night.

The reality of their daily life explained Gus and Lana's physical exhaustion quite well. The fact that both of them cared very much about what they did, and felt they weren't achieving their aspirations, explained their emotional and mental exhaustion far better than their own assumption—that they had fallen out of love with each other.

## WHAT IN THE ENVIRONMENT
## PREVENTS BURNOUT?

*Variety.*    The greater the variety, the lower the levels of burnout.[16] Variety can be found somewhere on the happy ground between overload and boredom. People function best at an optimal level of variety. Extremely high levels of variety create anxiety and strain, while extremely low levels create boredom and anger. The optimal level is different for different people and requires constant and continuous stimulation from the environment.[17] This is why no matter how exciting a marriage is initially, in the absence of variety, boredom and monotony can wear it down.[18]

The ways couples introduce variety into their relationships are as different as couples are. For some, variety means travel—every so often they just get antsy and feel they "have to go somewhere." That can mean anything from a hike in the woods to a drive to a beautiful sea resort to traveling in Europe. For some couples, variety is people-related. They like to meet new people, and if one of them meets someone new that person becomes a source of enjoyment for both. For some, variety means conquering new skills, taking classes, learning a craft. For some, variety means making certain times or dates special. One couple has lunch together every Wednesday—at a different restaurant each time, which they alternate responsibility for choosing. Another couple reserves Sunday mornings for a leisurely breakfast in bed with fresh bran muffins, coffee, and *The New York Times*.

Variety is in the eye of the beholder. For some couples "lunch every Wednesday" or "breakfast in bed every Sunday" doesn't sound very exciting. For those couples variety means doing things that are spontaneous and unplanned. They might hire a babysitter and go to a fancy motel and make love. They might sneak out of the house at night and go skinnydipping. One couple likes to go to a hot tub where they can "just focus on each other in an atmosphere that is sensuous and relaxing," where there are no telephones and no children to disrupt them. Another couple likes to play "pick-up" games in bars, in theaters, or in any other public place. They love to watch the response of onlookers and laugh about it later. For a gay couple, a romantic atmosphere is created by cooking a gourmet meal together and then eating it by candlelight with soft music playing in the background. For another couple a special atmosphere is created by wearing sensuous clothes and making love at different times of day and in different rooms of the house. For some couples variety involves physical activities—sailing, playing tennis on sunlit courts, skiing on snow-covered mountains, or jogging around the neighborhood. For others it involves playing bridge, giving parties, going to concerts, participating in sports events, supporting political causes—the list is endless.

Whatever form variety takes, it always makes certain times in the lives of a couple more exciting and thus increases emotional arousal and rejuvenates romance in the relationship.

*Appreciation.*    How much appreciation and recognition do you get for your contribution to the relationship? Appreciation, it turns out, buffers against burnout.[19] Feeling appreciated and respected makes us feel good—about ourselves and about the person who made us feel that way. On the other hand, feeling unappreciated, no matter how much we work, not only makes us feel angry and resentful at the person criticizing us; it makes us feel bad about ourselves. It is as though we see ourselves mirrored in the people around us. When such a mirror projects a positive image, an image of someone warm, generous, sexy, and fun to be with, that is the way we come to view ourselves and behave. When the mirror shows us someone cold, stingy, nasty, and obnoxious, that too becomes part of our self-image and influences our behavior.

Most of us have within ourselves the capacity to behave warmly or coldly, generously or stingily, in a sexy and playful way or in a nasty and obnoxious way. When people treat us as warm and playful, that, in and of itself, will bring out more of our warm and playful behavior than our cold and obnoxious behavior. The power of this self-fulfilling prophecy has a very practical implication. If you don't get enough appreciation in your work, you and your mate can make up for it at home. Minimize criticism (especially of those things that cannot be changed), and maximize mutual boosting and *honest* appreciation of each other. Appreciation that is given only when truly felt is not likely to be taken for granted or disregarded.

*Self-actualization.*    The more an environment provides individuals and couples with opportunities for self-actualization and personal growth, the less likely they are to burn out.[20] Abraham Maslow maintains that people have a drive toward actualization of their human potentialities. It is one of the basic human motivations and a central personality tendency.[21] Self-actualization is also a major theme in the writing of Carl Rogers. "There is in every organism, including man, an underlying flow of movement toward constructive fulfillment of its inherent possibilities, a natural tendency toward growth," writes Rogers. "It can be thwarted but not destroyed without destroying the whole organism."[22]

Environments that offer individuals and couples opportunities to achieve self-actualization, in which they are challenged to pursue spiritual growth and self-discovery, in which they can strive to fulfill their human potential, are environments that enhance the romantic spark. Lynne, a successful career woman who married in her late thirties, described the feeling:

> There is almost nothing I did when I was single that I can't do now because I am married, and so much more I dare to do and am able to do because I am married, which I could not do when I was single.

Self-actualization involves continuous change and growth, which for some people can be anxiety-provoking. It requires openness to new experiences in a positive, active, and creative way.

## OTHER STRESSES AND BUFFERS
## IN THE ENVIRONMENT

Overload, conflicting demands, and the pressure of family commitments are, quite obviously, not the only stresses enhancing marriage burnout. Other stresses include such things as boredom, heavy loads of household chores and responsibilities, constant demands to prove oneself, crowded living conditions, noise, and pollution.

If I were to ask you what are the most stressful environmental features in your marriage, what would you answer? In my experience, couples are able to describe these stresses rather easily. What is usually more difficult for them is making the connection between those stresses and the experience of burnout in their own marriages.

Variety, appreciation, and self-actualization are not the only environmental features buffering against burnout. Other positive features, according to the research data, include good personal relations with family, friends and coworkers; unconditional support in time of trouble; feedback on performance; autonomy; and a home that is comfortable, pleasant, and designed to meet one's needs, preferences, and personal taste. Positive features such as variety and self-actualization help maintain an optimal level of emotional arousal in the relationship, while such features as appreciation, good relations, and unconditional support help the development of trust and security, which strengthen commitment.

## OBJECTIVE VS. SUBJECTIVE ENVIRONMENTS

When talking about the effects of the environment on people's well-being, it is often assumed that the environment is an objective entity out there in the real world. The truth of the matter is that this is never the case. We never interact directly with the physical world surrounding us. We interact with the psychological world that was created through the mediation of our senses. We don't experience an objective reality, but rather our own subjective reality.

We are constantly bombarded by stimuli from the environment. In order to make sense of the world, we have to screen out some of these stimuli. Our senses select, organize, and interpret, and thus we end up with a personal and subjective view of the world. Our perceptions are not a passive reflection of the environment. They are the result of an active process in which we shape and create our environment.

In the research cited earlier, the environmental features that were found to cause or prevent burnout were not aspects of the physical world. They were aspects of the psychological world of the people who described them. They were not based on objective measures, but on subjective reports. People described overload the way they experienced it, and not in terms of the actual amount or difficulty of the work imposed on them. Conflicting demands, family obligations, variety, and appreciation were all subjectively defined as well.

The same environment can be perceived very differently by different people. It can be seen as full of variety by one person, as full of overload by a second person, and as boring by a third. It can be seen as stressful and burnout-causing by one person and as exciting and full of challenges by another. Whether you will burn out depends on the way you cope with your own subjective environment.

According to stress psychologist Richard Lazarus, a personal process of "appraisal" always mediates between the effects of the environment and the emotions they produce in the individual.

"Appraisal can be most readily understood as the process of categorizing an encounter, and its various facets, with respect to its significance for well-being." A situation can be perceived as either relevant or irrelevant to one's well-being, as already harmful, potentially harmful, challenging, or potentially positive in outcome.[23]

The same situation will affect different people in different ways, depending on their histories and their personality characteristics. One person may react with anger, another with depression, another with fear or guilt; still others may feel challenged rather than threatened under comparable conditions. For example, one person may cope with marital problems by denial and another by depression. One person may handle an insult by ignoring it, another may get angry and have a fight, another may plan revenge.

There are differences in the ways people approach life. Some people are dramatically affected by even the smallest stresses. These people tend to view the world as a place dominated by evil forces where one is best prepared if always ready for the worst. Each problem is exaggerated and seen as evidence that things are bad and will naturally become worse. Other people believe that when left to themselves, things will naturally turn out for the best. The most important thing for them is to be happy and experience life to its fullest. Consequently, they never exaggerate a trivial event into tragedy.

People differ in their appraisal of stresses and their ability to cope with them. These differences can influence when burnout will occur, how long it will last, and how severe its consequences will be. It is not necessarily objective conditions that cause misery or even happiness, but how we interpret those conditions. An old rabbinical story makes this point very well:

> A man came to the wise rabbi in great distress begging for help. "Rabbi," he said, "I am going out of my mind. With me, my wife, and the six children all living in one little room, there is no space for breathing. The noise and the crowding are making us all crazy. I don't know what to do." "Do you have a goat?" the rabbi asked. "Yes," the man answered. "Bring the goat into the house," said the rabbi. "What do you mean, 'Bring the goat into the house'?" the man asked with great shock. "I've just told you we have no air to breathe as it is." "You want my advice, don't you?" the rabbi asked sternly. "I do, I do," the man replied meekly. He went

home and brought the goat in. A week later the man returned to the rabbi, this time in even greater distress. "Rabbi," he said "life is not worth living. Now, in addition to everything else, we have to deal with this filthy goat. I can't take it anymore." "In that case," said the rabbi, "get the goat out." Next day the man came to the rabbi, kissed his hands and said, "Rabbi, thank you! What a pleasure it is not to have a goat in the house. There's so much air, so much space, and no goat filth. Life is wonderful!"

Self-imposed stresses are subjective even if people perceive them as objective reality. In order to reduce such stresses as overload, conflicting demands, and family commitments, every stress has to be scrutinized to clarify whether it is a real demand or a self-demand, whether it is a "have to" or a "want to." To do that, it is important to recognize the rewards that may be related to the stress. (Being always busy may be related to feeling important. It also is an excuse to get away from other, less desirable activities.)

For example, Susan's mother might like Susan to call her up occasionally, but she puts the demand on herself to call her mother every day. After a while Susan may act as if the "every day" dictum came from her mother. Only after close scrutiny will she realize that this was her own demand. Occasionally we can test whether a demand is real or self-imposed. Thus Susan could cut back the number of calls to her mother from seven to three a week and then wait for the repercussions. When Susan realizes that her mother does not really demand that she call every day, she has to examine what possible rewards she was getting from imposing that demand on herself. It is possible that Susan likes to feel needed, and "having" to call her mother every day makes her feel needed. It is possible that Susan's mother is a good listener and Susan simply enjoys talking to her. It is also possible that given how busy Steve is with his work, Susan has a need to fill her time with demands so she too can be exhausted at the end of the day.

## THE EFFECT OF
## EXPECTATIONS

Expectations about romantic love always exist as a part of most people's belief system. They are most influential when a couple makes a commitment to each other. These expectations can be conscious or unconscious, verbalized or unverbalized, culturally shared or private.

A couple who believed that getting married would give them a paradise on earth, and who then found that the sink got clogged every week and the car wouldn't start on cold mornings, is bound to feel disappointed—in the sink, the car, and the marriage. If a couple's dream is achievable, however, there can be a feeling of euphoria in having a dream come true. There is peace and security in knowing that one has found the holy grail of modern society—a marriage in which the romantic spark is still alive. Unfortunately, euphoria is always temporary, and reality is often less exciting than a dream.

A classic example of this is the couple whose romantic ideal involved being the first in their group to marry, marrying the most attractive person in high school (the homecoming queen, the quarterback), and settling down in a nice suburban ranch home. Once the dream has been achieved and the enjoyment from it exhausted, the couple may feel bored and bitterly disappointed, because achieving the dream, which was supposed to give their life a sense of meaning—forever—has failed to do so.

When romantic expectations are not achieved (even if the reason can clearly be attributed to environmental stress), the feelings of disappointment tend to be directed at the mate and cause the erosion of love and commitment. The disappointment is made more painful when the mate seemed to match a romantic image, thus promising that the ideal love can be realized. In time the positive emotional energy is drained out of the relationship, and gradually love burns out. The experience of burnout, in turn, weakens the couple's love and commitment toward each other. The negative, downward spiral continues until love is dead.

In order to ensure the continuous growth of love and commitment, expectations must be constantly redefined. This happens naturally when change is a part of the couple's romantic ideal and part of their expectations. An example is the couple for whom the ideal relationship is one in which they communicate openly about everything, in which they are committed to each other and to living life to the fullest, believe that change is an opportunity, and feel that the best place to grow is with each other. A relationship like this, in which the romantic ideal is achievable and growth-centered, can get better with time. It can deepen and become more secure (grow "roots"). It can also allow both mates to grow as individuals and as a couple (grow "wings"). That, in turn, will strengthen the couple's love and commitment, creating a positive loop that (at least in theory) can last forever.

## ROOTS AND WINGS

Since I discussed burnout so extensively in Chapter 1 it seems only appropriate to end this chapter with its opposite—"roots and wings." The most profound trait of marriages with roots and wings is that they not only maintain the romantic spark even after many years, but they actually get better with time. The roots symbolize security and mutual trust, a feeling that your mate knows you completely, with all your virtues *and* your faults, and loves you *just the way you are.* The wings symbolize the excitement of personal and spiritual growth, the feeling that together and alone you are getting the most out of yourself and out of life. Lynne says:

> We have been married for nineteen years and through all this time we've been talking nonstop. I can't tell you how many times we've missed an exit on the highway because we were too involved in a conversation. We are both very involved in our careers, but luckily our fields are close enough to understand what the other one is doing, so we can talk about it. Because we have been with each other all these years we understand each other's way of thinking. But since we come from very different backgrounds we are able to provide different perspectives and a challenge that a person in our own field could not provide.
>
> But it's not just talking about work that has improved with time. Everything has gotten better with the years: our sex life, our freedom with each other, our feelings of security, of belonging, and even our financial situation. . . . Given what I see around me with our friends and other people, our marriage is pretty unusual. I worried about it a lot before I got married. This is why I was in no hurry to get married, why I waited so long. But when we met we both knew that this was it. And we were right.

For a happy marriage it is essential that there be *both* roots and wings. When either one is absent, the result can be devastating.

A relationship that has only roots but no wings provides a

sense of security but is most often experienced as boring, stifling, and oppressive. A woman in a traditional marriage says:

> My husband is a good man and a good provider. I know he loves me and the kids and was never interested in other women. I have resigned myself to the fact that we are going to remain married. But there is no spark between us. The marriage is so boring that I find other people to do things with us so I don't have to spend time stuck with just my husband.

On the other hand, relationships that have wings but no roots tend to be rather short-lived. In such relationships both partners develop their own interests, their own circles of friends, and their own leisure-time activities, but they don't bring these interests back to the relationship. Consequently, the bonds that should keep the couple together are loosened. A young professional woman says:

> Eventually I realized that we had absolutely nothing in common. We weren't speaking the same language. We were awake during different times, and our lives were completely separate. We were passing each other like two trains in the night. Sooner or later I knew that one of us just had to bring up the question: What's the point of staying married?

Only relationships with *both* roots *and* wings have the foundation of commitment and security and the growth energy needed for keeping the romantic spark alive. Of course, even when both components are present, they are not always perfectly balanced. At times the commitment is at the center of attention; at other times growth seems more important. Yet overall, there is a sense of balance between the two and an awareness that even if they are not both operating at a particular moment, the potential for both is always present.

## FALLING IN AND OUT OF LOVE

For most people concerned about keeping love alive in their relationship there are two questions of paramount importance: *"What causes burnout?"* and *"How can burnout be avoided?"* My Love and

Burnout Model addresses both of these questions.[24] Everything discussed in this chapter—including the three facets of falling in love, the effects of the environment, and the effect of expectations—are parts of the model and were presented for that reason.

The model describes two paths, leading either to burnout or to roots and wings. The two paths start similarly with a couple in love. What is the difference between a couple that burns out and one that develops roots and wings? If we leave aside the possibility that the burned-out couple has serious emotional problems, we will have to assume that the difference lies in their differently perceived environments.

A stressful environment—or an environment that a couple perceives as stressful—prevents the one couple from making their romantic dream come true. Coping with the stress drains energy and love from the relationship. A supportive environment enables the other couple to grow and become self-actualized. Getting a sense of meaning from the marriage provides the emotional arousal needed for keeping the romantic spark alive.

# CHAPTER 3

# When You Look
# For a Marriage Therapist

Anyone who goes to a psychiatrist needs to have his head examined.

P. T. Barnum

The play *It Was the Lark,* written by the Israeli humorist Ephraim Kishon, takes place twenty years after the events recounted in Shakespeare's *Romeo and Juliet.* Somehow the star-crossed lovers have survived their rendezvous with destiny and settled into middle age. In the beginning of the second act, an overweight, balding Romeo and a querulous, nagging Juliet wake up in their drab apartment. Soon they start arguing, with much exasperation and annoyance, whether it was a nightingale or a lark that they heard on their first night of love. "Definitely a Nightingale!" proclaims Juliet. "A Lark!" Romeo shouts back, adding, "You were always like that! Just to provoke me, just to argue, just to tease! Black? White! Today? Tomorrow! Lark? No, definitely not . . ." "Oi, Momo, you're stubborn! . . . You're stubborn! *A Nightingale!*" retorts Juliet.[1] When they turn their backs toward each other, the silence of the dead stretches across time and bed.

The humor and sadness of the play is derived from the contrast between our sentimental image of the passionate, beautiful lovers and the drab familiarity of their middle-aged selves, their burned-out marriage. It would seem that the playwright is telling us that the only way to make love last forever is to die at the height of passion. Most of us, however, are placed in less dramatic circumstances than Romeo and Juliet; anyway, we prefer to look to places other than a crypt to preserve our love.

Even if marriage burnout is a new concept, the experience it describes is clearly not new. People have fallen in and out of love before, people have gotten married and divorced before, and people have asked for help with problems before. Never before, however, have so many people asked for help from psychotherapists. As Rollo May says, we are "an age of therapy."[2]

With the technological revolution came an ever-increasing reliance on experts and specialists. In the area of human emotions and relationships, psychotherapists are the experts. Many modern couples feel that their parents can't really help them with problems, because their parents' marriage (unlike their own) is based more on commitment than on romantic love. The religious answer they get from a priest or a rabbi (that their union is sacred or at least semi-inviolate because it was blessed by God) does not quite address the problem that love has died.

Not everyone who has marital problems seeks therapy. Some people avoid therapy because they don't believe that it (or anything else for that matter) can help bring back the romantic spark to their relationship. A man who left his wife for another woman after fourteen years of marriage said:

> I don't believe in this notion of "working on a relationship." You didn't have to work at falling in love. When a relationship isn't working, it means that love is not there anymore. It's better to admit that, and the sooner the better.

Other people see in seeking professional help an admission of failure. In addition, they know intuitively that the therapist is going to explain their problems as some kind of pathology. What they also know is that whatever neurotic traits they may have or share are not the primary cause for the disintegration of their marriage.

Clinical psychology, the field most involved in the treatment of marital problems, is defined in the *Dictionary of Behavioral Science* as "a branch of psychology devoted to the study, diagnosis, and treatment of behavior disorders," behaviors defined as "disturbed, abnormal, and deranged."[3] Clinical psychologists are trained to approach problems as a kind of disease, an abnormality. Some see marital problems as caused by the pathology of the individual, others see them as caused by dysfunctional patterns in the couple. One way or another some abnormality is identified. Abnormality implies uniqueness (abnormal in the sense of "not normal, not typical"). This assumption of the unique quality of marital unhappiness is perfectly expressed in Leo Tolstoy's epigraph to *Anna Karenina:* "All happy families are alike, but an unhappy family is unhappy after its own fashion." Indeed, the quote is a favorite among family therapists. The disease model of clinical psychology is appropriate in the case of seriously maladjusted individuals. The unique abnormality of a particular couple, however, can hardly account for the fact that over 50 percent of all marriages end in divorce, and that the majority of the rest have had at some point problems serious enough to make the partners consider divorce.[4]

## THE THREE MAIN APPROACHES TO MARITAL THERAPY

Marital therapy began as a professional specialty in the United States in the thirties, but only after World War II, with the dramatic increase in the number of divorces among young couples, did it start to grow rapidly. In recent years, with the growing acceptance of therapy as a way to address couples' problems, with the growing numbers of troubled marriages, and with the pressure to provide cheaper and shorter therapy, couples' therapy has been developing at an exponential rate.

Until the development of family therapy, therapists avoided and discouraged contact with their patients' mates. Therapy was based on the premise that psychological problems arise from unhealthy interactions with people close to the patient, and can best be treated by an intense relationship with a therapist. Seeing each mate separately continued to be the most common practice of marriage therapy for thirty years. It wasn't until the late sixties that the practice of seeing both mates together in joint therapy was established. Today most marriage therapists insist on seeing a couple together during some of the sessions or during a certain part of each session.

There are three major approaches to marital therapy—the psychoanalytic, the behavioral, and the systems approach.[5] If you and your mate are having a marital problem, and if you decide to seek therapy, these are the three basic styles of therapy you are likely to encounter.

### A PSYCHOANALYST

Sigmund Freud originated the idea of psychoanalysis; his followers expanded it in theory and application. Psychoanalysis emphasizes the role of innate drives, childhood experiences, and unconscious forces.[6]

In the context of psychoanalysis, the therapist provides for the patient a screen on which to project unresolved, and largely unconscious, childhood issues that are being replayed in the patient's adult life. The assumption is that the patient will "transfer" these past emotional attachments to the psychoanalyst because of a "repetition compulsion" in which the analyst becomes a substitute for the parental figure. Once a repetition compulsion has been worked through, once these unconscious processes become accessible to the conscious mind, once the connection between the present and the past is comprehended by the patient and the transference is resolved, therapy is over.

For example, if a man was abandoned by his parents as a baby, he is likely to have a compulsion to repeat the abandonment scenario by unconsciously alienating every woman who falls in love with him. In the therapy, this man will transfer his feelings toward his parents to the therapist—either by perceiving the therapist as rejecting or else by doing things that will force the therapist to respond in a way that can be interpreted as rejecting (for example, missing appointments without notice).

Unlike the women in this man's life, the therapist will understand the unconscious origin of his behavior and will point it out. When it becomes clear to the man that his perception of the therapist is a result of his own projections, he can deal directly with the pain and resentment he still harbors toward his parents. After these old feelings are resolved, he will be free to have healthy interpersonal relationships. Psychoanalysts see any other approach to this man's problem as treatment of the symptoms rather than treatment of the underlying cause.

With the popularization of psychoanalytic ideas in the mass media, people have absorbed much of the superficial material of psychoanalysis and have started using it to explain their own and other people's behavior. A woman may accuse a man of replaying with her his unresolved hostility toward his mother. Shifting the focus from a problem within the relationship to a problem with him makes the man the subject of blame and frees the woman from responsibility for the role she plays in the relationship.

It should be clear from everything said so far that for orthodox psychoanalysts the idea of working with couples together in joint therapy is unacceptable. They believe that transference, the most important element in therapy, is diluted in the presence of another person. As long as the unconscious issues that spouses bring into the marriage are not dealt with through transference, "real" improvement is impossible. Thus, when a couple has marital problems, the mate suffering more pain, or the one identified as having a psychological problem (in both cases most often the wife), is sent for individual therapy. By committing herself to therapy such a woman concedes that the marital problems are her fault.

Psychoanalytically oriented *marriage* therapists have had to make a major adjustment in order to work with couples. Most of them, however, still prefer individual therapy, and some manage to do some individual work even within the context of couple therapy. They emphasize unresolved childhood conflicts and unconscious motivations in the choice of marriage partners and in the maintenance of unhappy and destructive marriages. Mates are seen as driven by unconscious forces to create their life circumstances, including their marital problems. Conflicts between mates are seen as a reenactment, at a deeper level, of the unconscious conflicts within each mate.[7]

A psychoanalyst to whom you go for help with a marital problem is likely to assume that you chose your mate in order to gratify some unconscious needs that originated in your early childhood. Your choice will also be seen as influenced by some important similarity between your mate and the parent with whom you formed your primary childhood attachment. The therapist will presuppose that your marital problems are the result of unresolved conflicts in your family of origin that are unconsciously replayed in (or transferred to) your marriage. The therapy is likely to be very long because it is aimed at bringing all these unresolved conflicts into consciousness. Only after that will you be able to deal with your mate in a healthy and mature way, at which point you and your marriage will be cured (or else you will be cured and decide to get a divorce).

Psychoanalysis's contributions to marriage therapy include its emphasis on the power of childhood experiences and unconscious motivations in what would otherwise seem like irrational behavior. (Why does one stay in a victimizing relationship or push lovers to the point where they have no recourse but to leave?) Another major contribution has been the emphasis on the role unconscious motivations play in the choice of a mate and the creation of a marriage. Psychoanalysts believe that people are driven to create their life circumstances in order to satisfy some important psychological needs.

The main objection raised by opponents of psychoanalysis, in addition to its length and relative ineffectiveness with concrete symptoms, has been its tendency to attribute too much importance to early childhood experiences and not enough importance to the current environment. Other criticisms have been directed at the tendency to attribute too much power to the unconscious (thus diminishing the person's responsibility) and not enough power to the conscious mind, to spiritual needs, and to future goals; the tendency to assume excessive pathology (especially in women); and the tendency to attribute the reason for the suffering to the person in pain. Behaviorism responds to many of these criticisms.

### A BEHAVIORIST

Behaviorism focuses on overt behavior. Pathological behavior is seen as caused by learning and reinforcement. Behavior therapy specializes in methods of changing maladaptive habits. Therapists are not concerned with unconscious, unresolved conflicts because they see both the causes of problems and their solutions in the current environment. Behaviorism takes people's problems at face value. Therefore, if you choose a behavior therapist, you will be asked what *you* consider the problem to be. The therapist will then approach the problem as you defined it. A behaviorist is not likely to assume, as a psychoanalyst typically does, that since the roots of your problem are unconscious, you don't understand your "real" problem.

If, for example, your problem is a morbid fear of being touched by a person of the opposite sex, the behavior therapist will not spend time reliving the childhood trauma that created the fear, but will focus directly on relieving your immediate fear. You will be asked to make a list of all the activities relating to being touched that scare you and rank them in the order of the fear that they raise, from least to most scary. At the bottom of the list you may mention imagining a handshake with a person of the opposite sex; at the top, making love. Next the therapist will teach you to relax with the help of special relaxation exercises, as well as imagery of pleasant places and relaxing activities (lying in the sun on a white sandy beach or sipping a delicious milkshake).

Once you have learned to relax, the therapist will ask you, while in a state of complete relaxation, to imagine the item at the bottom of your list. If your relaxation is disrupted, the therapist will return you to the relaxation training. When you are able to remain relaxed even while imagining the item at the bottom of the list, you will be instructed to imagine the next item. This process of "desensitization" will continue until you are able to imagine the most scary items on the list without panicking. Actual physical contact is the final proof that your fear is gone and that the therapy is finished.

Behavioral marriage therapists assume that in every social interaction people try to maximize their rewards and minimize their costs. Happy marriages are characterized by a maximum of rewards for both mates. Problems in marriage occur when mates give few rewards to each other or make the costs of the relationship excessive. Problems also crop up when there is an imbalance, when one spouse is reaping most of the rewards while the other is paying most of the costs, or else when spouses use coercion to get the rewards they want. Based on this set of assumptions, the behavior therapist's goal is to teach couples how to provide each other with maximum rewards at a minimal cost. In order to do that, the therapist asks each spouse to state explicitly what he or she would like to receive from the other, and then helps the couple reach an equitable exchange of these desired behaviors or rewards.[8] An example will clarify this process.

One of the first attempts to apply behavioral principles to couples was made in 1969 by Richard B. Stuart.[9] Dr. Stuart treated four couples who were in the divorce court for similar reasons—the husband wanted more sex and the wife wanted more talking. The therapy consisted of helping each couple negotiate a contract in which the husband could earn a poker chip for every fifteen minutes of dialogue. When the husband earned eight poker chips, he could exchange them for sexual intercourse. As expected, the rate of talking went up significantly, as did the rate of sexual intercourse. After a few sessions, none of the couples wanted to continue with divorce proceedings.

More recent examples of the behavioral approach tend to be more sophisticated. An exchange may involve sexual activities that are pleasurable to each mate (one evening devoted completely to satisfying the sexual needs and wants of one mate; another evening devoted entirely to satisfying the other mate) rather than exchanging sex for talk. Yet the techniques are still aimed at helping mates learn more productive and positive means of effecting desired behavior changes in one another: how to negotiate fair exchange contracts and how to use rewards to modify each other's behavior instead of punishment or coercion.

The contracts that therapists help couples negotiate are very often written, so they can be easily renegotiated and modified. Placed in a visible location, they can serve as a constant reminder and reference. The two major forms of contract in use are *quid pro quo* and *good faith*.

In the quid pro quo (or tit-for-tat) contract, the desired changes of both mates are cross-linked so that if you change your behavior, your mate will also change in the requested way. For example, if Ruth wants David to spend more time talking with her and he wants her to spend more time with his colleagues, a quid pro quo contract might be written as follows: If David spends an hour talking to Ruth, Ruth will spend an hour with David's colleagues. In this contract, mates' behavior changes are contingent on one another. If you do not fulfill your part of the contract, your spouse is under no obligation to change, and vice-versa. The problem with this kind of contract is that mates can get into a "you go first" game. The good-faith contract is written so that a mate who engages in the desired behavior receives a positive reinforcer independent of what the other mate does. In the example above, it may be agreed that if David talks with Ruth for half an hour, he can choose which movie they are going to watch that week. In such a contract there is no benefit in waiting for the other to change first.[10]

The discussion of the two forms of contracts demonstrates the extent to which behaviorists take people's problems at face value and their marriages as straightforward business propositions. The behavioral marriage therapist assumes that couples know what their problems are. Therapy is indeed effective when that is the case. Problems arise in those cases where the psychoanalytic approach seems more applicable, when couples are not sure what their problems are.

Since behaviorists, unlike psychoanalysts, deal with observable behaviors, they can measure their effectiveness. Research indicates that behaviorists have been most successful when treating problems that are concrete and observable, such as premature ejaculation in a man or inability to reach orgasm in a woman. They have been less successful in cases where the couple's problems could not be reduced to an observable symptom.

The best way to demonstrate the difference between the approaches of a behaviorist and a psychoanalyst is to imagine a couple going to both for help. Ken (age 51) and Margaret (age 50) have been married for twenty-five years and have four grown children. Ken is a successful businessman, Margaret a housewife with many outside interests. Both of them are very attractive and elegantly dressed, and both feel pleased with their lot in life—except for the marriage, which is not working. They aren't communicating, and they feel frustrated and angry with each other. The only time they are able to express this anger, however, is when they drink too much alcohol, which they have been doing regularly.

The psychoanalytically oriented marriage therapist to whom Margaret goes for help (because she is more upset than Ken is about the fact that the marriage is not working and because her drinking is more of a problem) decides to see each one of them in therapy alone. He explains to them that their individual problems have to be resolved before they can benefit from joint therapy.

In Margaret's individual therapy, it comes out that her childhood had been traumatized by her father's alcoholism. When sober he was kind and loving, when drunk abusive and violent. The unpredictability of her father's behavior and the fear caused by his violent outbursts caused in Margaret a deep-seated distrust of men and an acute sense of her own powerlessness. Margaret's mother accommodated herself to the father's drinking in an attempt to gain some measure of stability in the family's life. She "mothered" him when drunk and worked hard to hide his drinking and to maintain a normal household where meals were served regularly and as much order as possible was maintained.

In Ken's therapy, it comes out that his childhood had been traumatized by his father's alcoholism and his mother's abandonment when he was very young. Ken and the other children were reared by an aunt who came to the house several times a week but who could not handle either the father's drinking or the household chores. She didn't cook regular meals, and the house was always a mess. Being the oldest son, Ken often had to get his father from bars when he was too drunk to get home by himself.

Because of her childhood experiences, Margaret was looking for a husband with whom she could reenact her childhood trauma of life with an alcoholic father. Because of his childhood experiences, Ken was looking for a wife with whom he could reenact his childhood trauma of abandonment by his mother. Ken and Margaret found in each other exactly what they were looking for.

For the psychoanalyst, the goal of therapy is to help Ken and Margaret realize how each one of them actively contributed to their marital problems by reenacting their childhood traumas in their marriage. Once this core issue is made conscious, the therapist can help Ken and Margaret work through their anger and resentment toward their parents. Only after these childhood issues are resolved in individual therapy can Margaret and Ken start dealing with each other as mature adults.

The behavior therapist wants Ken and Margaret to come to therapy together, since they define their problem as marital. From the start they are asked, directly, what their problem is. When they both say that there is "no communication" between them, the therapist wants to know what aspect of communication, exactly, is not working—the verbal, the sexual, or something else. Ken and Margaret identify their sexual communication as the main problem. Ken says that they don't have enough sex, that Margaret never initiates physical contact between them, that he feels frustrated and sexually deprived. Margaret says she can't be sexual in a vacuum. When there is no communication between them for days, when he never as much as touches her hand, how can he expect her all of a sudden to be sexual?

For the behaviorist, the goal of therapy is straightforward—to help Ken and Margaret improve their sexual communication. To accomplish this, he first asks them to make two lists: one of sexual activities they find most anxiety-provoking, the other of activities they find most enjoyable and relaxing.

During therapy Ken and Margaret are taught to relax by imagining items from the top of their second list. Next they are prescribed a treatment schedule at the start of which sexual intercourse will be forbidden. They are instructed to find time that is completely free of interruptions and take turns performing certain tasks. The first tasks are relaxing and nonthreatening sexually. Next they are instructed to give each other a half-hour-long sensual massage, the way they would like to get it. Once they learn in this way what each likes, they are instructed in the following session to give each other a massage the way the other likes it. In their meetings with the therapist, they discuss the experience: what was pleasurable, what was not, what was easy, what was difficult. They are asked what gives them pleasure and are encouraged to talk about their sexual desires and fantasies. After they are able to relax and enjoy touching each other sensually, the sessions gradually progress from less to more daring and anxiety-provoking foreplay in which Ken and Margaret take turns giving each other pleasure, the way they now know the other likes pleasure to be given. Only after this groundwork has been accomplished successfully are they permitted to make love. According to behavior therapists, this kind of approach, if done gradually and fairly (quid pro quo), can not only solve Ken and Margaret's sexual problem, but also improve their verbal communication and the overall quality of their relationship. This is done in brief therapy without ever addressing Ken and Margaret's childhood traumas or unconscious motivations.

As we can see, the psychoanalyst and the behaviorist make very different assumptions about the essence of human nature. Since for the psychoanalyst that essence is expressed in unconscious processes triggered by childhood experiences, these processes are the focus of therapy. Since for the behaviorist that essence is expressed in overt behavior, overt behavior is the focus of therapy. In both cases, when a couple comes for help, help is given in accordance with the therapist's theoretical perspective. This perspective may have little or nothing to do with the couple's own perspective. When couples give themselves over to "experts" in the hope of saving their love, they force their relationship to fit the therapist's perspective. More often than not, however, because they are focusing on each other in a new and different way, because they are trying to change old patterns of behavior, and because they believe that the therapy is going to improve things, some improvement almost always takes place.

Both psychoanalysis and behavior therapy were originally developed to treat troubled individuals. Only much later were they applied to the treatment of couples, and their basic approach to couples isn't much different from their approach to individuals—both assume an underlying individual pathology in couples' problems. Systems therapy, on the other hand, originated directly from work with troubled couples and families. This difference in origin is just one of the differences between the systems approach and the other two approaches.

## A SYSTEMS THERAPIST

If you and your spouse come to the office of a systems-oriented family therapist, your experience will be very different from your experience with either a behaviorist or with a psychoanalyst. The focus (and with it the focus of blame) is not on you or your mate, but rather on the new system the two of you have created during the time you have been together, a system that has life of its own and that is more than the sum of its parts. It is assumed that a change in one part of the system (or one mate) invariably causes change in the other part (or mate), which then causes change in the first part, and so on. For example, anger in one of you may cause a defensive withdrawal in the other, which increases the anger of the first, which increases the withdrawal of the second, which may lead to violent behavior in the first, which may make the second resentfully close off all attempts at communication.

While the psychoanalyst sees causes of events as linear (i.e., problems in the present are caused by events in the past), for the systems therapist causes of events are circular. Each spouse's behavior is seen at one and the same time as both a response to and the trigger for the other spouse's behavior. If you complain to the therapist about something obnoxious your mate has done, the therapist is likely to try to find out what preceded that event (whether there was something you did to provoke that behavior) and what followed it (what you did in response).[11]

The systems therapist assumes that between adults in a marital system there is no totally passive, victimlike position. This perspective prevents attaching blame to one person because both mates are seen as contributing to every interaction. Although in certain circumstances one mate *appears* the victim and the other the abuser, this is an "optical illusion" derived from an arbitrary designation by the couple as to who is the actor and who is the reactor. The therapist tries to change that designation. (One way to do that is to suggest that the victim is getting something from the role, such as being good.) To a systems therapist all relationships are structured with time into stable social systems that tend to resist change. Consistent patterns of interaction become the rules that govern the system. If you and your spouse are having problems, the therapist will assume that your interactions as a couple consist of some dysfunctional patterns. The therapist's goal will be to change those destructive patterns and bring your marriage system to a healthy state of balance.

A common example of such a dysfunctional pattern is the situation in which the husband sees his wife as demanding and intrusive while the wife sees her husband as cold and distant. The wife complains to her husband, but rather than making him spend more time with her and express more affection, her complaints win her the title of a "nag." He withdraws. She nags more. He withdraws even further. When such a dysfunctional pattern is operating, no one's needs are met. Therefore, the systems therapist will try to change the pattern. The therapist assumes that the way in which a sequence of events is described and understood results from arbitrary agreements by the mates. Does he withdraw because she nags (the way the couple describes it), or does she nag because he withdraws? A change in the description of this sequence breaks stereotypes and may radically alter rules of interaction and family myths.

One school of systems therapy uses paradoxical instructions. Rather than provoke the resistance to change of the system, the therapist uses the resistance as part of the therapeutic process, by prescribing the symptom. For example, the wife may be told that she is not nagging enough. She should nag much more and with greater vim and vigor. The husband may be told that he doesn't withdraw far enough. He should leave the house altogether. The assumption is that both of them will realize the absurdity of the suggestion and, disobeying the therapist's instructions, will stop the dysfunctional behavior altogether. Another systems therapist may instruct the couple that from that day on the husband is to ask for everything he previously received from his wife without asking (his meals, clean clothes, etc.). This is expected to change the rules governing the marriage. Once the rules are changed, or the rules about who makes the rules are changed, the dysfunctional pattern will be broken, and the couple's problem solved.

When Ken and Margaret come to the office of a systems therapist, they come with their four children, because the therapist wants to see the whole family system in operation. Observing the verbal and nonverbal interactions among the family members in the therapy room (who sits where, who says what to whom), the therapist notices certain patterns of interaction: Margaret mediates between the children and Ken. The children are treating Margaret as an equal, and Ken as distant and unapproachable. Margaret treats Ken with resentment. Ken's response is to withdraw. Margaret's response to his withdrawal is to get even more resentful. The therapist concludes that Ken is too isolated from the family, the cross-generational bond between Margaret and the children is too strong, and the marital bond between Ken and Margaret is too weak.

In order to reshape this dysfunctional family system into a healthier system, the therapist strives to emphasize the generational gap between Margaret and the children so she is treated as a parent and not as a sibling, improve the relationship between Ken and the children, and strengthen the marital bond. To accomplish this the therapist may suggest that Margaret be given control of a part of the family's money, that Ken spend time alone with the children, and that Ken and Margaret find an activity that they both find exciting and do it together. Each one of these changes is likely to change a dysfunctional pattern of interaction in the family. When several changes take place at the same time, their effect is likely to be multiplied and result in a more healthy and balanced family structure.

## THE PROBLEM WITH ALL THREE APPROACHES TO MARITAL THERAPY AND THE CONTRIBUTION OF LOGOTHERAPY

Even in this oversimplified description of the three major approaches to marital therapy, it is clear that each approach has certain advantages and certain disadvantages. Most marriage therapists use some combination of all three approaches while working with couples. Typically, a therapist explains the underlying dynamics of the couple's issues from a psychoanalytic perspective, describes what needs to be done to reverse negative patterns from a systems perspective, and uses behavioral techniques when appropriate.

In spite of the many differences among them, as clinical psychologists, marriage therapists all too often explain the causes for a couple's problems in terms of a disease or an abnormality. This is true whether they focus on abnormalities in the individual mates or whether they focus on dysfunctional patterns in the couple. The

disease model denies the situational context of the couple's problems, which includes, in addition to such stresses as illness, financial
difficulties, and demanding work, all the cultural trends discussed
earlier—the high rates of divorce, the breakup of the extended
family, and the changing roles of men and women. It also includes
the culturally sanctioned emphasis on romantic love as the most
important basis for marriage and the unrealistic expectations a belief in romantic love can generate.

A focus on pathology, by definition, implies a relative disregard for the healthy parts of the couple's relationship. This fact
was dramatically demonstrated in a recent conference for family
therapists presented by one of this country's leading medical
schools. The most important and exciting feature of the conference
was the showing of a series of videotapes made during actual therapy sessions. Four of the country's best-known family therapists
were videotaped treating the same couple. The therapists were able
to demonstrate their different therapeutic styles in individual lec-
ture sessions, during which they could stop the video presentation
at any point and comment on a particular intervention.

In a final review session with the two organizers of the conference, the couple was asked to evaluate each of the four therapists
and to explain what they had gained from each therapeutic intervention. The couple was very generous in their compliments to the
four therapists and described in great length and detail the insights
they gained from each one of them. In closing, the interviewer
asked if there was anything that they found missing, something that
they wish had been discussed but was not, something missed by all
the therapists. The couple answered without a moment's hesitation,
"No one asked us whether or why we love each other. No one
asked what was good about our relationship, what it was that kept
us together for ten years." The reason no one asked the couple
about love is quite obvious. They were having problems, which is
what brought them into therapy. All four of the therapists saw their
goal as alleviating those problems; consequently, problems were
the focus of their attention. It should be noted, however, that both
the man and the woman were attractive, articulate, and professionally successful individuals. What is even more important, they
behaved lovingly toward each other and were committed to the
relationship. These facts were never brought up in therapy.

Love is rarely the focus of family therapy, whether the therapy is performed by a psychoanalyst, a behaviorist, or a systems therapist. The reason is the same in each case: Since the couple presents problems, problems are the focus of therapy. When love does come up, it is addressed as a secondary issue. For couples who base their marriages on romantic love, however, love *is* a primary issue. Couples who are taught by the prevailing cultural values to believe in romantic love are trying to work out in their marriages an issue of major significance. They are looking for love to give life a sense of meaning. When they fail, they are devastated. This is why they go to a "marriage expert" for help, but the therapist, who is also socialized to believe in the same romantic ideology, doesn't see the problem of the failure of love for what it is.

Helping the individual find meaning in life is a major focus of treatment in the existential school of psychotherapy. It is *the* major focus in one of its branches, called *logotherapy.*

Victor Frankl, who developed logotherapy (Logos = meaning in Greek), describes it as focused on "the meaning of human existence as well as on man's search for such a meaning." According to Frankl, the striving to find meaning in one's life is the primary motivational force in man. He quotes a public opinion poll showing that 89 percent of the thousands of people polled thought that man needs "something" to live for. Logotherapy emphasizes the power of values, of expectations, of choices. Frankl denies that "one's search for meaning . . . is derived from, or results in, any disease. . . . A man's concern, even his despair, over the worthwhileness of life is a *spiritual distress* but by no means a *mental disease.*"[12]

On the basis of his experiences as a surviver of a Nazi concentration camp, Frankl argues that there is nothing in the world that can so effectively help one to survive even the worst conditions as the knowledge that there is a meaning in one's life. Thus, logotherapy regards its "assignment as that of assisting the patient to find meaning in his life."[13]

Frankl did not apply logotherapy to work with couples. For one thing, he saw the search for meaning as a unique and specific task that must be accomplished by each individual alone. In addition, he did not see romantic love as the primary solution to the existential dilemma, but rather as one of the experiences by which people can discover meaning in their life. Similar reasons explain why other branches of existential psychotherapy have not been applied to work with couples.[14]

## A FOCUS ON LOVE IN THE TREATMENT OF MARRIAGE BURNOUT

When a couple comes to therapy for the first time, they usually look grim and tense. Each mate carries a mental list of all the "Terrible Things" that the other one is doing, or has done, throughout their marriage. If we drew two balloons above their heads to indicate what they were thinking, both balloons would show them presenting the "Crime List" to a shocked and dismayed therapist who is leaping to their side, where together they will work to change the unreasonable (and stubborn) mate. Instead, the questions that I ask are: What attracted you to each other when you first met? What attracted you to this inconsiderate, cold, and uncaring man? What attracted you to this demanding, hysterical, and unsympathetic woman? The questions have an almost magical effect. Faces relax, and smiles replace angry looks as they tell me how they fell in love with each other. Dona describes her first meeting with Andrew and what made her fall in love with him:

> Andrew lived next door to me. When I got mad at my previous boyfriend, I invited him to a party. He was a very beautiful person and had many beautiful qualities, and I fell in love with him. . . . He was sort of the strong, silent type, you know. . . . He was pretty decisive about where he wanted to go. He usually went where he wanted to, and I liked that. He was a good lover, and he was nice looking. . . . He is a very elegant man and tidy. His image of himself is important, so he always looked good. He wasn't pennypinching; he would spend money on dinner and stuff like that, which I enjoyed. I thought that chemically we had a lot in common. . . . I mean, I fell in love with him. You can't explain why you fall in love with somebody; it's a ridiculous thing . . .

When I asked Andrew how he fell in love with Dona, he said:

> We were next-door neighbors. I remember bumping into her a couple of times at the mailbox, which was next door. And then she invited me to a party. . . . She seemed quite professional. At least that's the overriding term one would use. . . . I thought she was attractive . . . and she was quite friendly, not difficult to get to know.

. . . And she exhibited some emotional dependency, which was also very attractive to me . . .

One of my favorite exercises in workshops on marriage burnout is to ask participants what attracted them to their mates initially and then ask them what the three most stressful aspects of their relationship are. In every single case, of the hundreds of people who have participated in these workshops, there was a direct relationship between the original attraction and the current stresses. If you stop for a minute to consider what attracted you to your mate, and then consider what it is about your mate that gives you most trouble, you are bound to discover that the two are closely related.

Most often it is the things that initially attract people to each other that eventually cause their burnout. A man who is attracted to a woman because of her strength and energy says, when he burns out, that she is controlling and hysterical. A woman is attracted to a man because he is generous with his money. When she burns out he is a spendthrift. Dona fell in love with Andrew because he was the strong silent type. She burned out because he was controlling and didn't know how to communicate. Andrew fell in love with Dona because she was a competent professional woman. He burned out because she was manipulative and too involved in her career. Dona described her irritations with Andrew:

We were not building something together. We were just always going off in separate directions. There was no couple. There was no bond. . . . Whenever we would try to discuss something, I would get violently angry with him because I couldn't get through. . . . He is always, I think, protecting himself from being controlled. So if I ask him to do something, I've got to think how can I ask him to do it? I can't be direct. I've got to think. And it's exhausting. And what he began to detect in me is that I was manipulating, which I really was, because I could never say to him I'd like you to do such-and-such, because his response would be: Oh yeah? You know, something like that. . . . And his way with money is not my way either. He has no budget. He doesn't know—he's got a business but doesn't know what anything costs him. . . . He doesn't take the trouble. It makes me feel insecure . . .

Andrew, describing his side of the story, said:

> I have a great deal of respect for her professional qualities and always will. On the other hand, what I like in people and admire in people is to be well rounded and do more than one thing, which is why I've been willing to take a crack at this and a crack at that. Dona will never do that. Ever. There comes a point where, you know, the good news turns to bad news. . . . I think she found me unstable . . .

And on the issue of control Andrew said:

> She is very . . . manipulative, maybe a little bit too strong, but she was always trying to get me to do something. Most of the friction was because she wanted to do something and wanted me to go along, when I was perfectly content to sit at home, or I wanted to go do my own thing. . . . It got to the point where she realized that she couldn't control me . . .

Because of the strong connection between the things that attract and the things that cause burnout, addressing the original attraction can serve an important diagnostic purpose. After hearing from a couple what attracted them to each other, it is quite easy to predict the things about each other that will give them the greatest difficulty.

For people who believe in romantic love, the things that attract and the things that distress are both reflections of an existential search. They are related to an internal image of the ideal life in which one's fears of isolation will be removed and one's uniqueness cherished. When a love relationship fails to fulfill this ideal image, the pain and rage focus naturally on those aspects in the mate that caused the most acute disappointment. In other words, while the attraction represents the existential hope, the stress represents its disappointment. The things that attract don't *always* become the things that distress. They do so in those cases in which romantic love has failed to fulfill people's expectations.

When mates see how they themselves desired the things they now find so objectionable about each other, they realize their own role in shaping their relationship and their power to affect it. When a stress that has been labeled "a problem caused by my spouse" is relabeled "a frustrated hope" or "a blocked expectation," it does not seem quite as overwhelming. This is especially true when the problem caused by the spouse is seen as related to the very thing that made him or her so desirable initially, because, while the spouse's personality is not in our control, our own hopes, dreams, and romantic goals are—at least to a certain degree. (The degree of control increases with the increased awareness of the internal workings of our minds.) Relabeling stresses as frustrated hopes reduces helplessness and hopelessness, which, as we know, are the hallmarks of burnout.

The search for meaning through romantic love can take very different forms for different people, or during different periods of life. Yet the dreams a couple had at the beginning of their relationship can continue to play an important role in their lives for years after. I had a demonstration of that in my work with a couple introduced earlier in this chapter.

Ken and Margaret came to see me because they felt burned out in their marriage and were seriously contemplating divorce. Margaret's main complaint was that Ken was always so involved in his work and that he was never available to her, even during her times of greatest need. "I don't see the reason for staying married," she said. "I am alone all the time anyway." Ken, while agreeing that he might have been too involved in his work in the past, still insisted that things were changing, that he wanted to be closer to Margaret but felt rejected by her, both emotionally and sexually.

When I asked Ken and Margaret about their original attraction to each other and their hopes for the marriage, I discovered that in addition to being attracted to each other's looks, Ken was attracted to Margaret's warmth, and she was attracted to his strength. Since both came from very poor and unstable family backgrounds, their dream was to be financially secure and have a comfortable, warm, and stable home. During their twenty-five years of marriage they made their dream come true. They were very comfortable financially, had a beautiful home, a lot of "nice things," and a close-knit, stable family.

But working to achieve the dream was not easy. It required a lot of hard work from both of them: for Ken in his job, for Margaret at home. Both felt that they had put more into the marriage than they had gotten back from it. My own sense was that Ken and Margaret were suffering from the fact that now that their dream had come true, they felt that their lives were empty, but instead of attributing their sense of disappointment and emptiness to an "existential crisis" (which is to say a crisis concerning lack of meaning in life), they attributed it to each other.

I asked Ken and Margaret what would be their one wish if they met a good fairy that was able to fulfill any wish. Ken's response was, "I would like Margaret to love me." Margaret said, "I want to have a wild, crazy, passionate love affair with Ken." What these two people, who were on their way to the divorce court, wanted more than anything else was a romantic relationship—not with a fantasy stranger, but *with each other.* It would probably come as no surprise that Ken's and Margaret's wishes were related to what they experienced as most lacking about each other. Ken complained that Margaret was cold and rejecting. ("She never comes and gives *me* a kiss or a hug spontaneously.") Margaret complained that Ken was doing things without consulting her, and seemed much more interested in his work than he was in her. ("He never asks my opinion about anything, and is always much more interested in spending time discussing a business deal than he is in spending time with me.")

Predictably, their greatest stresses were related to what Ken and Margaret found most attractive about each other when they first fell in love. In those early days he loved her warmth and sociability, and she loved his strength and stability. Now she was too sociable (toward others) and he was too strong and stable. Once they became aware of the relationship between what they found most difficult and what they found most attractive about each other, as well as between their greatest stresses and their frustrated hopes, and once they became aware that they had the same romantic dream, making that dream come true became the focus of all their efforts. Once, when trying to explain how important romantic love was for her, Margaret said, "Finding a love like that (like the love I have been dreaming about and hoping for) is like finding God."

During my work with Ken and Margaret, all the information presented earlier about them came out. Like most other couples therapists, I am using elements from all three major approaches to marital therapy in my work. Yet what Ken and Margaret demonstrate is the powerful effect a search for meaning can have on a marriage above and beyond the effects of all the variables addressed by the clinical approaches.

There is one more field of psychology that in my opinion has great relevance to couples' therapy, even though, to the best of my knowledge, it has never been used for that purpose—social psychology.

## THE CONTRIBUTION OF SOCIAL PSYCHOLOGY: TWO DIFFERENT EXPLANATIONS

Social psychology is the scientific field that seeks to comprehend the nature and causes of individual behavior in social situations. The situational context of problems, which is underemphasized in clinical psychology, is overemphasized in social psychology. Social psychologists are not therapists and are not concerned with treatment, but rather with understanding the situations that shape the behavior of individuals toward each other.[15] In the case of marital problems, the question for a social psychologist is: What are the situations that cause problems for all couples? A rather different question is asked by a family therapist: What are the unique problems presented by this couple? The first question emphasizes the shared aspects of marital problems; the second question emphasizes the unique aspects and thus fosters the misconception termed earlier the "fallacy of uniqueness."

For a social psychologist, one of the most effective ways to help couples is to let them discover, with the help of other couples, the fallacy of their perceived uniqueness. When I run such couples' groups I ask participants to describe their expectations of their relationships, their major stresses, and the ways they cope. During this process couples inevitably discover how universal both their hopes and stresses are. Realizing the universality of their experience helps break the fallacy of perceived uniqueness. This, as we know, reduces guilt and blame and frees emotional energy for more positive coping.

We are active participants in creating the world we experience. During our interactions with the environment we constantly form impressions and explanations for events we observe. In social-psychological terms we are "making attributions" for these events. The attributions different people make, even for the same event, can vary widely.

Seeing a man slip and fall, for example, can be attributed to all sorts of causes: to the slipperiness of the ground, to the slipperiness of his new shoes, to the man's innate clumsiness, to absent-mindedness, to a state of physical exhaustion, or to intention—falling on purpose to amuse a child. When the focus of the explanation is on the environment, the attribution is called *situational* (e.g., the man slipped because of the slippery ground); when the focus of the explanation is on something in the person, the attribution is called *dispositional* (e.g., the man slipped because he is clumsy).

People all too often explain their own and other people's behavior in dispositional terms. For example, when they experience certain feelings and physical symptoms in response to a jealousy-triggering situation (such as their mate having a love affair), they say, "The reason I am experiencing this jealous reaction is because I am a jealous person." Another person, given the exact same set of circumstances, could say, "The reason I am feeling jealous is because my lover is going to bed with someone else."

The interesting thing is that both those who define themselves as jealous and those who define themselves as nonjealous actually experience jealousy very similarly in terms of both physical and emotional symptoms, and in similar situations, when there is a perceived threat to a valued romantic relationship.[16] The difference between dispositional attributions and situational attributions is not semantic. It has far-reaching implications for the individual making the attribution or about whom the attribution is made. Individuals making dispositional attributions are explaining events by the fact that they are "those kind of people." That explanation puts them in what social psychologist Philip Zimbardo calls "a prison of their own mind," a mental prison from which there is no way out.[17]

The person who wants to be a lawyer but does not apply to law school because he or she is shy has created a self-made prison of the mind. The person who marries someone whose only redeeming quality is faithfulness, because he or she is jealous, has created a self-made prison of the mind. The couple that experiences problems, and is convinced that these problems are the result of each other's innate personality characteristics, is also creating a mental prison. The lists of "Terrible Things" mates keep about each other help keep them in these mental prisons. Because they assume that "they are the way they are, and that's all there is to it," people who are making dispositional attributions are not very motivated to change.

Individuals who make situational self-attribution, on the other hand, are explaining events by the fact that they are reacting "to the particular situation," which means that in another situation they might react very differently. For example, such people may note that they are nervous in front of large audiences, feel excluded when their mate is flirting with a good-looking stranger, or feel different since the three children came along. Such people are not very likely to explain their response by the fact that they are "those kind of people" and "nothing can be done about it." They are much more likely to see their response as caused by a particular stressful situation and, consequently, to focus their efforts on changing that situation. Rather than accepting the situation as a given, such people actively seek to improve their lives and their relationships by changing the situation.

In my work with burned-out couples, a very important goal is to help mates make the transition from dispositional to situational attributions. Typically, marital problems are defined dispositionally: "He is a cold, closed person. He is simply incapable of communicating his feelings." "She is insatiable in her demands; nothing I ever do is enough for her." In response, I typically ask whether there has *ever* been a situation in which he communicated his feelings or she appreciated something he did. As luck may have it, there is always at least one circumstance in which both mates agree that that was indeed the case.

Even if there was only one instance of this atypical behavior, it still means that he is not a closed person, but rather a person who opens up more easily in certain situations; and she is not an insatiable person, but rather a person who is more easily satisfied in certain situations. The challenge is to try and identify what it was about those particular situations that enabled him to open up and her to be satisfied. As difficult as that task may seem, it is much easier than trying to make a cold person warm or an insatiable person satisfied.

A similar shift from a dispositional to a situational explanation can be made in the case of a problem such as jealousy. When a person comes for therapy because of jealousy, most often the dispositional attribution of "a jealous person" has already been agreed on by both mates. In order to challenge it, I usually ask, "Have you been *that* jealous in all your intimate relationships?" The answer to this is most often no. My next question is: "What is it about this particular relationship that triggers your jealousy?" Or else: "What was it about the relationship in which you were least jealous that made you feel different?" These questions are rather different from: "Why am I a jealous person?" and "How can I change myself to stop being jealous?" Instead of attributing the jealousy to a pathology in one mate, it is attributed to a jealousy-producing interaction or situation. Instead of individual therapy for the jealous mate, both mates are encouraged to try to change things so that jealousy is not triggered.

Dispositional attributions can be made by couples about couples. Such attributions can also be challenged by an alternative—situational—attribution. When a couple says, "We never communicate," I typically ask in response: "Was there ever a time or a situation in which you did communicate?" "What was it about that situation that made it easy for the two of you to talk to each other?" When a couple says, "We never do fun things together," they are begging to be asked: "What did you ever do together (no matter how long ago) that both of you considered fun?" "What is it about that activity, or the circumstance in which it happened, that enabled both of you to have fun?"

Although social psychology has not been applied directly to couples therapy, the examples above demonstrate that it can provide an important addition to the current clinical approaches. Of course, real life is a mixture of attributions, some situational and some dispositional. We fall in love because of endearing characteristics of our beloved, and certain dispositional attributes about ourselves give us a consistent and secure sense of self. Social psychology, while emphasizing the interaction between people and their environments, does not deny the importance of individual traits and dispositions. Rather, it suggests that human experiences such as shyness, jealousy, marital troubles, and burnout, have an important situational component that is more amenable to change than people's personalities.

### COUPLES' VS. OBSERVERS' ATTRIBUTIONS OF MARRIAGE BURNOUT

Environmental pressures such as money problems and work stresses can erode relationships based on romantic love, while environmental support and growth opportunities help feed the romantic spark. Nevertheless, even couples who carry a heavy burden of such stresses and pressures are often far less likely to see them as the major reason for the deterioration in their relationships than are objective outside observers. In spite of the obvious cost of such misattribution, they tend to attribute their marital difficulties either to each other's personality deficiencies or else to some inherent incompatibility in their personalities. Similarly, couples benefiting from environmental support, more than outside observers, tend to attribute its positive effects on the relationship to themselves. For obvious reasons, this misattribution is far less costly psychologically to the couple than the tendency to attribute to themselves the blame for the negative effect of environmental stresses.

How easily people can see the effect of environmental influences on *other* people's marriages! In two of my studies on marriage burnout, three hundred subjects were presented with eight short marriage scenarios and asked in each case to guess the couple's level of burnout. The eight scenarios are presented in the box on p. 87, together with the scale used to evaluate the levels of projected burnout.

As you can see, some of the scenarios emphasize *personality compatibility,* such as the case of Mark and Mary, who have very similar personalities and who enjoy similar activities. Some of the scenarios emphasize personality *incompatibility,* such as the scientist David and the social worker Dalia whose personalities and preferred activities are very different. Some of the scenarios emphasize *environmental stresses,* such as Tom and Tina, who have four young children, or Joe and Judith, who have been married for five years but because of Joe's hard work can never afford to take a vacation. Some of the scenarios describe *positive home environments,* such as Gary and Gina, who just got married and entered their new home.

Results comparing the average burnout scores attributed to all eight scenarios showed that in both studies in which they were investigated, the rank orders for the burnout levels were identical.[18] The highest levels of marriage burnout were attributed to the couple experiencing the most stress: the hard-working Joe and his wife, Judith. Tina and her husband, Tom, with their four young children, came in a close second. The newlyweds Gary and Gina, living in the pleasant environment of their new home, received the very lowest burnout scores. In other words, the situation explained both the highest and the lowest burnout scores: Stressful environments explained the two highest burnout scores, and a positive environment explained the lowest score. Compatibility or lack of compatibility also had an effect on observers' evaluations of burnout. The compatible Mark and Mary were seen as less burned out than the incompatible David and Dalia. Yet the difference due to compatibility was much smaller than the difference due to environment.

---

Try to imagine the following couples and, in spite of the limited information provided, guess their levels of marriage burnout using the following scale:

| 1 | 2 | 3 | 4 | 5 | 6 | 7 |
|---|---|---|---|---|---|---|
| not at all burned out | | | somewhat burned out | | | totally burned out |

- John and Jacky have been married thirty-five years. They have three children and four grandchildren.
- Mark and Mary are very similar in terms of their personalities. Both love reading, hiking, and listening to classical music.
- Joe and Judith have been married for five years. Joe works very hard. He comes home very late and continues working into the small hours of the morning. Because of his work, they can never afford to take a vacation.
- Gary and Gina got married three months ago and this week have entered their new home.
- David and Dalia are very different in terms of their personalities. David is a scientist who enjoys most of all spending time with his scientific books. Dalia is a social worker who enjoys most the company of people.
- Tom and Tina have four young children. The oldest child is six years old; the youngest one is still a baby. Tina does not have help with the house or the children.
- Benjamin and Beth have been married five years. They have an eight-month-old baby and a nice suburban home.
- Eli and Iris love doing things together, but each one of them also has a very full and rich life as an individual.

---

What these findings show is that objective observers, when presented with brief descriptions of marriages, tend to attribute burnout more to stresses in the environment than to personality incompatibility. It is interesting that those same "objective observers" were all subjects in a study on marriage burnout. When asked about their own marriages, they tended to attribute the cause of their own burnout to personality incompatibility! A woman who, like Tina, had four young children and not enough money to afford help with the house or the kids gave Tina's marriage the highest burnout score. Yet she explained the cause of her own marital difficulties by the fact that her husband "is a cold and uncommunicative person who does not have the same needs for intimacy and sharing" that she has. The fact that most evenings she was so wiped out that the only thing she could do before falling asleep was to watch television somehow did not seem as important in her evaluation of her marriage as was her husband's supposed coldness and inability to communicate. Now, it may very well be that her complaint about her husband is a legitimate one, but she fell in love with him "as is," and there is a much smaller chance that his personality will change than that the environment will change.

*In summary,* I have presented the five approaches that, in my opinion, have the greatest relevance to the issue of burnout in love and marriage. The three clinical approaches—psychoanalysis (which explains the origin of marital problems in childhood experiences that are reenacted in marital conflicts), behaviorism (which emphasizes techniques for changing behaviors that cause marital discord), and the systems approach (which treats marriage as a stable system where the causes of events are always circular)—have the important advantage of well-developed theories and techniques for working with couples. Their greatest disadvantage is an overemphasis on pathology and a relative disregard for the existential and situational context of couples' problems. The existential approach (which emphasizes people's search for meaning) and the social-psychological approach (which emphasizes the situational context of people's experiences) have the big disadvantage of not having been applied specifically to the treatment of marital problems. In my own thinking about marriage burnout, and my work with couples, I incorporate the contributions of all five of these approaches. This integrated approach served as the theoretical foundation for this book.[19]

The next three chapters are devoted to an exploration of marriage burnout in three of the most important facets of life—work, home, and sex. Work involves the couple in their interaction with the outside world; home involves the couple in their interaction with the smaller circle of family; sex involves the couple in their intimate interaction with each other.

# CHAPTER 4

# Work and Marriage: The Balancing Act

The ability to love and the capacity for work are the hallmarks of full maturity.

Sigmund Freud

If I were to ask you, "What is more important: your work or your marriage?" what would you answer? If you are like the thousands of people I asked, your answer would be: "My marriage!" Then there is the question: "What is your favorite day of the week?" My data suggest that your most likely answer is Saturday. ("The weekend is here!") Your next most likely answer is Friday. ("The whole weekend is still ahead.") Your third most likely response is Sunday. ("It's good to have a day off, but it's getting too close to the work week.") Most people prefer weekends ("family times") to workdays.[1]

Yet if I asked you how much of your prime time—time you are not totally exhausted or preoccupied with something else—you spend at work, and how much of your prime time you spend at home, chances are that work would come out ahead. At work, the people you interact with get the best parts of you. To those strangers you are polite and attentive. By the time you come home to the person who is supposedly most important in your life, you have neither the energy nor the patience to be polite and attentive. So you dispense with tact and other niceties, and tell yourself that "at least at home I can be myself." Why is it, though, that being oneself almost never implies being one's best?

All too often, once people feel assured of their mate's love and commitment, they start taking this love for granted. They make demands they would not think of making during the early stages of the relationship, demands they would never make of other people. The mate becomes the one person in their lives who is "supposed to" understand their work stress. "Who can I ask to be understanding and supportive if not my mate?" they ask self-right-eously. Leah, who has been too often on the receiving end of this attitude, says:

> When my husband was a student, he said he was under terrible stress because he had to study. I was supposed to understand. When he was a junior faculty member, he said he was under terrible stress being junior faculty. I was supposed to understand. When he became a senior faculty member, he was under terrible stress being senior faculty. And I was supposed to understand.
>
> It seems that every period in our fifteen years together has been "the most difficult period" in his life. And I was expected to be sympathetic, understanding, and never make demands. When I realized that this was the way things were going to be forever, I knew I had to get out of the marriage.

By the time Leah's husband realized his job was destroying their marriage, it was too late. A romantic relationship can withstand only so much pressure. This is not to say that a marriage can't survive, or even benefit from, a short dose of crisis-at-the-factory. In short doses a mate can provide loving support. But when crisis becomes a daily event, it imposes stress on marriage that erodes love. Dealing with continuous stress at work is, in effect, making work a higher priority than marriage. No romantic relationship can withstand that kind of assault for long.

## COMPARING JOB AND MARRIAGE BURNOUT

In a good marriage the job doesn't come first, and such a good marriage can prevent job burnout. That's what I discovered in three studies in which 1,187 participants described their work, marriage, and levels of burnout. People who were stressed at work, but felt supported by their mates, were able to cope with situations that were otherwise intolerable.[2] A young lawyer who was involved in a lengthy and complicated divorce trial describes it:

> I am almost at the end of my rope. The pressures of a court trial are immense, and this one has been dragging on for weeks with no end in sight. I feel very responsible to our client, and I think that the senior lawyer working with me on the case is totally incompetent and

irresponsible. Not only that, but the other side is one of the biggest law firms in town. Our team is no match for them under the *best* of circumstances, and these are definitely *not* the best of circumstances. . . . It is very important for me to know that I can come home at night and be with someone I love who loves and appreciates me. It keeps intolerable things in perspective.

If, on the other hand, people are in a bad marriage, the stress involved can have a very negative effect on their work. A computer consultant whose marriage of fifteen years was ending says:

I sit in front of the computer and I see blank. Since I am a free-lance consultant, and consequently am never sure about my next project until the contract is actually signed, the pressures of supporting a family have always been very difficult for me to bear. Now that my marriage is on the rocks, the tension is draining all my creative energy. And being creative is essential to my work. It is the essence of what I do, of what I sell to my clients. For weeks now, since the problems between us became intense, I haven't been able to work. I know what needs to be done, but I can't concentrate enough to be able to do it. I am so drained I feel like throwing everything away.

Findings of the three studies comparing job and marriage burnout show that overall burnout was more related to marital problems than to work stress.[3] Apparently, the overall quality of people's life is more affected by the quality of their marriage than by the quality of their work. This is an important finding considering that most of us concentrate our best energies on our jobs—perhaps in a belief that we have to work at our jobs while our love relationships will somehow take care of themselves. The greater importance of marriage was also documented in national surveys showing that only a small percentage of people rank work as the central factor in their lives. Family life is consistently described as more important than work in most people's lists.[4]

Participants in the three studies described their marriages not only as more important to them, but as more satisfying emotionally and as less pressured than their work. They had better personal relations at home than at work; they got more emotional rewards, more support, more sharing, more opportunities for self-actualization, and a greater sense of meaning. Work, on the other hand, was a source of bureaucratic and administrative hassles; people felt pressured to make decisions without enough time or information, they had few opportunities for influencing decisions that could have direct impact on their lives, often they had little respect for the people they worked for and with, and, in addition, the work environment tended to be more uncomfortable and impersonal than that at home.

What saves some people from going crazy at work is their family life. David, a fifty-year-old training expert at a large government agency, was married and the father of six children. He tells how his family protected him during a crisis:

> After thirteen years in the same department, I was told I was going to be transferred to another department *the next day.* I felt devastated; I felt a total lack of self-worth. I did not trust the person I was transferred to and resented the unfair and inconsiderate way the transfer was done. But I had no choice. I know this is not at all uncommon, but it's devastating when it happens to you. I found it very hard to take. I felt that the company was playing games with my life.
>
> I felt angry, humiliated, and used; they were going to pick my brains and then dump me. The experience was eroding away my soul. I felt like I didn't exist. I was doing my job like a machine, like a warm mannequin, not a person. . . . I felt trapped. That was the worst thing . . . I wanted to escape at any cost, but there was no way out. The obligations of a large family didn't give me the latitude to simply walk out. And there was the pressure of having put all those years into a retirement system that I knew I was far enough into so that I couldn't go somewhere else. I knew that if I left I was throwing a lot of my future away. . . . The most devastating thing was the feeling of worthlessness. And I couldn't get out of it. I was so miserable, I couldn't see any of my friends. I was in no shape to be a loving husband and father.
>
> At times I thought I was at the point of murder. The pressure builds up and builds up until something has to give and you've got to cash in all your stamps. And then you just do it. You simply have to escape.
>
> We are a good, warm, and loving family, and this is the thing that got me through all this. . . . That's the thing that has held me together. The love and support of my wife and children prevented me from committing an act of violence, either on someone else or on myself—which I contemplated seriously. The pleasure of the day wasn't worth the pain.

David's story demonstrates, better than all the data presented earlier, the difference between work and marriage in causing and in preventing burnout.

I am often asked which is more prevalent: job burnout or marriage burnout. While estimates of burnout (either in marriage or at work) in the population as a whole are as yet unavailable, I was able to compare the levels of burnout on the job and in marriage in the samples I studied. In a combined sample of 960 men and women, the average score of marriage burnout was 3.3. This score was identical to the average score of job burnout obtained in a combined sample of 3,916 men and women. Similarly, the average marriage burnout score in a study of 200 Israelis—2.8—was identical to the average job burnout score in a combined sample of 393 Israelis. The similarity between levels of burnout in marriage and on the job, in such very different samples, is less surprising when one considers the fact that they are both measured using a very similar self-report test (see the Burnout Test on p. 257). Since both tests ask how frequently the individual has had a series of negative experiences, a certain similarity in response can be expected. The similarity between job and marriage burnout is also less surprising when one considers the fact that these two areas cover most of an individual's life in our society, and are also the two primary paths for finding a sense of significance in life. Because both work and marriage so often fail as answers to the existential dilemma, job burnout was described as "the social epidemic of the eighties" and the modern institution of marriage as being in "a state of calamity."

From the similarity in people's levels of burnout on the job and in marriage we can assume that there is a similarity not only in the intensity but also in the subjective experience of both. Indeed, just as in marriage burnout, people experience job burnout as a state of physical, emotional, and mental exhaustion caused by long involvement in emotionally demanding situations. People burn out on their jobs for the same reason they burn out in marriage: Their experience doesn't match their ideal. Just as young lovers fall out of love because married life isn't like the fairy tale they imagined, workers fall out of love with their careers because they can't achieve what they expected. How many social workers have burned out because they thought they could make a profound difference in every case they handled? How many nurses have burned out because they thought their ministrations would keep patients alive? How many teachers have burned out because they believed they could save every marginal student? How many doctors have burned out because medicine cannot reliably fight pain and disease? How many lawyers have burned out because, no matter how superior their skills, they could not win every case— and worse, often lost the cases they cared about most?

Not surprisingly, the process leading to job burnout is very similar to that leading to marriage burnout.[5] Just as marriage burnout can happen only to couples in love, job burnout can happen only to idealistic and highly motivated individuals. Highly motivated people don't work hard because of money (even though it's always nice to get paid well). They don't work hard because of the threat of discipline or censure either. Idealistic people work hard because they expect their work to make their lives matter in the larger scheme of things and give meaning to their existence. They don't need either a "carrot" or a "stick" to motivate them. They are motivated enough as it is because they identify with their work.

In a supportive environment (where they have the autonomy, resources, and support needed to accomplish their goals without the frustration of bureaucratic hassles and red tape), such highly motivated workers can reach peak performance. Reaching peak performance increases their sense of significance and success, which, in turn, increases their original motivation. When the same highly motivated workers are thrown into a stressful environment (where they are overloaded with work; where their ambition is stifled by bureaucratic interference, poor communication, and paperwork; where they can't get the resources they need to get the job done well; where they feel stuck below their level of competence; where they feel unappreciated and where they don't get a sense of meaning from their work), burnout is almost inevitable. This can be clearly seen in situations where failure is built in. A case in point is jobs in which there is no way to have the quantity of work demanded done in the quality it should be done. For motivated people whose egos are tied to their performance, failure is a most powerful cause of burnout.

All the things I said in the last paragraph can be as true of a marriage as of a job (as we know from Chapter 2). A stressful environment (say three kids and a dog in a station wagon on the way to the beach in 90-degree weather with "Peter and the Wolf" playing over and over on the tape deck), too much work (all the beds to be stripped, sheets and towels to be washed, diapers to be soaked), poor communication (a wife who can't understand why her husband gets so mad at the kids on the way to the beach; a husband who can't understand why his wife complains so much about dirty towels), too much paperwork (bills), being stuck below one's level of competence (driving kids to the beach; doing laundry), not having adequate resources (juggling the checkbook), not feeling appreciated (by each other), and feeling like a failure will lead to burnout in marriage, too.

Job and marriage burnout not only parallel each other, they also affect each other. It is very difficult to isolate the experience of burnout, either at work or in the marriage. When people start burning out on their jobs, typically, they pull back from co-workers and begin to feel isolated. They don't think they are getting enough appreciation for their work, or that the work is challenging enough. Consequently, they start putting increasing demands on their mates for professional appreciation and challenge. Such demands are both unfair and unrealistic since the mate is probably not well enough informed or qualified to fulfill them. Frequently the atmosphere of disappointment and regret becomes associated with the marriage; it erodes love and contributes to burnout.

Noticing the close connection between burnout on the job and in marriage made me, after ten years of studying job burnout, shift my focus to the study of marriage burnout.

Burnout can work the other way as well, spilling over from the marriage into work. Most often this involves people who escape marital problems by totally investing themselves in their work. People like that usually come to work very early, leave very late, and take work home with them, to avoid the possibility of having to talk to their mates. As long as work gives them a sense of significance, of making a difference, of being successful, of belonging, they are able to avoid burnout. But if a problem comes up at work, if they experience a crisis or a big failure, they have nothing to fall back on at home. Consequently they start feeling burned out in their work as well as in marriage.

The final result is often very similar, even when the overinvolvement in work is not motivated by a need to get away from a burned-out marriage. In recent years, the term "workaholic" has appeared frequently in both popular and scientific literature. The term was coined by Wayne E. Oates, a priest and a religion psychologist, in his 1971 book *Confessions of a Workaholic.*[6] It connotes addiction to work. Typically, workaholics are people for whom work has become a single, all-involving preoccupation. It is the only thing in life that seems to matter, the only thing that makes them feel alive. They invest all their time and energy in it, so there is little or nothing left for other people or activities.

Since they get their sense of "cosmic significance" from work, most workaholics, like most devoutly religious people, don't need to get it from love. Consequently, many of them never marry, limiting themselves to dating people who won't interfere with their work. When they are forced for some reason (such as pressure from their company or their family) to marry, unless the mate is also a workaholic, the demands for more time the mate makes (sooner or later) eventually start the pattern of escape into work described earlier.

When both mates are workaholics, their involvement with each other and the relationship is more like dating than marriage. Such couples may keep separate apartments and may even live in separate cities; they keep different hours and know different sets of friends. Their limited involvement in the marriage leaves them plenty of time to be involved in their careers. Needless to say, burnout at work for a workaholic is a traumatic, devastating event, far worse than the breakdown of a marriage that has been kept, firmly, in second place. This leads to the worst case of all, when people who get their sense of significance in life from both work and love burn out simultaneously in work and in marriage. The physical, emotional, and mental exhaustion become so all-encompassing that in some cases the individual is completely immobilized. Things are as bad as they can be and there is no hope for anything to improve. Nothing seems to matter, and there is nothing worth living for.

A probation officer, burned out in his job and recently separated from his wife, says:

> I sat all through the night with a gun pointed at my head. I couldn't see a reason to live. My wife left me, and I couldn't blame her. I was really impossible to live with. She needed to get away to save her own sanity. And I felt like a total failure at my job. It all of a sudden dawned on me that I was trying to do an impossible thing. I couldn't really change anything in the lives of the kids I was responsible for. And besides, I no longer felt they deserved help. I couldn't believe

I had sacrificed my marriage for them. What a stupid fool I'd been.
. . . I felt all alone in the world, trapped in a corrupt and inefficient
system . . . my whole life had been wasted. What reason was there
for me to go on living?

After this lengthy discussion of the similarity and direct relationship between burnout on the job and in marriage, it may be
worth noting that neither the similarity nor the relationship is obvious to the people who experience both of them. Many a time, after
an intensive burnout workshop, a participant would confide in me,
saying: "If I knew then what I know now, I would still be married."
What they mean is that with the insight they gained during the
workshop they realize that they were too quick to blame their
spouse for their problems at work, and too quick to give up on the
marriage—when the real problems lay elsewhere. People don't see
the obvious not because they are unbelievably dense or lacking in
sensitivity or insight. They have simply focused on the closest thing
at hand: When they burn out, instead of focusing on the situational
stresses that caused their burnout they focus on their own failings
and on the presumed failings of the person closest to them—their
spouse.

## MEN AND WORK

Balancing work and marriage is equally important for men and
women, yet traditionally men are more invested in their work and
women in their marriage. Consequently, in traditional marriages
the balance between work and marriage occurs more between husband and wife than within the individual man or woman.

Lillian Rubin, author of *Intimate Strangers*, asked hundreds of
people of all ages and from all walks of life, "Who are you?"
Almost invariably, she discovered, a man will respond by saying
what kind of work he does: "I am a salesman," "I am a physician,"
"I am a police officer." Having identified himself by his career, he
then, sometimes as an afterthought, may mention something about
being a husband or a father. A woman, on the other hand, is far
more likely to start by saying "I am a mother and a wife" and only
then mention something about her career.[7]

So, in spite of all the recent changes in sex-role definitions, the
majority of men and women still define themselves in terms of

traditional sex-role stereotypes. Men are socialized to identify with their work to the extent that both professional success and professional failure are seen as personal success and failure. Women, on the other hand, were socialized, until very recently, to define personal success and failure more in terms of their roles as wives and mothers. For men (as well as for modern career women) who believe in romantic love, finding an answer to the existential dilemma in work contradicts the alternative—romantic—solution.

The inherent contradiction between the idealized image of romantic love and that of a successful professional career does not become apparent until one tries to actualize both simultaneously. Take the senior faculty member whose wife, Leah, left him because she hadn't signed on to be a faculty wife, with all the stresses and rewards involved in that role. For him, becoming a successful scientist was supposed to be not only *his* dream, but their joint dream. He expected his wife to identify with his professional ambitions and take personal pride in his successes. He expected her to enjoy his international reputation and all the benefits it offered them in travel and in leading a richer and more exciting life. All he wanted in return was her trust and support while he worked to make that dream come true. The problem that eventually destroyed the marriage was the fact that Leah did not share his dream. Her own sense of meaning in life was tied much more to the quality of their daily communication than to the idea of being married to a successful scholar. She did not identify with his success and was acutely aware of the personal price she was paying for that success. Leah remained in the marriage as long as she believed that her own dream of closeness and intimacy would come true some day. When it became clear to her that the sacrifices demanded of her and of the marriage for the sake of his success were not temporary, when it became clear that there was a basic discrepancy between her husband and herself in what they both wanted from life, she saw no choice but to leave the marriage.

Obviously, the situation is different when both husband and wife identify with the husband's achievements. Sarah and her husband are an example. Sarah grew up in a very poor family, trained as a nurse, and married a successful doctor. Her life, as the wife of a well-to-do man, fulfilled her wildest fantasies. She was happy to quit her job as a nurse and to take on the job of supporting her husband's career. Her greatest joy at the beginning of their marriage was decorating their big beautiful house. Sarah spent time every day taking care of the house and the big garden surrounding it. She took great care of her own appearance and always looked slim, tan, and elegant. She was thrilled to entertain her husband's colleagues, and saw herself as a fairy-tale figure—perhaps Cinderella.

What was the difference between Sarah and Leah? Both of their husbands had achieved top positions in their fields. Both of their husbands made a good living, although, granted, the doctor made more money than the professor. Sarah, however, identified with her husband's career and was happy to stand in his reflected glory, while Leah did not and was not. Sarah and Leah show that the impact on the marriage of a very stressful career depends to a large extent on the subjective costs and rewards the career provides for both husband and wife.

Everything said so far has assumed that a man is successful in his career. But not all men are successful professionally. What happens to a man who finds that he is a failure at work? Whit, a thirty-three-year-old mechanical engineer, is an example.

Whit chose engineering because he liked to build things with his hands and was good at it. For twelve years his work at a large oil company gave him ample opportunity for success. The work involved creating new instruments and improving old ones. Whit loved the excitement of each new challenge. He even enjoyed the stress involved. Sometimes he worked twenty hours straight to meet a deadline. He was often so absorbed in his projects that he ignored his wife and children, but he believed that his wife understood that he was working for both of them.

Whit made a lot of money, which enabled him and his wife to buy a lot of expensive "toys," things they both enjoyed. He felt respected and successful in his work. Whit was happy with his life and felt it gave him everything he wanted. Then things started to go wrong. Whit was promoted to a managerial position. It was the natural career step for him, but he had never been trained in management. It was not something he wanted to do, except for one thing—it was an important promotion, and all of his colleagues noted that "if you don't get promoted, you're actually getting demoted."

The first few months on his new job were stressful for Whit because he didn't know exactly what he was doing. But there was something exciting about managing a team to get a project done, and he enjoyed the new challenge. After this brief period of getting acquainted with the new job, he got a project that was beyond his budding skills as a manager: He needed to guide sixty people through a $5 million dollar project in just nine months. Whit started working twenty hours a day, the way he had when, as a hands-on engineer, he needed to get something done, but he found that his subordinates didn't care as much about the project as he did. He also found that they resented his authoritative style of management. Their dissatisfaction grew with time until they rebelled openly by going over his head and demanding his removal from the project. To his great shock, top management sided with them. Three months before the project was to be finished he was transferred.

Whit was devastated. He had failed in his work, the thing that meant the most to him, and he had failed royally. Everyone in the whole company heard what had happened. Every day he ran into people who had once been on the team, people who knew about his failure. The embarrassment and humiliation were almost too much for him to bear. When he first got the news about his dismissal from the project he contemplated quitting the company, but his wife urged him not to, at least not until he had another job to replace it. (His professional position was very important for her own sense of significance and security.) Whit, in fact, didn't start looking for another job. His ego was so crushed by his failure as a manager that he couldn't summon the emotional energy he needed to go job hunting. He felt depressed and emotionally depleted, had difficulty concentrating and difficulty sleeping. Life had lost its meaning. Eventually his wife, who tried for as long as she could to be strong and supportive, said she couldn't take it anymore.

At the same company, Whit reached peak performance and then burned out. Reaching peak performance increased Whit's sense of significance and success, which in turn increased his work motivation. He remained in this positive loop for twelve years and probably would have remained in it indefinitely if he hadn't been promoted. When he was given a job in which he was bound to fail, he burned out in less than a year. Because his marriage was secondary to his career, his marriage couldn't give his life the sense of meaning work had given it.

Although Whit's involuntary removal as head of the project, like David's involuntary transfer to another department (which was described earlier in the chapter), is not uncommon in large bureaucratic organizations, they are extreme events. For most people, burnout is caused by a slow and gradual process of erosion. Rona and Ben are an example of burnout caused by the daily tedium of work. When they first met and fell in love, Ben had a good union-protected job that provided a secure and comfortable income. Unfortunately, the secure job was also very boring, and after fifteen years in it Ben decided to quit. He wanted a business of his own, and chose to open a restaurant. He wanted Rona to help, at least at the beginning, until they could afford outside help. Reluctantly, Rona agreed. After five years of hard work, which was neither exciting nor financially rewarding, both felt burned out in the job and the marriage, but there was no easy way out.

Burnout is not always caused by external events as it was for Whit, Dave, and even Ben. Sometimes job burnout is triggered by a mid-career crisis. Like burnout, the mid-career crisis tends to happen to people who are highly motivated, with great ideals and enthusiasm. It happens particularly to people who have made their career choices at an early age—say, when they were in their twenties. They start out convinced that being a lawyer, a doctor, an architect, a teacher, a police officer, means making a major contribution to society. By mid-career they either realize that their contribution may be far smaller than they had hoped, or else they begin to think that society doesn't deserve the sacrifice they are making. They start feeling empty and disillusioned, painfully aware of their mortality and the passage of time—time remaining and time spent. Someone once said we should look at our lives as days of the week, with each day representing a decade. Well, these people suddenly look up from their work and they discover it's Wednesday, or Thursday, or even Friday morning, and they say, "Wait a minute. This isn't what I want!" William Bridges describes it:

When the dream has been gained, the vice-presidency, the book, the three kids and the handsome home—there is the moment of realization: "O.K., I've got it, now what?" And even: "Is *this* it? Is *this* the destination that I've sacrificed everything for?" The discrepancy between public image and private awareness can be excruciating at this point in life. And what of the person who didn't make it? The denied dream is the other gateway to reality. There one is faced with the nevers. "I guess I have to face the fact that I'm *never* going to be the head of the company . . . *never* going to be the parent of four happy, well-adjusted children." And with that acknowledgment comes the strange sense that one has been chasing a carrot on a stick, that the sunset into which one was riding was painted on the other end of the train car.[8]

Burnout is less likely to happen, and if it happens is less likely to be devastating, if work is balanced by marriage. The balance between work and marriage is a difficult one to achieve, and a difficult one to maintain. One of the ways to identify the balance—or imbalance—between them is to list side by side, on a piece of paper, what is demanded of you at work and what is demanded of you at home. Doing that can help you ascertain to what extent these demands are essential, current, legitimate, and reasonable and to contemplate your priority in responding to them. Let's take the example of Phil, who is thirty-four years old, has three young children, and works as an attorney at a large law firm. Phil's lists looked like this:

| WORK | HOME |
|---|---|
| 1. Be a brilliant lawyer. | 1. Be a good husband and father. |
| 2. Not make any mistakes. | |
| 3. Protect my clients. | 2. Support my family financially and, of course, emotionally. |
| 4. Keep up with new laws/court decisions. | |
| 5. Bring in new clients. | 3. Take care of the yard. |
| 6. Pal around with my colleagues without making it seem like I'm malingering. | 4. Be a role model for the kids and a good disciplinarian. |
| 7. Get along with my bosses without making it seem like I'm toadying. | 5. Share chores. |
| 8. Be a good boss to my secretary and the back-office support staff. | |
| 9. Dress appropriately. | |
| 10. Be entertaining, charming, someone other lawyers like and respect. | |
| 11. Be a team player and represent the firm well. | |

You will notice that Phil not only has many more items in his work column, but that the work column is more specific and well thought out. Phil feels that all the things he does at work are important and that he must exert a great deal of energy meeting these demands if he is going to make partner at his law firm, which is his paramount concern. Compared with this, the demands imposed by his family are extremely light. I would further wager that if we had asked him about any of the items on his work list—say, "How can you be a 'good boss to your secretary?' "—Phil could tell us exactly what that meant, from being clear in his instructions to taking her to lunch during National Secretary Week. But if we would have asked him what it meant to be "a good role model" for his kids, it might have taken him quite some time to come up with an answer.

Interestingly enough, as is often the case, Phil seemed to resent far more the relatively small demands made by his family than he did the huge list of demands made by his job. Moreover, Phil considered his family much more important to him than his job. What Phil learned from making the lists was that he was short-changing his family. In addition, by scrutinizing his lists in a careful and honest manner, he came to realize that some of the demands he listed as imposed by his job were actually self-imposed. In other words, under close inspection, he gained insight into the fact that he was making demands on *himself* as a lawyer, boss, and colleague far in excess of what his law firm expected of him.

Phil's experience is not unique. It tends to characterize high achievers: top-level executives, politicians, lawyers, doctors, psychologists, scientists, and all other professionals who get involved from a very young age in a demanding and ego-involving career. Unfortunately, many of them don't stop to evaluate their self-imposed demands and priorities until it is too late. Typically, they start their careers very early. In elementary school they work very hard to be accepted into the best high schools. In high school they work very hard to be accepted into the best colleges. In college and in graduate school they work very hard to get the best possible position, at the best company, political office, law firm, hospital, clinic, university. Once they get that desired position they work very hard to be promoted and stay on top of the field.

During those years they typically also fall in love, marry, and have several children, but since the job has the highest priority, they rarely have time for family. It usually takes a dramatic event to shake up this single-minded involvement with work. The dramatic event could be positive, such as a major achievement, or it can be negative, such as a major failure, a life-threatening illness, an accident, or a divorce. In all cases, the precipitating event makes what seemed to be a substantial world look fragile and unreal. The dramatic event many times happens when the individual is around the age of forty to fifty. As a result of it they begin to question the value of their work and life.

## WOMEN AND WORK

If their professional identities are more important to men, and if their domestic identities as wives and mothers are more important to women, and if people burn out because they are disappointed in their expectation that the role with which they identify most will give meaning to their lives, then it follows that more men will burn out on work than women. (Following the same line of reasoning, we can make the equally obvious prediction that women will be more burned out in their marriages than men. We will return to the second prediction in the next chapter.)

In spite of this "obvious" prediction, studies show that it's not true. Studies of sex differences in job burnout indicate that women report higher levels of burnout in their work than do men. For example, in one study I did with Ditsa Kafry, involving 96 professional men and 95 professional women, the women reported extreme levels of burnout four times as often as the men.[9] Women also reported higher levels of burnout in other studies I did, for example: a study involving 205 professional men and women, a study involving 220 professionals, a study involving 118 human service professionals, a study involving 89 schoolteachers, and a study involving 66 managers.[10] In every study we attempted to find professions in which the precentages of men and women were similar. In business, that meant looking at middle management; in medicine it meant looking at family medicine and pediatrics; in education, it meant looking at the higher grades of elementary school or at high school.

Why do women report more job burnout than men? While it is possible to explain it by the "fact" that women are innately weaker, less able, have a special vulnerability to stress, use inade-

quate styles of coping, or are more willing than men to acknowledge weakness, it is also possible to explain the sex difference in
burnout by different expectations and different stresses the two
sexes have in their work environments. Many of these differences
can be traced back to the greater difficulty women have in achieving
a balance between their work and home responsibilities.

The apparent reason for women's higher levels of burnout is
the relative absence of rewards in their work (worse pay, worse
work conditions, and so on) and the prevalence of stresses when
compared with men. Women felt they had less freedom, less autonomy, and less influence in their work, as well as less variety, less
challenge, and a less positive work environment. They felt they had
fewer opportunities for self-expression and self-actualization and,
on the whole, fewer rewards for their work. In addition, studies
show that women suffer from discrimination and harassment in
male-dominated professions.[11] No wonder they report higher levels of job burnout. For many women, the most stressful aspect of
work was the demands from people around them—both at home
and on the job—that made them feel harassed and overextended.
Women's attempts to respond to all these demands left them feeling
overloaded, torn, and conflicted.

In addition to the different stresses they encounter, men and
women often bring with them into work different sets of expectations. Studies of sex differences in work attitudes suggest that
women are more emotionally involved in their work than are men,
and tend more to see their careers as a source of personal growth
and emotional fulfillment.[12] When these high expectations are not
met, women burn out. Women's higher emotional involvement in
work can be seen as a result of their sex-role socialization. This
socialization has the greatest impact on women's roles as wives and
mothers, but it also influences their work roles. This is most clearly
evident in the helping professions, in which women are dispropor-
tionately represented (such as nursing, social work, teaching, counseling).

Working in the helping professions puts women in a high risk
group for both job burnout and marriage burnout. The reason has
to do with three basic traits shared by most of these professions,
traits that are also typical of marriage: (1) They are emotionally
taxing; the emotional demands of the work are often similar to the
demands of parenthood or of marriage; (2) the professionals share
certain personality traits that made them choose work with people

as a career, and that make them see marriage as the most important relationship in their lives; (3) the professions share a "client-centered" orientation that is modeled after the parent-child relationship. Each of these traits is among the primary causes of burnout. When combined, they multiply each other's individual effects.

*Emotionally Taxing Work.*    Working with people always involves a certain degree of stress. The specific degree and kind of stress depend on the particular demands of the job and the resources available to the professional. It always means dealing with people's idiosyncrasies while at the same time remaining both professionally skilled and personally concerned. Marriage requires similar skills. In some jobs the emotional demands of the work and the marriage are so similar that their stress is multiplied. A psychotherapist told me:

> After eight hours of listening to people in my office, I simply don't have the patience to listen to my husband when I come home. I love him. He is the most important person in the world to me. I know he has more right to my time than all my patients. But at the end of the day I am so emotionally drained, that I simply can't be available to him. It's very sad.

*Self-selection.*    If working with people is emotionally taxing for everyone, it is particularly disruptive for people who choose such work because they like people, have great empathy for their needs, and value themselves most as being sympathetic, understanding, and helpful. Whenever I ask such professionals to list their reasons for choosing to work with people, whatever their occupation, their reasons always include some variation of "I like people," "I am a people's kind of a person." Many of these professionals see being people-directed as the essence of themselves. It is an essence they express not only at work, but even more in their intimate relationships. This positive self-perception is shaken when such a person burns out either on the job *or* in the marriage.

A counselor in a community mental health center, who specialized in working with couples and who burned out in her thirteen-year-old marriage, described the devastating effect it had on her perception of herself as a person and as a therapist:

Even when I knew that I didn't love him anymore, that I couldn't stand his touch, that I had to get out of the marriage, I continued fighting the knowledge. I simply couldn't face the fact that I, of all people, was failing in the relationship that was the most important one to me. How could I continue counseling other couples if I couldn't counsel myself? How could I help others when I couldn't help myself?

*A "Client-centered" Job.*    Most long-term human relationships are symmetrical; both partners are expected to do their fair share. Two of the major exceptions are parenthood and client-centered jobs. In the client-centered job the professional gives a service of some kind, and the client receives it. The professional's work is justified only so long as there is a client to be helped. All training focuses on the client's needs and the best ways to serve them. Very little attention is paid to the needs of the professional or the stresses imposed on the professional by serving clients who are particularly difficult or demanding. Parental love, which is the model for many helping professions, is ideally unconditional; it does not depend on reciprocation. Parents whose love is conditional (on the child's performance, for example) are criticized, as are professionals who satisfy their own emotional needs through their clients.

An asymmetry in relationships can be very stressful. The stress is doubled when combined with the emotional demands of work with people *and* of marriage. It is particularly stressful for idealistic people who choose to work with people and marry for love. All of this is, of course, equally true for men and for women. The difference is that more women go into the helping professions, and women tend to feel frustrated at their jobs.

It is not just in the helping professions that women suffer. Most working women have difficulty combining career and family. A successful businesswoman describes it:

The work of a professional woman who is also a wife and mother is never complete. There is always more that can be done and should be done—a pair of pants that needs mending, a closet that needs cleaning, a child that needs that special time with you. . . . I carry all these "shoulds" in my head all the time and that means that I can never come home from work, flop down in a chair, and just unwind. I've got to make dinner.

In a study done by my Israeli colleague, Dalia Etzion, twenty-nine women and twenty-nine men holding middle-management positions were compared regarding their job burnout, life and work satisfaction, and various life and work features. The men and women were matched in age, seniority, and managerial level. As in all previous studies, results indicated that the women were more burned out than the men. It was also found that with the same level of education a man was likely to climb to a higher managerial position. For women, burnout increased with education; for men it decreased. Apparently, the higher expectations associated with getting a higher education were more easily achieved by men, and at a lower price.[13]

Women also paid a higher personal price for their careers in terms of family life. Thirty-one percent of the women in this group remained unmarried, yet not one of the men was single. In addition, the more successful a woman manager was in her career, the less successful she felt about her home life. For men, success at work was not related to either success or failure at home. In interviews I did with women managers, they talked with great pain about the personal sacrifices they had to make for the sake of their careers; many times they doubted whether it was all worth it. A public relations director in a government agency said:

> Now that I am getting close to my fiftieth birthday, I spend a lot of time thinking about my life, evaluating things, wondering. . . . If a young woman would come to me today and ask whether I recommend this life to her I would have to say no. The price you pay is just too high. Look at me. I may be the head of the department, but I am home alone at night. My marriage just couldn't sustain the pressure of my career. And it wasn't even that the household chores were not taken care of, because they were. I always made sure that the house was clean and food was on the table on time. What got to my husband was the fact that I was more successful than he was. At parties people knew who I was and knew him only as my husband. He just couldn't take it. My marriage was literally the price I paid for my success, and now I am no longer sure it was worth it . . .

In spite of all the recent advances in the status of women, and the changes in sex roles for both men and women, the reality is still that most women who combine a home and a career are carrying the double burden of two full-time careers: the regular duties of a job as well as most of the duties of child care and housework. The career woman/housewife/mother is frantic trying to respond to all her competing demands. Typically, she is the first one up in the morning, preparing breakfast for her family. During lunch and on her days "off" she takes care of family errands. She shops for groceries on her way home and, while her husband and children relax in front of the television, she works in the kitchen preparing dinner. Afterward, while her husband retreats, she cleans up and then helps the children with their homework. On evenings and weekends she cleans the house, does the laundry, and drives the children to their various activities.

Women's daily routines also have many domestic interruptions. It is usually the mother who takes the children to the pediatrician for their physicals and shots and to the dentist to get their teeth cleaned. It is the mother who stays home with them when they are sick. It is the mother who goes to parent-teacher conferences and is called when there is a problem. Thus, it should come as no surprise that one of the most consistent sex differences in my research on burnout has been the greater conflict between work and home experienced by women. In Dalia Etzion's study, the conflict between work and home was correlated with burnout—but only for women, not for men.[14] The best interpretation for this is that the conflict between the demands of work and the demands of home life is more intense for women and thus more stressful. This interpretation was supported by the findings of the study I did with Ditsa Kafry, in which the conflicting demands women had both at work and at home were more frequent and more stressful than those men had.[15]

In addition to the job stresses that working women share with men, and the heavier burden of housework and child care that they tend to take on themselves, women are burdened by other stresses that result from the cultural prescriptions of their sex role. These stresses originate in external or internalized social mores that put women in a double bind in which they are doomed if they do and doomed if they don't. Rose's case is a perfect example.[16]

Rose was twenty-nine, attractive, warm, sensitive, and exceptionally bright. She had graduated Phi Beta Kappa from an Ivy League college. She met her husband while working on her Ph.D. in science, which she received with the highest honors. Throughout her education she was supported by the most prestigious grants, fellowships, and scholarships. She was not just a grind. She played competitive tennis and appeared with a local amateur orchestra playing the violin. When her husband took a position with a law firm on the East Coast, there was no question that Rose would pull up roots and follow him. Soon after they settled in their new home Rose discovered, to their great delight, that she was pregnant.

Several months after the baby was born, Rose, who was preparing her dissertation for publication, was offered an assistant professorship at a prestigious university located sixty miles away from home. It was a great professional compliment and the ideal job for her. But now she had a baby with whom she wanted to spend as much time as possible. Rose was torn.

When she stayed home with the baby she felt she was disappointing all the mentors who believed in her enough to recommend her for the job. When she worked at the library she felt guilty about leaving her baby with a sitter. The more Rose thought about her two choices, the more she felt trapped.

Since Rose seemed unable to resolve the conflict, I suggested that she get some feedback from a group of strangers. In order to get this feedback Rose agreed to be videotaped showing the two sides of her role conflict. Both tapes started with Rose talking about her background, her education, and her interests—but the endings of the two tapes were different. In one tape she presented only her career plans, saying she wanted to accept the university position, teach, do research, and publish scientific articles. In the second tape she presented only her family plans, saying she wanted to stay home with her baby for a few years, and fix up their new house and garden. Male and female college students were shown the two tapes. After viewing the career tape, they described Rose as more success-oriented, ambitious, aggressive, dominant, and independent—adjectives traditionally ascribed to career-oriented males. By contrast, after viewing the family tape, they described her as less competent overall and less able to withstand pressure. In spite of or because of her reduced competence, women liked Rose less while men liked her more in the family tape. Men found her more feminine, open-minded, sincere, intelligent, well adjusted, kind, sensitive, and warm and wanted more to spend time with her.

It is possible that men are somewhat threatened by career

women, especially a woman as brilliant as Rose. It is possible that men saw Rose, in the career tape, as being able to provide less emotional support and care for a man than a woman who was a homebody. It is also possible that a woman who stays home with her baby is more closely following a sex-role stereotype and is, consequently, more understandable and more likable. Whatever the explanation, it seems clear that even among students—who are more liberal in their attitudes toward career women than most other groups—a career woman is in a double bind: If she chooses a career she will be seen by men as less feminine and less desirable. If she chooses a family, both men and women see her as less competent professionally. Such conflicting cultural messages can affect a woman only if she internalizes them. An exceptionally bright woman, Rose internalized both messages. That was why she was conflicted. She believed she could have both a career *and* a family. She expected both roles to give her life meaning, although, of course, not of the same kind and not at the same time. The two idealized images did not conflict until she had to make a choice between them. What did she do? Did she take the job, because superb child care can always be found and it was her big chance to make a splash in academia? Or did she stay home, because her baby was going to be young only once? Rose stayed home. She had another baby and started teaching part time at a local four-year college.

If you are a woman, you may well feel disappointed with her decision. Why? Because women want to believe that a woman can, in the catch phrase of the eighties, "have it all." Although Rose might tell us she does have it all—she has a loving husband, two children, and a teaching job—it is also clear that she didn't try to become a superwoman, she didn't go for the brass ring. Every choice means giving up on an attractive alternative, and disappointment causes burnout. This is equally true for men and for women. The difference is that women are presented with more of these conflicts and therefore tend to burn out more.

People who successfully combine a career and a family find a way to achieve balance between them, and that balance protects them from overinvolvement with either role. When they feel they failed at one, the other gives meaning to their lives. A professor of chemistry who is married to a man who is also a professor of chemistry in the same department, with whom she has two children, says:

> When I feel like a failure as a wife and mother, I say to myself, "Well, at least I am a decent chemist." When I feel like a failure as a chemist, I say to myself, "At least my husband and children think I am wonderful."

This balance can be achieved by the individual—man or woman—and it can be achieved by the couple. While all couples have to deal with issues related to the home-work conflict at least to some extent, those couples where both mates have a career about which they care deeply represent a special category termed by social scientists "dual-career couples."

## DUAL-CAREER COUPLES

The term "dual-career families" was coined in 1976 by Rhona and Robert Rapoport

> to designate a type of family in which both heads of household—the husband and the wife—pursue active careers and family lives. "Career" is sometimes used to indicate any sequence of jobs, but in its more precise meaning it designates those types of job sequences that require a high degree of commitment and that have a continuous developmental character.[17]

Studies show that dual-career couples have a number of advantages over traditional couples (in which the husband works and the wife stays home).[18] The most obvious advantage is a considerable financial edge gained by having two incomes. Dual-career couples also have stronger marital relationships; marital satisfaction is increased, and self-esteem rises when both partners have careers. In several studies, women who work report greater self-esteem, effectiveness, well-being, and marital satisfaction than do housewives. Similarly, husbands of women who work full-time report happier marriages, have fewer infectious diseases, and are less prone to psychiatric impairment than husbands married to housewives. While the gains felt by the wives were more in terms of self-actualization, the gains felt by the husbands were more in terms of the egalitarian relationship. Several of the husbands whose wives started working after being housewives for many years discovered, sometimes to their own surprise, that not only were they—the husbands—skilled and competent in their new domestic responsibilities, but they actually enjoyed the extra time they were spending with the kids.

As for the careers of dual-career couples, several studies find that couples who share the same career, or the same field, benefit. In a study of eighty-six sociologist couples who held appointments at the same academic departments, it was found that sociologist wives were more successful than women sociologists in general. They obtained higher degrees and more promotions, and continued with their careers longer.[19] In another study of two hundred psychologist couples it was found that when compared with a group of men and women who were not married to fellow professionals, the psychologist pairs produced more publications than their same-sex counterparts. (A psychologist woman married to a psychologist published more than a psychologist woman not married to a psychologist.)[20] Similar findings were obtained in a study of dual-career lawyer couples.[21] The husbands of professional women were more likely to respect professional competence and achievement not only in their wives, but in women in general.

Children (especially daughters) also benefit when both parents work. It was found, for example, that daughters of working mothers were more likely than daughters whose mothers stayed home to choose their mothers as role models and as the people they most admired. Adolescent daughters of working mothers were active and autonomous and admired their mothers but were not unusually tied to them. For daughters of all ages, having a working mother meant seeing the world as a less restrictive place.[22]

While dual-career couples have many advantages over traditional couples, they also have a higher divorce rate than traditional couples. Clearly, dual-career couples are pressured to make adaptations that are not required within more conventional marriages. The psychiatrists Carol and Theodore Nadelson say that dual-career couples are often faced with difficult choices:

> For example, the husband who is transferred to a new location may have to consider not only his wife's social adjustment and interests,

his children's schooling and relationships with peers, but, to a greater extent, his wife's career possibilities. *She* may not be able to obtain a position equal to her present one, or her career advancement may, in fact, be jeopardized by a change in location. Wives share a complementary dilemma. The wife may be offered a potentially gratifying career opportunity, only to recognize that this shift might put added pressure on her family, especially if a location change may be required. She may decide to decline the offer, or she may seek another apparent solution: that one partner commute. This latter pattern has become frequent in recent years. The costs of these changes may be significant enough to cause a rupture in the marital relationship.[23]

The Nadelsons also say that dual-career couples may be forced to reconsider their family roles (what is an appropriate activity for a man/husband/father as compared with a woman/wife/mother) and forced to adapt emotionally to new roles and expectations. Among the areas of conflict in dual-career couples they mention competition, envy, and unrealized expectations.

In my work with couples, the main complaint of dual-career couples was lack of time. This was especially true when both mates had careers they valued and that demanded a lot of their time. When asked about stress in his marriage, Anthony says:

> *Most* stressful is the inability to resolve the conflict between money and time. Making the kind of money I want to have obliterates the emotional connection that I want to have. But I don't want to give up the income of a good job. Yet, I am working too much for it to really make sense if I'm going to balance my life the way I believe I want to—and the way I believed it would be when we fell in love. . . . While there is no question in my mind about what I would choose if I had to make the choice between my work and my relationship with Ellen, luckily (or maybe unfortunately) I don't have to make a choice. So I end up giving the best part of my days to my work.

Ellen's response reflects a similar sentiment:

> I love my work. It is, and has always been, a very important part of my life and of my definition of myself. Tony has not always been as happy in his work, so I am delighted that he enjoys and is successful

in it now. Yet the time commitment both jobs require is the greatest strain on the relationship. It takes so much out of us that when we are together, in the evening or on weekends, we are totally wiped out. Even though I have complete confidence in our love for each other, I know from personal experience the accumulative effect such continuous stress can have on a relationship. I know that if we want the romance to remain in our relationship we have to be on guard and make sure it doesn't get lost.

Certain conflicts around issues of time management are inevitable when both mates are constantly negotiating the demands of an important career and the demands of an important relationship. Time is one resource that cannot be recouped or expanded. No matter how energetic, clever, and skillful a couple is, they can never have more than twenty-four hours in a day. One way to address issues such as time is for both mates to list their work and home demands side by side and for both of them together to examine each other's lists. Even when couples have been together for many years and claim to know each other intimately, this process can produce some surprises.

A wife may discover that the demand to have dinner on the table by a certain time and the guilt feelings associated with going out for dinner with the family are values and judgments she carries in her own head that were imprinted there in her childhood. She may discover that for her husband going out for dinner has far more positive and exciting associations and that he would love to do it more often. A husband may discover that being a good provider, which he believed to be the most important responsibility of a husband, is not so important to his wife. For his wife, the time spent together as a family may be more important than the raise her husband might get if he spent extra time working after hours.

Even when a certain demand is recognized as having been real by both mates, after close scrutiny they may decide that, given their current priorities, the demand is no longer essential. In other cases they may decide that even if a demand was legitimate and reasonable in the past, it no longer is. Listing the home and work demands, examining those demands together, being willing to recognize self-imposed demands, and being open to negotiating all demands are the important first steps in achieving a marriage-work balance. A balance between work and marriage enables people to get a sense of meaning from both. This solution to the existential dilemma has (at least in theory) twice the chance of succeeding as relying on either work or marriage alone.

Work can be very ego gratifying. It enables some people to be "heros" in a culture-prescribed "hero system" (to use Becker's terminology).[24] For those people, work can have a transcendent value. A politician who manages to get to the top of a political structure can get his sense of "cosmic significance" from his political power; a businessman who manages to get to the top of a financial empire can get it from his monetary power; a successful artist can get it from his art and the recognition it gives him. For such recognized "heroes" of society, having power, money, and recognition can provide enough meaning to life so that the romantic solution can be skipped. Only in those rare cases in which people are totally self-actualized in their work can they forswear love. Unfortunately—or maybe I should say fortunately—our culture's hero system works only on rare occasions. In addition, there are very few places at the top (and some of the people who make it to the top still feel empty). For the majority of people, the most intense, most moving, most meaningful experiences are those related to love. Even for people who are successful in their career, often work is not enough to give life meaning unless there is love too.

# CHAPTER 5

# Marriage: His, Hers, and Theirs

In marriage, a man "enlarges into a husband," while a woman "by degrees dwindles into a wife."

William Congreve
*The Way of the World*

*Who is more burned out in marriage, men or women?* Men believe that they are the ones who suffer in marriage. In popular literature and movies, plot after plot describes how men desperately want to escape the trap of marriage set for them by women. Men do have the lion's share of the burden of financially supporting a family. Warren Farrell, in his book *Why Men Are the Way They Are,* complains that marriage defeats men's basic drive in life: to have sex with a large number of young female partners.[1] Male comics have, for centuries, complained about the general incomprehensibility of women.

If we ask women which, of the two sexes, is most likely to burn out in marriage, their answer is invariably "Women!" Rosemary, a thirty-three-year-old woman living in a small northwestern town, puts it this way: "The reason is that women carry more of the burden at home, they expect more from their marriages, and their marriages are more important to them than they are to men." The vast majority of the women whom I asked this question agreed with Rosemary.

Since men and women have such different perceptions of who, in a sense, gets a rawer deal in marriage, I took a look at some research on men and women and marriage. Data suggest that marriage benefits men more than women, both physically and emotionally. Rates of mental disturbance, for example, indicate that while married women have higher rates of mental illness than married men, single men are more likely to be mentally disturbed than single women.[2] When marriages break up, divorce tends to have

123

more adverse impact on the health of divorced men than it does on the health of divorced women.

The eminent sociologist Jessie Bernard presented these and other statistical data in her book *The Future of Marriage.* The data document that married men are happier and healthier, both physically and mentally, and live longer than do single men. Married men are less likely to commit suicide, have fewer mental and physical health impairments, and have fewer serious symptoms of psychological distress than their single counterparts. They are more likely to earn good money and less likely to get involved in crime. (It can be said, of course, that women *choose* to marry the kind of men who earn more money and don't commit crimes, rather than that being married *makes* men earn more money and commit fewer crimes.) In spite of all protestations to the contrary, men seem to be aware of the benefits of marriage and their dependency on women. Even if their marriages end in divorce, men usually try marriage again right away, or as soon as an appropriate marriage partner becomes available. Bernard argues that in spite of the bad press that marriage gets from men, "whether they know it or not, men need marriage more than women do." She suggests that men resent marriage *because* they are so dependent on it.[3]

For women, marriage is not nearly so positive an experience. Actually, for many women who view marriage as their ultimate goal in life, marriage seems to be a health hazard.[4] Bernard cites studies indicating that wives lose self-esteem and a sense of personal identity because they conform to their husbands' needs and expectations. Married women are more likely than married men to experience psychological distress, including depression, passivity, anxiety, phobias, and nervous breakdown. Since single men showed more distress in these same areas, when compared with single women, the conclusion seems justified that marriage is harder on women than it is on men. Further, more wives than husbands report feeling frustrated and dissatisfied with their marriages, while fewer wives than husbands report enjoying positive feelings of companionship; more wives than husbands seek marriage counseling and therapy; more wives regret their marriages; more wives consider separation and divorce, and more wives than husbands actually initiate divorce proceedings. After a divorce, women are far less eager than men to get married again.[5]

As I noted during the discussion of changing sex roles and their effect on marriage burnout, family therapists report that most couples coming into therapy do so because of the wife's dissatisfaction.[6] In addition, the results of a large survey indicate that when a woman's expectations for her marriage are not met, *and* it is possible for her to leave the marriage, she will.[7]

Of course, it is not always possible for women to leave a marriage, because most women are financially dependent on, if not the husband's income, at least the husband's and wife's joint incomes. Barbara Ehrenreich, in her book *The Hearts of Men,* mentions Jessie Bernard's work, but argues that while Bernard may be right about men's dependence on the loving care of women, her analysis of marriage missed a far more important factor: women's financial dependency on men. Why is a financial dependency more important than an emotional one? Because, says Ehrenreich, a financial dependency is likely to last longer.[8] Ehrenreich says that women's financial dependence traps men in marriage and burdens them with the struggle to support wife and children. Indeed, there are data that document the health hazards of men's breadwinner role. A number of studies found, for example, an increase in peptic ulcers, heart attacks, and strokes among unemployed middle-aged men.[9] One study found that one hundred men whose jobs were going to be terminated had significant increases in blood pressure, cholesterol level, and norepinephrine level, changes that have an adverse effect on the cardiovascular system.[10] According to Ehrenreich, ever since the 1950s, medical opinion noting the lower life expectancy of men started explaining it by the fact that "there was something wrong with the way men lived, and the diagnosis of what was wrong came increasingly to resemble the popular (at least among men) belief that men 'died in the harness,' destroyed by responsibility."[11]

So who is right—Bernard or Ehrenreich? Are men more burned out in marriage because they are trapped by their financial burdens and suffer the health hazards of the breadwinner role? Or are women more burned out in marriage because they carry a heavier burden of household chores, experience more emotional and psychological stress, and find their needs for intimacy are less well satisfied?

To find the answer I did four studies involving 458 men and women. The sex difference in marriage burnout in all four of these studies was the same. Interviews and clinical work with burned-out couples showed the same sex difference: *Women report higher levels of burnout than men.* [12] The first study involved one hundred men

and women from the San Francisco Bay Area who have been together for an average of eight years. The relationships varied from
very traditional to very nontraditional. Women in the study were
more burned out than men. They reported feeling "depressed
about the relationship," "emotionally exhausted," and "wiped
out" more often than did men, and felt more often that they had
"nothing left to give." Men reported only three burnout symptoms
more often than women: feeling trapped, pessimistic, and anxious.[13]

In my clinical work with burned-out couples, I discovered that
when marriages broke up, men often seemed to be in the dark
about what had happened. These men frequently said in interviews
things like:

> I don't know what happened to her. We were very happy, or at least
> I thought we were happy. Then one day, out of the clear blue sky,
> she said she wanted a divorce. I still don't understand what went
> wrong.

The women, on the other hand, had been aware for some time
that there were problems in the marriage, but they had been unable
to make their husbands understand:

> I tried to explain it to him for years. He just wouldn't listen. I could
> never talk to him and make him understand. Finally, I just gave up
> trying and asked for a divorce.

The question that remained unanswered at the end of the San
Francisco study was whether these findings were unique to the
particular group of people who participated in it. Were the findings
influenced, for example, by the liberal attitudes toward sex and
marriage the Bay Area is notorious for? (One might argue that
because of these liberal attitudes women had higher expectations
that were more likely to be frustrated.) So I repeated my study in
the conservative Israeli port town of Haifa (by coincidence, a sister
city of San Francisco). There I gave the Burnout Test to one hundred couples who had been married an average of sixteen years.
Israeli women reported significantly higher levels of burnout than
did Israeli men. Out of the twenty-one symptoms included in the
Burnout Test, the wives reported experiencing nineteen more
often than did their husbands, including feeling "depressed,"

"emotionally and physically exhausted," "whole body hurting," "weak," "troubled," and "anxious."[14]

With the single exception of anxiety, the sex differences I found in the Israeli sample were identical to those I found in the American sample. With regard to anxiety, Israeli women reported feeling anxious more often than did Israeli men, while American women reported feeling anxious less often than did American men.[15] This difference might be explained in part by the stereotype of the Israeli man as a "tough soldier," which develops as a result of the lengthy military service and frequent wars and which inhibits the expression of anxiety. Women also reported higher levels of burnout in two subsequent studies on marriage burnout. One study involved one hundred Israeli adult college students. The other study involved fifty-eight Americans who participated in a marriage-burnout workshop in the southwestern United States.

In spite of the consistency of these findings, an important question still remained: Were women indeed more burned out in their marriages, or did they only *report* higher levels of burnout? Is it possible that women, in fact, suffer the same level of burnout as men, or even less than men? When data are based on questionnaires in which people are asked directly to describe how they are feeling, the way they were asked in the marriage-burnout studies, the researcher is always left with the problem of interpretation. In our culture, for instance, it is more appropriate for women than for men to be weak and vulnerable. Does that mean that it's easier for women to admit that they are burned out?

John Nicholson reports in his book *Men and Women: How Different Are They?* that if you ask people how they feel in an emotional situation, women will typically say they are more deeply affected. Yet, when hooked up to machines that measure blood pressure and heart rate, men actually show the greater physical response. On the other hand, when erotic films are shown, men typically report higher levels of sexual arousal, but women's bodies react just as strongly.[16] In other words, men and women respond verbally the way they think they are supposed to respond.

Sometimes people aren't aware of how burned out they really are. They may know how physically, emotionally, and mentally exhausted they feel but attribute it to something other than the real cause. (Think of the man who believes that his long commute to and from work leaves him exhausted when he gets home, but who in fact dreads facing his family and uses his "exhaustion" as an excuse for retreat.) This psychological deception happens most commonly in situations where admitting burnout will require actions people don't want to take, like getting out of the marriage. Perhaps men have more reasons to suppress their burnout and have an easier time doing it, or else women are more in touch with their feelings and quicker to attribute them to burnout.

Should we trust what people say? Should we look at people's physiological responses? Should we listen to the insights of a psychotherapist who interprets their unconscious motivations? Every choice has its advantages and disadvantages. The advantage of self-report data, in the case of marriage burnout, is that it provides information about people's subjective experiences. This is very valuable information in and of itself, whether it is the "whole" or the "true" interpretation or not. Even if their physiological responses to stress are the same, for example, the fact that men and women interpret them differently is very likely to affect their chances of burning out.

In my research, I made it easy for people to admit to being burned out by telling them that only those who were once on fire can burn out. Consequently, I felt I could trust the honesty of their responses. Another reason that made me trust the questionnaire data about sex differences was that it was confirmed by my experience as a therapist. I saw many burned-out couples over long periods of time, and got to know them rather well. In the majority of cases, the wives were more burned out. One last point here: If a woman says she is burned out, there is a greater likelihood that she will seek a divorce *because* she feels burned out. Self-report can be an indication of future action.

If we accept that women are, in fact, more burned out in their marriages than men, we are still left with the question *why*.

Why are wives more burned out? Jessie Bernard would say it is because women carry the heavier burden of stresses in marriage. Barbara Ehrenreich might point out that current marriages are an unfair test of burnout for men and women. Men who burned out on marriage have already left the marriage because, unlike their wives, they could afford to. In other words, there is a selection process that leaves in marriages the husbands who are *less* burned out and the wives who are *more* burned out. Another proposition made by Ehrenreich that can be used to explain women's higher levels of burnout is the notion that some men—men who can't face breaking up the marriage themselves—make life so miserable for their wives that it is the wives who end up walking out of the marriage. Looking only at the self-report data, we are likely to find that these wives have higher levels of burnout, since the deterioration of the marriage was something they did not wish or cause.

I assumed that there are two other reasons why women burn out in marriage: First, women enter marriage with higher expectations than men do that the marriage will give their life a sense of meaning. Second, the hassles and stresses married women have to deal with in their roles as wives and mothers are significantly higher than those married men have to deal with in their roles as husbands and fathers. Some of the data generated by my research had a bearing on these two assumptions. I will present these data next.[17]

## MEN, WOMEN, AND ROMANCE

Women do not necessarily have higher expectations of romantic love than do men. Women do, however, seem to attach their expectations of romantic love to marriage more than men do. For most women—because of the way they have been socialized—finding true love *in marriage* means security, companionship, and happiness everafter. My research findings reveal that women describe their marriages as a more significant part of their lives, and as more important than work. Women also report expressing themselves more in their marriages than men do. Men, on the other hand— because of the way *they* have been socialized—view marriage as a trap. The research findings show that one of the few negative emotional experiences men report more frequently than women is feeling trapped.[18] When women make marriage so important, it is that much easier for them to burn out. Men, who see their wives and families as important to their life but not central to it, find themselves less disappointed in marriage.

The sex differences in expectations of marriage are also evident in data on romantic ideals. When asked how important different aspects of romantic love are (see box on p. 130), women's ratings were higher on nine of the ten items, including trust, understanding, friendship, emotional attraction, security, intellectual attraction, life sharing, romance, and money. Of the ten items, only one—physical attraction—was rated slightly higher by men than by women.[19]

Why do women expect marriage to give meaning to life more

than men do? A historical explanation is offered by the sociologist Robert Bellah and his colleagues in their recent book *Habits of the Heart*. The authors suggest that since the early nineteenth century, "while men's work was turning into a career or a job, women's work had the old meaning of a calling, an occupation defined essentially in terms of its contribution to the common good." While the role of men emphasized "self-aggrandizing individualism," the role of women emphasized "unselfishness and concern for others." While men were identified with the head, women were identified with the heart. The contrast between the sexes was not "wholly disparaging of women, since the romantic movement exalted feeling above reason as the wellspring of genuine humanity." This was especially true in the area of love and marriage, an area that required the participation of both sexes. Love, which was a matter of the heart and not the head and was an essential basis for marriage, was otherwise woman's sphere. Women accepted much of the ideology of family life and women's sphere.[20]

---

How important, to you personally, is each of the following aspects of romantic love? Please use the following scale:

|  1  |  2  |  3  |  4  |  5  |  6  |  7  |
|-----|-----|-----|-----|-----|-----|-----|
| not at all important | | | somewhat important | | | extremely important |

Physical attraction ____         Trust ____
Emotional attraction ____        Understanding ____
Friendship ____                  Romance ____
Long acquaintance/life           Security ____
  sharing ____                   Money ____
Interest, intellectual           Some other aspect (please
  attraction ____                  explain) ____

It may be interesting for you and your mate to compare your responses. Are your responses similar? Is your rank order of the ten items similar? What are the differences? Why do you think you see things differently?

Modern psychoanalytic theory provides an alternative—personal-history—explanation for the greater existential significance marriage has for women. The psychoanalytic explanation for the development of sex differences was discussed in the works of Dorothy Dinnerstein and Nancy Chodorow and most recently in Lillian Rubin's book *Intimate Strangers.* [21]

According to Rubin, there are some deep-seated psychological differences between men and women in our society, differences that are not born in nature but result from the fact that a woman is almost always the primary caregiver during infancy. Since it is a woman who "feeds us, shelters us, comforts us, and holds us in her arms to allay our fears,"[22] it is a woman with whom we form our first and most important emotional attachment.

In growing up there are two tasks of paramount importance: the development of an independent and coherent sense of self and the development of a clear gender identity as either a man or a woman. These tasks are different for boys and girls, because a woman mothered them both. For a boy, developing a clear masculine gender identity requires renouncing the emotional attachment to mother and seeking instead an identification with father. Accomplishing this difficult separation enables boys to establish strong ego boundaries. Therefore, boys have a stronger sense of being unique and separate. For a girl, developing a feminine gender identity is much easier because it requires identifying with mother, with whom she already has the primary emotional attachment. Because of the strong identification between mother and daughter, however, it is much more difficult for a girl to separate and develop an independent sense of self. These differences between the sexes in early development have, according to Rubin, a profound effect on the psychological makeup of men and women and on the relationship between the sexes, making them in effect "intimate strangers."

Because boys have to repress their feelings toward their mothers at an early age, before their ability to express complex feelings has fully developed, as adults men have difficulty connecting words with feelings. For most men, therefore, words are not a major aspect of intimacy. Since women never have to renounce and repress their emotional attachment to mother, they are more in touch with their feelings and more comfortable talking about them. This, says Rubin, is why talking about emotions is easier and more important for women than it is for men. Sharing their inner life is at the center of most women's definition of intimacy. These early-child-hood experiences can explain why women attach more significance to all aspects of communication than men do. Indeed, as the romantic ideology data showed, trust, understanding, friendship, and emotional attraction were more important to women. Other data indicated, similarly, that self-expression in marriage was more important to women than it was to men.

When women fall in love and get married, they expect their intimacy needs to be satisfied in marriage. Unfortunately for those needs, women marry men who often don't have the same needs. Dara describes her frustration:

> Ben just doesn't seem to have the same need to talk that I have. He reads the newspaper every day but never wants to talk about anything he has read. I, on the other hand, want to talk about things that I read, things that I feel, things that I think. And I can't do it with him. And it's terribly frustrating. I find it so easy to talk to my friends. We can talk for hours and hours. Why can't I talk in this way to my husband, who should be the closest person to me?

Ben is frustrated because, basically, he doesn't understand what Dara wants:

> She tells me she wants to talk about a problem. I listen, and then I tell her how she can solve the problem. I don't know what else you can do with a problem but try to solve it. But instead of being grateful, she gets furious with me.

Men and women are equally different in the way they feel about sex. For women, argues Rubin, there is no satisfactory sex without an emotional connection. For men, the two are more easily separable. The reason, again, has to do with those early stages of development in which the boy had to repress his emotions toward his mother but did not have to repress the erotic aspect of his attachment. The girl, on the other hand, had to repress her erotic attraction to the mother but could maintain the full intensity of her emotional attachment and identification. As a result, writes Rubin, "for men, the erotic aspect of any relationship remains forever the most compelling, while, for women, the emotional component will always be the more salient."[23]

From the perspective of marriage burnout, these differences in childhood experiences make emotional attachment a more salient component in women's romantic images, while making the erotic aspect a more salient component in men's romantic images. As a result, men and women enter relationships with different romantic images and with different sets of expectations, which can't but influence their probability of burnout.

In my studies, poor sex life, lack of physical attraction, and boredom were more highly correlated with burnout for men than they were for women.[24] Physical attraction was the only aspect of romantic love rated higher by men than by women. Also, men described themselves as more desirable sexual partners, and sex life as better, than women did. Kathy, who had been married for sixteen years, describes the difference between her and her husband in their approach to sex:

We may have a terrible fight and not talk to each other, but when we get to bed he wants to make love. How in the world he can even be thinking about sex with so much tension between us is beyond me. When we fight I get all tight inside. I need to feel close and loving before I can relax enough to open myself up for lovemaking.

Murray, her husband, sees things differently:

To me sex is a way of getting close. After we have a fight, I think that making love is the easiest way to make up. Unfortunately, Kathy doesn't see it that way. She would rather continue sulking.

If women, more so than men, expect marriage to give meaning to life, if the major component in women's romantic image involves emotional attachment and communication, and if the major component in men's romantic image involves sex, then it is impossible for both men and women to have their romantic images come true in the same relationship, and women's expectations are more likely to be frustrated. In other words, sex differences in marriage burnout are obvious, and burnout is inevitable. I devote a whole chapter (Chapter 7) to a discussion of this pessimistic conclusion. For now, let us leave it and move on from a discussion of expectations to a discussion of stresses.

## MARITAL STRESSES—MEN'S AND WOMEN'S

What are the most stressful, burnout-causing aspects of marriage for women? Are they the same as the most stressful aspects of marriage for men? According to my research findings, the answer to the second question is a very clear no.[25] Conflicting demands, for example, which had the highest correlation with burnout for women, ranked only seventh on the men's list. For women, the ideal of "unselfish concern for others," of loving and being loved, is a more important part of the role definition and romantic ideal than it is for men. In addition, women are socialized far more than men are to actualize their romantic ideal in marriage. The feeling that they are failing is very painful. Susan describes the stress of conflicting demands:

> The hardest thing for me is the feeling that I am disappointing people who depend on me and trust me. They include both my family and people in my work. It's not that their demands on me are unreasonable or unfair. It's that there's only one of me. I only have twenty-four hours in each day and I feel like I'm being torn apart.

Feeling pressured by family commitments, which was the second highest burnout-causing stress for women, was fifteenth on the men's list. Susan gives an example:

> Weeks before Thanksgiving I am beginning to worry about whom to invite for dinner. My brother can't stand Steve's sister and her husband, but Steve's mother would never come if his sister didn't come. And even though I find his sister a bore, I think that the family should be together for the holidays. So I talk to everybody for hours, trying to make them accept each other, in addition to shopping, cooking the meal, cleaning the house, and all the rest. Steve could not care less who comes for dinner, and since the holidays are the busiest time of the year at his work, he doesn't help much with the preparation of the meal either.

Conflicting demands and family commitments have an important thing in common. As noted before, they both reflect a failure to perform according to some standard or expectation. The perceived failure generates feelings of guilt and anxiety over not doing things the way they "should" be done, a very powerful cause of burnout for women, which ranked a mere fourteenth for men.[26]

When discussing the stress of conflicting demands, family commitments, and guilt, parenthood deserves a special mention. Books, songs, television commercials, and sitcoms all celebrate the cotton-candy world of parenthood. Their archetypal images are of cherubic little children, wearing soft nighties, all washed and combed, with rosy cheeks and cheerful smiles, coming to give Mom and Dad a good-night kiss. But, as every parent knows, parenthood is far from being a state of constant bliss. You have to feed children, wash them, dress them, shop for them, keep them healthy, keep them happy and take care of them when they are not. You have to give all of yourself, all of the time, without expecting anything back. In other words, you ideally have to love with no strings attached. There is no training for your role as a parent, a role that for many people (especially women) is the most ego-involving. Not only that, you can't get out of being a parent the way you can get out of a bad marriage or a bad job. You don't get weekends off. You can't postpone a child's need the way you can put off unpleasant paperwork. You can't quit parenthood, you can't take a sabbatical, and you can't trade a difficult child for another.

Under the weight of these stresses some parents burn out. The parents who are most likely to burn out are those who had unrealistic expectations of parenthood, who expected their child, even as a baby, to love them unconditionally and give meaning to their lives. It tends to happen more to those who are isolated, ignorant about the tasks involved, and lacking in resources and support. It happens most often during difficult periods in the child's or the parent's life. In a study involving seventy-three mothers, for example, a significant correlation was found between their burnout as mothers and the impulsivity of their school-age children.[27]

The most tragic consequence of burnout in parenthood is child abuse. In interviews with professionals and volunteers working on parental stress "hot lines," I learned that burnout is one of the fundamental causes of child abuse. Parents calling on those hot lines often say that they have reached their limits: "I can't take it anymore." "I am totally wiped out." "My child is driving me crazy." "I am falling apart." "I can't cope." The triggers of abuse, like the triggers of burnout, are rarely dramatic events. They are most often mundane daily problems of child rearing, especially with children from birth to five years of age. During these years parents are most likely to feel trapped in the house and bound by all that is required in the care of a young child. Socially isolated, unable to separate themselves from the child, and ignorant of what can be expected of their child, they feel a deep sense of failure and guilt.

In a pilot study of twelve abusive parents we found that the burnout level of these parents was the highest of any group we have ever studied.[28] Virtually all the abusive parents in the small sample suffered from financial hardship, poor family relations, and lack of support from spouse or friends. They expressed an inability to cope with their emotional and economic problems and resorted to violence because they had few skills to help them face the demands of parenthood. In light of the stresses that parenthood can entail, it is interesting that the number of children a couple had and the number of children still living at home were not correlated with burnout in marriage.[29] This suggests that while in some marriages children are a stress, in other marriages they are a joy and part of the glue holding the couple together. Whether they are one or the other depends on the couple's expectations, stresses, and available resources.

The stresses of parenthood do not discriminate between the sexes. Single fathers are as stressed as single mothers. But since, in our society, women still carry the lion's share of the parental role in most families, they end up carrying more of the physical and emotional burdens that come with that role. Since societal norms define motherhood as the most important role in a woman's life, feeling that she is not performing to the high standards of the role can cause a worse feeling of personal failure in a woman than a similar less-than-perfect performance can cause in a man.

From everything said so far it seems that women's stresses in marriage are related to their higher expectations both of marriage and of themselves. They are stressed by conflicting demands because they accept those demands as legitimate. They are stressed by family commitments because they accept them as their responsibility. The feeling that they are not performing to the high standards they imposed on themselves causes them tremendous guilt—the severe internal judge that decrees they have failed. For many women an ideal life often means a perfect marriage—with a shared inner life, shared goals, mutual recognition, appreciation, and self-actualization. Their emotional involvement in the marriage (which in most marriages is bigger than the men's) makes them take on the job of "the keepers of the spark." They work hard always to do what is "right." When they feel they have failed and the marriage is not all it is "supposed" to be, they burn out. Women, it seems, burn out because they care too much.[30]

This is not to say that marriage burnout is exclusively a woman's experience. Some men report higher levels of burnout than some women; in some marriages the husband is more burned out than the wife. As is so often the case, statistical averages don't always apply to the individual. The reason for men's burnout in marriage is the same as the reason for women's burnout—the marriage has failed to give their life a sense of meaning. Two couples I worked with are an example.

One couple was in their thirties, the other in their fifties. The husband in the younger couple was an engineer; the husband in the older couple was a high school teacher. Both men had once enjoyed their work but were, by the time I saw them, disillusioned and bored with it. Both described their relationships with their wives as the most important thing in their lives. In both cases, the wives started careers late in life. The younger woman had gone back to college after working to put her husband through. She had been extremely successful in school and had obtained a good academic position. The older woman had started working for a local politician after the three children left home. With intelligence, maturity, hard work, and enthusiasm, this woman had become the politician's campaign manager. Both women loved their work, were excited about their success in it, and were delighted to have a chance to prove themselves, to work up to their potential. Their marriages were important to them, but not more important than their work. These women derived their sense of meaning in life from their work as much as from their marriages—but they were married to men who now put the relationship first. This situation caused great tension in the two relationships. The tension was aggravated by the mates' realizations that they were reversing traditional sex-roles. The men were afraid they were caring "too much" about the marriage; the women worried they were caring "too much" about their work. These couples show the destructive effect of divergent interests, no matter whether it is the husband or the wife whose interest is focused elsewhere, outside the marriage.

For men who are in more traditional marriages, the most

stressful and burnout-causing aspect of marriage is overload. Overload ranked third on the women's list.[31] Steve describes the stress overload imposes on his marriage:

> When I come home at night, after a long and very stressful day in the office, I am exhausted. I don't have either the emotional or the physical energy Susan expects me to deliver as a husband and a father. I need a few minutes of peace and quiet before I unwind enough to be able to listen to her or the children. When I am not available emotionally or I am not supportive enough, she gets resentful. I wish she could come to work with me some day and see what it is like. That might help her understand the stress I deal with and maybe make her slightly more supportive of me.

For men who were socialized to expect success at work, in addition to love, to give their life a sense of meaning, men whose professional identity is the most important part of their self-definition, the romantic ideal is different from that of women. After spending a whole day in "the jungle out there," these men expect home to be a refuge and a haven. Similarly, men who were socialized by what Barbara Ehrenreich called "the breadwinner ethic"[32] expect in return for the economic support of their families to receive the nurturing and care wives are "supposed" to provide. When these idealized images of marriage don't turn out the way they expected, these men burn out.

Sexual variety is another aspect of most men's romantic images that seems less important for women. Indeed, the second most stressful aspect of marriage for men was boredom. Boredom ranked only sixteenth on the women's list.[33] Harvey, a businessman married twelve years, explains:

> I am a very sexual person. I just love the sexual energy between a man and a woman, even if it doesn't involve sexual intercourse. I have many sexually charged (yet unconsummated) relationships with women I come in contact with. But not with my wife. With her there is no sexual energy left at all, just boredom.

All these findings indicate that very often men and women enter marriage with different romantic ideals and experience, even in the same marriages, very different stresses. This conclusion was reached by other scholars as well, most notably Jessie Bernard, who went so far as to differentiate between "His marriage" and "Her marriage."[34]

Men and women, not surprisingly, see marriage differently. In all my studies on marriage burnout, men perceived their marriages more positively than women did. In the San Francisco study, for example, men described their communication with their mates as better than women did. They were more likely to describe their mates as their best friends and as the one person in their lives they could completely open themselves up to. (Women were far more likely to have a female friend with whom they talked about "everything," including problems with their mate.) Men described themselves as sharing more of the household chores than women gave them credit for. (Women described themselves as carrying more than their share of chores.) Men described sex as better and themselves as more desirable sexual partners than women did. All in all men seemed, indeed, happier in their marriages than did women.[35]

One day I was on a radio talk show. After I had spoken for a time on marriage burnout, the host invited listeners to call in. One of the callers, who sounded extremely upset, told us that he had been married for over fifty years. He said that until very recently he and his wife had had "a wonderful marriage." They were both "very happy together," their "communication was very good," and "sex has been wonderful." He had been perfectly content in the marriage until he discovered, to his great shock and dismay two weeks before, that his wife "was a whore." When I asked him to explain what he meant, he said that he found out she had been seeing other men all through their marriage, and was sleeping around even before they got married. He described himself as "terribly upset and burned out." "Wouldn't you be?" he demanded. I did not have the opportunity to talk to the man's wife, but my clinical experience leads me to believe that if I did, I would hear a very different description of their fifty years of "marital bliss." If she indeed had been involved with other men throughout the marriage (which might or might not be true), she most probably would have described the quality of their marriage, their communication, and their sex life as far less wonderful than her husband did. Because of the different perceptions that husbands and wives have of marriage, one of the first things I do in working with couples is to tell them that in my office there is almost never an absolute truth—but rather two versions for everything.

The findings that women have higher expectations from marriage and carry a heavier burden at home were confirmed in several studies.[36] These findings are also supported by prevailing cultural stereotypes and by the findings of other investigators showing that a wife's general life happiness and overall well-being are more dependent on marital happiness than are her husband's. Consequently, when problems occur, women tend to be more distressed.[37]

For a long time women's responses to life stresses have been attributed to their dispositions rather than to their situations. For example, the higher frequency of depression among women was said to be caused by women's psychological vulnerability and a weakness of character. Only recently have scholars begun to attribute the higher levels of women's complaints to the reality of most women's lives. It has been noted, for example, that depression is greatest among low-income women with young children—a group and a period of time characterized by the greatest kind of pressures. Contrary to the myth of legions of hyper-depressed "empty-nesters," women whose children have left home are relatively unlikely to suffer from depression. Much of the stress in their lives has flown the coop along with their children. Single women and married men, who are burdened by the least amount of stress, are least likely to suffer from depression. Only those "supermothers" who defined themselves in terms of their maternal role suffer from depression when their children leave home.[38]

## HOW WOMEN AND MEN COPE WITH BURNOUT

If too high expectations and the daily accumulation of stresses cause burnout, the obvious cure for women's higher levels of burnout is to puncture their balloon of high expectations, and to teach them to reduce the perceived stress in their lives.

For most women—for most couples—the idea of lowering their expectations for love and marriage is unacceptable. When two people fall in love, they don't want to hear that the chances of their marriage enduring will improve if they don't believe in the magic of love. During infatuation, when expectations are formed, both mates want the best and the most for themselves and for each other. Someone has to be designated the keeper of the spark, even at the risk of higher vulnerability to the dangers of burnout. Women tend to take on the job more often because of their sex-role socialization. But the task of keeping the spark alive is not exclusively a women's domain and can be defined as a man's responsibility as well—or instead. The best possible solution seems to be a *"joint custody" of the romantic spark,* in which both mates form together their expectations for the relationship, and in which both mates see to it that the relationship does not depart too much from their shared ideal. In relationships where this is indeed the case—whether the task is done simultaneously by both mates, or is alternated between them—the romantic spark has a better chance.[39]

Perceived stress in marriage can be reduced in two ways: by reducing the stress itself and by improving buffers against it. Some husbands and wives discuss their perceived stresses and negotiate sharing of tasks. The sharing can include earning money, paying bills, taking care of the children, and keeping house. This solution is increasingly evident among dual-career couples who have a companionship marriage, but it is also possible among traditional couples where husbands have avoided domestic responsibility because they grew up in a family that defined it as "women's work." Research indicates that when these men have to share child-care duties with their wives, they often discover that it can be rewarding. (They also begin to understand what their wives are complaining about when they say the children are driving them crazy.) Marriages in which there was a sharing of household and child-care responsibilities were described as happier by both mates.[40]

The second solution of improving the buffers against burnout is best accomplished by an effective social-support network. Women, I discovered, value and use social support more than men do. In a study involving eighty men and women in which six functions of social support were examined, five of the functions were rated as more important by women: having someone who listens, having someone who acknowledges work well done, having someone who accepts and supports unconditionally, having someone who confronts on emotional issues, and having someone who shares one's view of reality. The only function valued more by men was professional challenge, which many women tended to see as criticism.[41]

In another study involving 220 professional men and women in which coping with job stress was investigated, we found that talking to a supportive friend was a much more frequent and effective method for dealing with stresses for women than it was for men. Men preferred to confront the stress directly. When they could do nothing about the stress, men preferred to ignore it.[42] I discovered similar sex differences in coping in my studies of marriage burnout. I found, for example, that talking to a supportive friend was a much more frequent method for dealing with stresses for women than it was for men. Men tended to ignore the source of stress (even when the source of stress was their wife) and avoid it as a way of coping.[43]

There was an interesting reversal in the way the sexes coped with job stress as opposed to marital stress. On the job women were more reluctant than men to confront the source of their stress directly. ("Confront the boss? Me? Oh, no! I don't think I can do that. I am not assertive enough.") Yet in their marriages, women used confrontation more frequently than men did. They were the ones who most often demanded that a problem be acknowledged and discussed; they were the ones most likely to complain about not having enough quality time together.[44] Similar findings were reported by the psychologist John Guttman. Guttman discovered that wives were more likely to complain about problems in the relationship and that in good marriages when such problems were raised, wives managed the negative emotions so they didn't escalate.[45]

The largest difference between men and women in their coping style, however, had to do with the way they used friends. Women used a network of friends—both at work and at home—more frequently and more effectively than did men. Women found it easier than men to talk to a good friend about doubts, problems, and conflicts, and found talking more helpful. While talking to a supportive friend can be very comforting to one's ego, it is not the best way to confront problems with one's mate. A woman who talks to her best friend about her husband's beastly behavior is likely to receive all the needed support for her contention that the behavior in question is indeed beastly, but she is not likely to gain much insight into the husband's reasons for that behavior. This is why, research findings show, the more one talked to a supportive friend the more burned out one was likely to be. This finding was true for both sexes, but more so for women.[46] I might even argue that women's tendency to talk with their friends instead of with their husbands is in part responsible for their higher burnout rate.

Even if the temptation is big to use the easy way of getting support for one's perspective, it is much better, in the long run, to take the harder approach and talk directly to one's mate. This kind of discussion is most effective if done in the spirit of mutual exploration and learning, rather than confrontation. ("Why is this behavior so upsetting to me?" "What have I done to provoke, condone, or encourage this behavior?")

In spite of all the sex differences discussed throughout this chapter, the recommendation to deal with marriage problems directly is equally true for both men and women. While it is very valuable for women (and for men) to have a social-support network of other women (or other men) who share their particular kinds of stresses and role conflicts, who view the world the way they do, and who provide feedback, emotional sustenance, and assistance in times of need, such a network will not help prevent marriage burnout and may in fact enhance it, unless the insights gained in the support group are used to improve communication with the mate.

While women report higher levels of burnout, thereby creating a temptation to offer solutions that apply more directly to women, *burnout is a couple's problem and can be solved only within the context of the couple.* If burnout is a couple's problem, and the recommendations for dealing with it are the same for both husbands and wives, why devote a whole chapter to sex differences in burnout? I had two main reasons for doing that: First, the question, "Who is more burned out in marriage, men or women?" is one I am asked very often and therefore seems to be of interest to many people. (This whole book is organized around responses to the most frequent questions I am asked about marriage burnout.) Second, awareness of the sex differences in burnout is necessary in order to help men and women in relationships appreciate the universality of the other's perspective.

When a woman expresses frustration with the fact that her husband does not care about the marriage as much as she does, that he is involved in his work to the exclusion of everything else while she is left to carry the full burden of their home and family responsibilities, the knowledge that they are not the only ones who have this problem is helpful in reducing blame and guilt. Both men and women often have difficulty appreciating the differences in their perspectives. As a result, couples provide each other with less support than they might have, had they clearly understood what both wanted.

In the first three chapters of this book, the focus was on falling in love, the fantasy part of an intimate relationship. The last two chapters focused on the more mundane aspects of a relationship. I tried to convey the vital significance of the reality of people's day-to-day lives. Work and marriage address what most people's lives are really like, how most people try to find meaning in their lives using our culture's prescribed solutions. The actual process of living is what beats most people down, whether they are successful in what they do or not. This is why established relationships are not as exciting as the first stages of falling in love. The day-to-day existence is also what makes love relationships stable; it is what gives them their "roots." As we will see in the next chapter, sex is what gives many relationships their "wings."

# CHAPTER 6

# Sex in Marriage:
# The Slow and Steady Fire

Just because you don't see shooting stars,
Doesn't mean it isn't perfect . . .
It's the stuff that dreams are made of,
It's the slow and steady fire.

Carly Simon,
"The Stuff That Dreams
Are Made Of"

The best aphrodisiac is a passionate
partner.

Anonymous

During the break in a workshop I led recently, a woman in her late forties came over and said:

> After listening to you I no longer think I am burned out in my marriage. I still love my husband, and I know he loves me. Our communication is good, and we both consider each other our very best friend. The problem is that sex has become so boring and listless that it's almost not worth the effort. Mind you, it's not because we don't know what to do in bed. We know each other's bodies so well that we can always make each other come. But why bother? We both would rather read a good book or watch TV than make love. Our sex is efficient but soulless . . . like peeling potatoes.

What this woman wanted to know can be summed up by one of the most common questions marriage and sex therapists hear: *"Can sex be good even after many years of marriage?"*

Some people, who believe the only honest response to this question is no and yet who want the security of marriage, look for sexual excitement in illicit affairs. (Such people will end their marriage only on those rare occasions when an affair gets out of hand.)

If you are reading this book, chances are that a life spent living with one person and looking forward to sex with another is not a desirable solution for you. If sex is the most important thing in life to you, you are likely to remain in a relationship only as long as the sex remains exciting. When sex becomes less exciting, you will become restless and, sooner or later, leave. If your main goal in life is exciting sex, you are likely to end up with a long series of brief love affairs with little or no emotional bonding. You will become a latter-day Don Juan or a perennial vamp.

Illicit affairs are based on lies, yet most people want honesty in their relationships. Some people try to combine affairs and honesty by having an open relationship, where affairs are permitted within certain rules. The rules agreed on differ widely. For some couples the rule is "only when one of us is out of town." For some couples there is a condition such as: "Never spend the whole night with someone else." Since the advance of AIDS, there is an additional rule: "Always practice 'safe' sex." For one couple the rule is "every Tuesday and Thursday night." On those nights the wife brings her lover home, while the husband goes over to his lover. Such agreements are aimed at limiting the emotional involvement outside the marriage and protecting the priority of the marriage. However, keeping feelings in check is not easy; more often than not couples eventually choose to close an open relationship because "it was just too much hard work."

A San Francisco–based commune calling itself Kerista Village developed an unusual method for keeping sex exciting in intimate relationships. The Keristans, who at present number nineteen adults, have been together for thirteen years. They maintain a rotating sleep cycle in which every night another man sleeps with another woman according to a prescribed schedule. This arrangement, the Keristans argue, assures a high level of sexual variety without the otherwise inevitable loss of trust, security, emotional depth, and commitment. (And yes, they do have children; two children are raised by "joint parenting.")[1]

Other cultures have found different ways of keeping sex exciting. Orthodox Jews must practice partial abstinence. Because of the purity laws, which prohibit intercourse during and a week following the woman's menstruation, sex is permitted for only about two weeks a month. The forced abstinence, I was told by Orthodox couples, ensures that sexual intercourse will not become a boring routine. The most extreme practice of this "abstinence makes for passion" occurred in eleventh-century courtly love. Developed and idealized by troubadours and poets in the courts of the aristocracy, courtly love required that the exalted passion between a man and a woman remain unconsummated. Only unfulfilled and unsatisfied desire could fuel passion and bring it to its ultimate heights. In their tales, consummated affairs—like those between Lancelot and Guinevere or between Tristan and Isolde—always ended in great tragedy.

Open marriages, sexually liberated communes, Orthodox Judaism, and the ways of the troubadours probably seem to you like pretty remote prescriptions for normal married life. Like most married people, you would probably prefer to have a passionate sexual relationship with the person you love, the person you plan to spend your life with. You would probably rather not resort to forced abstinence, an open affair, or illicit affairs. In our culture, sexual attraction is a very important component of romantic love. The media, which reflect our cultural values and act as a powerful socializing force, offer an image of romantic love that has a very strong erotic component. It is difficult to imagine falling in love with someone to whom we are not sexually attracted. Conversely, sex is most exciting when done with someone we are in love with.

This connection between sex and love, which to us seems so natural and necessary, is very recent. There have been many cultures and social systems in which sex played an important part, but romantic love played no part at all. In those societies people had sex, most likely enjoyed it, and saw it as normal and natural—without the overlay of love. In other societies, love played an important part but was completely divorced from sex. For the Greek scholars, for example, true love was possible only between men, because only such love could be spiritual. Sex with a woman was procreative and thus could not be connected with true love.

In our culture, birth control has taken sex out of the realm of procreation and romantic love has made sex spiritual. We feel we are missing something important when sex is without love. We don't want sex to be just a biological function; we want it to be love and to have a spiritual meaning.

Ernest Becker, in his book *The Denial of Death,* argues that sex is part of man's "animal nature."[2] Man has always struggled to overcome his animal nature because it is tied to his mortal body. Sex is of the body, and the body is mortal. As in Greek mythology, Eros and Thanatos are inseparable; death is the natural twin brother of sex. People who exclude sex from their definition of romantic love, according to Becker, are people who deny the reality of the human body and its animal nature. The reason they do it and why that kind of an approach has appeal is because it helps deny the ultimate mortality of the body. A recent case in point is Scott Peck's best-selling *The Road Less Traveled*. In it he argues that sexual attraction is not a component of true love, that falling in love is nature's way to trick people [men?] into getting married, and that romantic love is a great lie. He defines "true love" as "an act of will," as "discipline," thus totally removing it from the realm of the body and into the realm of the spirit. Peck's distaste for sex is understandable. Sex is a lower function and love a higher function. People in love, however, raise sex from a biological function to a spiritual act of bonding, from "intercourse" to "making love."[3]

## THE ROLE OF EMOTIONAL AROUSAL

When people fall in love they are sexually as well as emotionally aroused. We are socialized to equate love with intense sexual arousal (unless we have a reason not to: say, we know that the person is completely wrong for us). Once the connection has been made, it becomes functionally autonomous and continues operating independently. Sexual arousal has a definite physiological basis, and can affect and be affected by any other arousal, physical or emotional. Lillian, an attractive woman in her mid-thirties and married ten years, describes it:

> As must be typical, the symptoms of the problem come up most glaringly in the bedroom. I no longer feel sexually attracted to or excited by Dave. Dave says he is still attracted to me—and that the lack of enthusiasm comes from me rather than him—but the predictability and low-key style of his lovemaking cause me to think that perhaps our lack of enthusiasm is shared. I have no complaints about his willingness, frequency, sweetness, or consideration and givingness during the lovemaking. It is the lack of creativity, genuine excitement, and passion that I refer to. And I do nothing to introduce these elements myself, since I no longer feel any passion or strong attraction. I do not find myself motivated to exhibit feelings I am not having—although some pretense on my part might get the ball rolling, perhaps. It's just not something I want to force myself to do. Passion can exist only in a circuit between two people . . . truly, I don't think either of us feels it . . . though we both want to.

Is it too much to expect sexual passion after over a decade of living together? And if so . . . does that mean that you give up having it so as to preserve the marriage?

We will explore Dave and Lillian's case in great detail throughout this chapter, but even at this point we know that they are probably matched in terms of background, attitude, and personality. We can also assume that when they fell in love, they fitted each other's romantic images.

After being married for many years, however, some men and women find that their spouses no longer fit their romantic images, either because the spouse has changed or because the image has changed. This, at least at first glance, was not the case with Lillian and Dave, who still loved each other, were committed to the marriage, and desperately wanted to recreate the exciting sex of their early years together. They did not want to break up, even though the idea kept returning. "When I contemplate life without Dave and his love," said Lillian, "I can almost feel myself shriveling up." What seemed to be missing in the marriage that was there during infatuation is the emotional arousal that comes from the newness of a relationship, from the uncertainty of the other person's love, from the excitement of finding someone who so perfectly meets one's hopes and needs. After ten years the relationship isn't new, and since the commitment to the relationship has been made, the uncertainty and insecurity are gone. Most important is probably the fact (well known to the courtly lovers) that once our hopes and needs are fulfilled, they lose their intensity and power. When certain needs are satisfied, they stop being needs, and other needs emerge to replace them. Lillian:

> Maybe I am no longer the same person who fell in love over ten years ago. I have blossomed and grown confident under the steady sunshine of Dave's love. Certainly I have very different needs today than I did when I met him. A decade ago I needed his nurturing and love so much that I was not aware of having any other needs. He was the answer to all my prayers.

Lillian was saying, in effect, that she expected Dave's love to give her life a sense of meaning, which it did, but only for a time. Once achieved, the fulfilled dream had gradually lost its power to reward and energize. Her need for nurturing and security was replaced by a new need for passionate sex:

> As a thirty-five-year-old woman, no children, successful career, I find that passionate sex, or the lack of it, is far more important to me than ever before. I am no longer working to build a career. I enjoy my work and feel successful. I think this is the age when a woman is supposed to reach her sexual peak . . . perhaps that is why I crave passionate sex in a way that I did not use to do.

Her dissatisfaction and boredom with the sex in her marriage precipitated Lillian's involvement in a passionate illicit affair:

> About six months ago I became involved with another man who elicited passion in me that I did not know I was capable of feeling. For years I had just figured that I was not a very sexually oriented person. Though my husband and I had had much more exciting sex before we were married and during the early years, we had not had passionate sex for at least three years prior to my affair with this other man. Although my affair was with a strange and crazy man whom I no longer have any interest in or desire to see, it elicited some very powerful feelings at the time . . . so much so that it was impossible for me to hide the fact that I was having an affair. Indiscretions on my part aroused Dave's suspicions, and I ended up telling him in stages the full extent of my extramarital involvement.
>
> Dave was wounded to the core. His infinite trust in me dissolved, and he said he lost the capacity to trust completely. It would do him no good to divorce me and try to find another woman he could trust, since he had lost the capacity for complete trust in another person. If I—whom he loved and trusted so completely— could betray him that way, then anyone could at any time.
>
> When I was so close to losing Dave, my emotions swung back powerfully toward him. I no longer cared about the other man or the affair, but cared only about repairing the damage I had done to the man I love—my husband. I felt that I would kiss his feet for the next ten years if that was necessary to win back his love and trust . . . to restore the bond and comfort that I had ruptured.

The drama surrounding the affair and Dave's discovery of the betrayal not only served to remind Lillian of the sense of meaning her marriage gave her, but also was, in and of itself, emotionally arousing:

> It was mostly my intense desire to right the wrong and stay on the good-wife path in the future (as well as his love and need for me and perception of my love for him) that convinced Dave to give me another chance. And the passionate desire I felt in wanting so much to heal Dave's pain and repair the damage I had done . . . and not lose the man I had loved all these years and still loved so much . . . all those feelings created at least a semblance of sexual desire and passion . . . so I thought it might all be restored.

During the aftermath of the affair Lillian and Dave talked, for the first time, about the stagnation in their sex life:

> At that point—while I was caught up in the passionate desire to repair the damage I had done and restore his trust—we talked about the sexual stagnation that had driven me to an affair. Dave said that I should have told him about my boredom with sex, and we would have found a way to make it exciting between us again. He said it just takes some time and attention and communication. He said he had noticed that I did not seem very interested in sex anymore. Even though that bothered him, he loved me so much that he was willing to sacrifice passionate sex in order to continue our marriage. He figured that passionate sex was small in relation to all that we did have between us. Neither of us realized that the lack of passionate sex caused a growing hunger in me that left me open for this devastating affair. Now that we knew, we both set about "working" at having better sex between us. So we took these steps:
>
> We got a layer of foam to soften our too-hard bed.
>
> I got an I.U.D. so that the inconvenience and unpleasantness of my diaphragm would not continue to get in the way of spontaneous sex.
>
> I told him that sometimes his breath bothered me and turned me off sexually and personally, and we identified the food items that caused this problem and eliminated it with 90 percent success.

Dealing with the "bad breath" issue pointed to a problem in the communication between Lillian and Dave, a problem that, as they later discovered, was evident in other areas of their life as well:

Dave was angry that I had not told him this for fear of hurting his feelings, when in fact his feelings were not upset. He took it like any other problem where you identify the cause and come up with the solution. I myself would have been devastated if he complained about my breath, which is why I did not say anything for the past few years. . . . We took some other steps as well:

We tried to make love at times other than late at night when we would be too tired for passion . . . we tried to do it more during the day, or early.

We went to a sex store in search of some interesting sex toys but did not find anything new!

We did much less genital sex (a pattern we had gotten into) and much more face-to-face sex . . . to have a greater feeling of intimacy. By more attention to forceful movements and proper placement of pillows, we found that I could have reliable orgasms even without direct oral or digital stimulation.

Unfortunately, the technical improvements were effective only in the context of the renewed emotional arousal. Once the emotional arousal temporarily generated by Lillian's affair was diminished, even the improvements in sexual technique couldn't maintain the sexual spark:

All of these steps seemed relatively successful in the beginning. They made important (though mechanical) improvements in our sex life. And when combined with the passionate desire I felt to repair the damage I had done, I thought that the steps we were taking might work. But I find that sex between us has again become boring for me. I am not sure what Dave is feeling. He gives lip service to interest, but his sexual actions demonstrate affection and technique rather than passion for me.

## THE EMOTIONAL AROUSAL OF RESOLVING CONFLICTS

How can emotional arousal be generated and maintained in a marriage? One answer, according to Jordan and Margaret Paul, is by resolving conflicts as they emerge in an open and nondefensive way aimed at learning.[4] Conflicts, as we all know, are inevitable in any long-term intimate relationship, because people are different. Whenever two people in a relationship want different things, or feel differently or think differently, a conflict occurs. It can be because one wants to make love and the other wants to sleep, because one feels like talking and the other feels like being alone, or because one person thinks their neighbor Joe is neat and the other person thinks Joe is a jerk. According to the Pauls, it is not the conflict itself but how couples handle that conflict that creates difficulties.

The Pauls believe that all responses to conflict can be reduced to two intents: to protect or to learn. When people try to protect themselves, they do it in one of three ways: compliance (giving up to avoid the conflict), control (trying to change the other's mind or behavior), and indifference (ignoring the conflict). When both partners protect they create what the Pauls call "protective circles." These circles (e.g., one mate always controls and the other mate always complies, or both mates ignore the conflict or both try to control each other at the same time) are the cause of such things as communication problems, emotional isolation, angry arguments, and—most relevant to our topic—infrequent and listless sex.

The intent to learn requires a willingness on the part of both partners to be open and nondefensive. (Not an easy order, by any means.) It can facilitate an exciting process of mutual exploration and discovery. The process of exploration can use whatever conflict emerges, and in it both mates have to face questions like: What reason did my mate have for doing that? What part did I play in creating the problem? How did my mate's behavior make me feel? Why is that so? What childhood fears, internalized values, and subconscious expectations were triggered for me? How is my behavior affecting my mate? Why is that so? What are the consequences for the relationship? The process of exploration can produce pain and fear, especially when the issues discussed are very sensitive, but ultimately, the Pauls say, the feelings it generates are those of love:

> As we share pain, the weight of our protections is lifted and we feel lighter and clearer. We see our mate with a heart so full of love it wants to burst. We want to be as close as possible, to be one with, to be inside of. Our entire being comes alive with the intensity of our passion.[5]

I would argue that mutual exploration into sensitive areas of conflict has such a positive effect because it is emotionally arousing. The emotional arousal generated can intensify and rejuvenate sex. As the Pauls note:

> In a long-term relationship intense sexuality will endure only if partners continue to share and explore. When each person begins to pull back to protect, loving feelings and passion fade. The physical aspect of sex alone cannot keep it exciting, no matter how practiced the techniques, how beautiful the partner, or how perfect the bodies. Without emotional intimacy sex eventually becomes boring and infrequent (or nonexistent).[6]

When Lillian and Dave began exploring why sex had become boring, it came out that for several years Lillian had been angry at Dave but had a great deal of difficulty expressing that anger directly. She was afraid that if she were to express the full extent of her anger and disappointment (if she let her emotional monster out of the closet) something terrible would happen (Dave would be so upset that he would leave her and her whole world would collapse). Dave felt that something was wrong but also preferred not to confront the issue. In the Pauls' terminology, Lillian and Dave created a protective circle in which both of them ignored the conflict.

When Dave and Lillian first met, Lillian was living an unstable ("flaky") life-style and felt very insecure about herself. She was attracted to Dave's strength, stability, and self-confidence. Dave, for his part, was attracted to Lillian's energy and emotional intensity. Their marriage fulfilled both of their romantic ideals. During the first years of their marriage, Dave was a good provider and a stable breadwinner, which enabled Lillian to go back to school and get a degree. After about six years, however, Dave decided he needed a change, so he left his secure and lucrative job to become a stockbroker, a career Lillian deemed "gambling and not a real job." Shortly after Dave became a stockbroker, the market slid, and the two of them found themselves dependent on Lillian's salary. During all this time Lillian told Dave it was "all right," in order not to hurt his feelings, but deep down it was not all right at all.

Dave's career has not been successful. For the past four years I have been the steady breadwinner while Dave has tried to break into the field of high finance. Although he did have one fairly good year, he brought in a total of about $40,000 during a four-year period. Even when he made some money, neither of us felt it could be freely spent because there was no way to know when or if he would make another commission. Being a broker, especially during these hard times for the stock market, can be very stressful work. Dave has put out a lot of effort, undergone a lot of stress, and gotten very little back for it.

Lillian understood that what she perceived as Dave's "failure" was "due to a series of bad-luck conditions, rather than a symptom of inherent failure tendencies or inadequacies in Dave." Still she felt "emotionally impacted by a sense of his 'failure.'" It triggered childhood fears and insecurities that were, at least in part, related to the fact that her own father was "a total and complete failure in the business world." Her feelings of security in Dave and in the marriage were shaken and with them the sense of meaning the marriage gave her life. The experience had an effect on her sexual feelings toward Dave:

> The sexist woman in me expects a man to be stronger and steadier and more financially successful than I am. Someone inside me wants to be a delicate, charming little girl . . . with a big powerful successful man to take care of her and overwhelm her with his forcefulness, his sureness, his sure-footed successfulness. I think I expect a husband to be successful just as Dave expects a wife to be faithful. We have both disappointed one another. Although I don't consciously make his career success a condition of my love, I am sure that on an emotional level I am experiencing deep disappointment in him. I have wondered if this disappointment is behind my lack of sexual attraction. . . . Dave's financial dependency is the crux of my anger and disappointment. . . . The whole failure issue—men should succeed; my father was a failure—has a lot of emotional energy around it and generates its own dynamic.

Clearly, Dave's supposed career failure disappointed Lillian's romantic image to such an extent that it could no longer give her life a sense of meaning. The disappointment had a very concrete manifestation in Lillian's sexual feelings:

And then there is the size issue. Dave is relatively short for a man (about 5 foot 5 inches; I am 5 foot). He is also very slender. I am fairly slender but more solid then he is. I never used to think about it at all, but lately I have been craving largeness in a man. Dave is wonderfully endowed sexually—and fills me up as no other man has ever done quite so well. But in terms of body size and weight I have lately found him lacking. I crave bigness and power on top of me when we make love these days. I feel cheated because my arms wrap so easily around his slender body. I feel like a protecting mother/companion/comfort-giver, when I want to feel like a nymphet overwhelmed by a large, powerful, and passionate man who is driven to frenzy by my loveliness.

Her disappointment in Dave had an effect on Lillian's romantic image:

I wonder why, after over a decade of marriage, I am suddenly disappointed and turned off by Dave's slenderness and shortness. I used to love the way he seemed on my level, my size. I liked the fact that he was not overwhelming. I was trying to express myself and achieve confidence and power in the world in my own right. I was sick of being overwhelmed by egocentric men. Dave was, and is, the most caring, loving, giving, wonderful man I have ever met. And I used to love his body. It hasn't changed a pound or an inch. Where have I changed, and why?

Is this body-disappointment based on the "failure-disappointment" that I feel emotionally? Have I got his smallness of body mixed up with his smallness of income? Will this body-disappointment go away when Dave gets a new career underway and has success? And will sexual excitement ignite between us then?

Lillian started examining some other questions having to do with the meaning of her life in the larger scheme of things:

Or am I just going through some mid-life crisis, wanting to re-create the fun, the dating, and the exciting sexual encounters I never had before I was married because I was insecure and miserable? . . . Or am I experiencing the downside of deciding not to have children . . . the emptiness—the "so, what's next?" feeling. . . . The lack of forward movement in life. . . . The lack of a major shared project to bring Dave and me together around something meaningful to both of us. Or are we experiencing the downside of not sharing some basic interests? Dave is more of an outdoors person; I am more of an abstract armchair philosopher type. . . . Perhaps we have each deadened ourselves by not pursuing independently the basic interests that we do not share. Desperately clinging to one another, perhaps we are losing ourselves as well as each other.

The "emptiness," the "lack of forward movement in life," the lack of a "meaningful major shared project" were all manifestations of Lillian's "existential" disappointment in her marriage. But the overgrown roots, the strong commitment to each other, compensated for the undergrown wings, the absence of excitement, growth, and sense of significance in the marriage:

> Will we continue to cling to one another—though rigid and frigid— too scared of losing each other to voice the feelings and fears and disappointments that prevent us from the passionate experience of one another? Or—through painful-yet-loving communication—can we break down the walls now stifling our love and need of growth?

Having focused so much on Dave's supposed career failure, I need to emphasize that Dave did not share Lillian's negative assessment of his career as a stockbroker. Dave, who is a very likable, bright, energetic, and emotionally solid person, mainly spoke of how much money he *did* make and described his continued prospects in rather rosy colors.

As I noted earlier, in spite of the intensity of her disappointment and rage, Lillian still valued very much the security her marriage provided and could not imagine life without Dave. She was afraid of what Dave might do if she expressed her negative feelings openly, so she repressed them. But it is impossible to block emotions selectively. Once you put on an emotional shield, it inhibits all emotions. Consequently, with her repressed anger Lillian repressed her feelings of love and passion toward Dave. Dave, at the same time, while not admitting his failure as a stockbroker, was still worried about his financial future. He wanted to protect Lillian from his fears and feelings of insecurity and inadequacy, which were caused by his "unmasculine" dependency on Lillian's earnings. Dave couldn't admit those feelings even to himself, so he blocked them out, blocking with them his love and passion.

When Dave and Lillian started talking about all those strongly-felt-yet-unexpressed emotions, they focused first on the most obvious issue of conflict between them—Lillian's affair—and discovered some interesting things:

> My affair needed to be looked at as a communication to Dave, rather than as an inability to restrain my impulses. I needed to look at what I was feeling toward Dave and trying to communicate to him by having an affair—and by being so obvious about it.
>
> Clearly the affair had more to do with what I was feeling toward Dave than what I was feeling toward the other man, especially given that the other man is of absolutely no interest to me anymore. Now that I am not acting out affair-type behavior, feelings about Dave are surfacing that I was not allowing myself to experience before.
>
> Perhaps the affair was a way of doing something to prevent myself from knowing what I was feeling toward Dave, since these are very threatening feelings. I experienced anger, resentment, disappointment, concern, fear . . . I am beginning to see the affair as a way of not having to experience these feelings.

When in a teary and highly emotional session Lillian and Dave were able to open up and discuss all of their feelings, they both experienced a tremendous relief. Lillian discovered that in spite of her "terrible feelings," Dave still loved her and actually was delighted to have found out what had been troubling her all along. Dave discovered that Lillian's feelings toward him were not altered because of his "unmasculine" feelings. With the emotional relief they felt came the excitement of finding, once again, how important their marriage was and how much meaning it had in their lives. With this realization came a powerful surge of the old passion. As they both reported to me later, "sex has never been better."

Dave and Lillian were able to confront the sensitive issue of money and come up with a solution that was comfortable for both of them: They rented out a room in their house, which provided an added monthly income and allowed Lillian to cut down on her work. This was something she wanted very much to do but felt unable to do earlier because of her financial obligations. Even after the money issue was resolved Dave and Lillian made a conscious effort to continue handling their conflicts in the same open, nondefensive way. Working through sensitive issues maintained a high level of emotional arousal in the marriage, which in turn kept the sexual spark alive.

## THE EMOTIONAL AROUSAL OF JEALOUSY

In addition to demonstrating the power of an open and honest discussion of conflict issues, Lillian and Dave's case demonstrates the power of jealousy to arouse emotions. Jealousy is a protective reaction to a perceived threat to a valued relationship.[7] If your mate is having an affair, but you don't perceive it as a threat either to your ego or to your relationship, you are not going to be jealous. If you have stopped loving your mate, and you no longer value the relationship, you are also not going to be very jealous. If you value the relationship, however, and your ego is invested in it, you are likely to find your partner's involvement with someone else threatening and to respond with jealousy.

Jealousy can drive people to do things they would never do otherwise. One man started spying on his lover in a fit of jealousy. One night he hid in bushes under her window for hours in the freezing cold. He sounded incredulous when he told me about it. "I am a stable, well-adjusted person," he said. "I don't know what is happening to me. I have never done anything as crazy as this in my whole life." A woman told me that on seeing her ex-lover with a "gorgeous Los Angeles type blond," she lost all control. She snatched the hat off the fellow's head—a hat she had given him—and kicked him in the groin. Then she ran to his car and locked herself in it. "As I sat in the car panting," she said, "I asked myself who that wild woman was. I wondered if I had gone completely out of my mind."

Jealousy can be extremely painful. A woman who participated in one of my workshops that was devoted to an exploration of "Emotions of Intimacy" said that sexual jealousy was the most painful emotion she has ever felt. "I've tried everything to get some control over it," she said, "but nothing, nothing, nothing works. The only thing left for me is lobotomy. And believe me, I am tempted. I don't think I can live much longer with this much pain." Sexual jealousy exists somewhere in the gray area between mental health and mental illness. As we have seen, people who feel intense jealousy often feel as if they're going out of their minds. At times they also do extreme things as a result of these feelings.

Most people have great compassion for those in the grips of jealousy. Nowhere is this better demonstrated than in the response to those who commit violent crimes as a result of jealousy. In my work with prisoners who committed "crimes of passion," I discovered that people (as well as juries) tend to be rather lenient toward these criminals.[8] Their hot-blooded murders seem somehow more human (and more excusable) than the same murders committed in cold blood, say, for money. My guess is that people empathize more with passionate criminals because they can identify with the powerful force that motivated them.

Jealousy appears to be universal. It is experienced even in cultures that condemn it and was experienced at some point even by people who managed to overcome it.

Because of the great pain associated with jealousy for most people, it is interesting to note the positive effect it sometimes has on the quality of sex. I met Jim and Stacy at one of my intensive five-day "Emotions of Intimacy" workshops. Jim was fifteen years older than Stacy. They had met as boss and employee and Stacy still perceived Jim as her mentor. Jim had been divorced for over five years when they became involved and during that time had had many affairs. While Stacy had several boyfriends, she was still a virgin when she met Jim. The difference between them in age and sexual experience created, at least for Jim, a problem. Sex, he said, had become boring. While he still loved Stacy and was flattered by the fact that such a young and beautiful woman was in love with him, and while he still felt committed to the relationship, he said that Stacy's lack of sexual experience made their love life unexciting. Because of that he wanted to be able to see some of his former girlfriends. He encouraged Stacy to get involved sexually with other men, an experience, he said, that would be "good for her and good for the relationship." He argued, "It would help her become more experienced and sophisticated sexually." Stacy, for her part, was very jealous of Jim's former girlfriends and felt inferior to them. Even though she was extremely attractive and had ample opportunities to date other men, she was not interested in anyone else. She said she would have been happiest in a monogamous relationship with Jim. Knowing that Jim didn't consider having sex with her enough excitement was very painful.

During the first days of the workshop the group's attention focused several times on Stacy's "jealousy" and "insecurity." On these occasions Jim was very understanding of "Stacy's problem" while at the same time openly pursuing other women in the group. Then, one sunny afternoon something happened that changed things considerably. Following a particularly intense session, Stacy was comforted by an attractive man in the group. This man had indicated several times that he was attracted to Stacy, but so far she had not responded. His nonsexual comforting hugs gradually changed to more sexual caresses. They went off to his room to "talk" and eventually they made love. Since the sexual encounter was spontaneous neither of them used contraceptives.

Jim was furious. He could see Stacy and the other man getting physical with each other, and he felt disregarded and betrayed. "How could you do that?" he demanded. Interestingly enough, the focus of his anger was not the fact that Stacy had had sex with another man (which is what he claimed all along he wanted her to do), but rather her carelessness about contraception. "You hurt me more than any other woman has ever done," he said, "and I trusted you to protect my feelings."

While processing the experience, I asked them whether there was anything positive about the experience. I was not at all surprised to hear Jim say, with great amazement, "When we made love it was the most passionate sex we had ever had. It was unbelievably intense and exciting . . . I can't figure it out." Stacy, with tears rolling down her cheeks, nodded in agreement. The reason sex was so exciting, of course, is that it happened in the context of intense emotional arousal. For both Jim and Stacy (as was the case for Dave and Lillian), the safety of the committed relationship was shaken. All of a sudden the certainty of their world and their feelings of security in the relationship were called into question. The feelings associated with jealousy—fear of loss and abandonment, envy, rivalry, feeling excluded, and feeling betrayed—were intensified. And, as we know, emotional arousal is a prerequisite for passion.

Jim and Stacy's story is not unusual. I have seen many similar cases in which one partner pushes to open up the relationship because sex became boring, and then is shocked and hurt when the other partner starts enjoying sex outside marriage. That shock and hurt, "for some reason," help to revive the sexual passion in the relationship. The reason, as Dave and Lillian's case also demonstrated, is that passionate sex, even more so than love, depends on emotional arousal. Love gives the biological function of sex a higher, existential significance. A jealousy crisis reaffirms this higher significance. This is probably why I have never heard any-one complain about boring sex when in the midst of a jealousy crisis.

Noting the emotionally arousing effect of jealousy is not meant as a recommendation to use jealousy to keep the sexual spark alive in long-term relationships. Rather, it is aimed at demonstrat-ing the powerful effect of emotional arousal—even negative arousal—on the intensity of sex.

I asked twenty-four men and thirty-four women who took part in a day-long seminar on marriage burnout: "How often do you experience intense jealousy in your relationship?" Analysis of the data revealed that the more frequently one experienced intense jealousy, the more burned out one was likely to feel.[9] It is possible, of course, to interpret this finding as indicating that people who are open about their feelings and who are not afraid to admit things that might present them in a negative light are more likely to admit both jealousy and burnout than people who are not open or who are invested in presenting a positive image. Extensive discussions with the seminar participants, as well as clinical experience with people who had jealousy as a problem, make me believe that even if such response biases exist, they account for a very small part of the finding.[10]

If jealousy has such a powerful effect in rejuvenating sex, how can it also cause burnout? The answer has to do with the difference between short-term and long-term arousal. While people vary tre-mendously in their tolerance for arousal, most like it when it is short. Almost everyone enjoys, for example, hearing a moving story, participating in an exciting adventure, or even being scared by a film or a fast-moving roller coaster, not to mention being passionately in love. Long-term arousal, on the other hand, is un-pleasant and stressful. When the arousal is extreme, over a long span of time with no relief in sight, it can cause physical, emotional, and mental exhaustion. Jalapeño peppers can give food an exciting taste in small measure but can burn when excessive.

In a relationship with a strong foundation of trust and security, jealousy can serve both as a reminder to mates of how important they are to each other and as a trigger for growth. In a relationship controlled by the routines of daily living, in which the mates take each other for granted, jealousy can put the relationship back in its place as their number-one priority. It can remind mates of the significance and security the relationship gave their lives. On the other hand, when jealousy is an ongoing problem, it threatens the very fabric of security and trust that is the foundation of a relationship. The constant need to cope with jealousy can be physically and emotionally exhausting and thus lead to burnout.

Jealousy and conflict arouse emotions that are primarily negative. Positive emotions can also be arousing. According to Stanley Keleman, who studies the body and its connection to psychology, emotional arousal had similar physiological consequences whether positive *or* negative.[11] This suggests that positive emotional experiences can have the same energizing effect on sex that negative experiences have. Positive emotions can be generated by outside events (imagine making love during the ecstasy of a big professional success) or by events inside the relationship. A woman, married eight years, says:

> At times, when we are in the middle of a particularly good conversation, when all of a sudden we understand something we've been struggling with for a long time, I am overcome with a flood of warm gushy feelings of love. I always dreamed about having this kind of intimacy in a relationship, and I actually have it. The feelings of love have a very strong sexual connotation for me . . . that the two of us are like one.

## EXPECTATIONS

When they talk about the quality of sex deteriorating with time, couples often use the first stage of falling in love as a yardstick. When they talk about rekindling the sexual spark in a marriage that has lost its passion, this is what couples want back. Even Ellen and Anthony, whose marriage is still vital and exciting, look back with nostalgia at this stage. Ellen recalls:

> We used to make love five times a night and as many times a day as our schedules permitted. We didn't want or seem to need sleep; we felt so energized by our mutual passion. When we took a week

off and went to a fancy beach resort, all we did most of the time was make love. We would go and get something to eat and then come back and make love, go for a swim, then come back and make love, get some sleep, then make love again. Nothing else mattered, not really. . . . We lived for the time we could be together. We didn't know how long the magic would last, so we wanted to take advantage of every possible minute.

Now things are different. Both of us are back to being the great sleepers we have always been. Sex is still wonderful, but it is a far cry from those early days. Sometimes we are both tired and several days will go by without our making love. When we do, we remember the great joy our bodies can give us. And we keep wondering why it is that we are letting the trivia of life deprive us of this joy. But no sooner do we make a resolution to give sex the high priority it deserves in our lives than some emergency comes up and again sex is pushed back in order of importance. This could never have happened during our earlier days together.

Sex hasn't been such a wonderful experience during courtship for all couples. Looking back at the early stages of their sexual relationship, some couples don't remember the thrill of passion, but rather the awkwardness, the insecurity, the nervousness. For those couples the quality of sex, many times, not only does not diminish with time, but actually improves.

Mimi married her husband relatively late, less because of passionate love and more because she saw him as a man she could share her life with and be happy. Talking about sex she said:

I don't really understand what people are talking about when they complain that sex gets boring. For me personally, after eighteen years of marriage, sex is much better than it ever was. Now I feel relaxed and comfortable during lovemaking. I don't need to pretend or impress. I feel secure enough to try out anything I want to. . . . We both know our own bodies better, and we know each other's bodies better. We know better how to give and receive pleasure.

For Bill, a systems analyst, who has been married for nineteen years to a woman who is thirteen years younger than he is, sex has also improved with time:

Before I got married I had been a bachelor for many years. During that time I had many wild affairs with exciting and unusual women. But I never considered marrying any one of them. When I met my wife I knew there was something different about her. I knew she was someone I could share my life with. And the years have proved I was right. During those years sex has become much better than it was when we first met. It is more than just a sexual act because it happens in the context of the whole relationship. It's like a rich, complex, many-layered fabric. I feel none of the pressures to perform sexually that I used to feel. Since I feel secure I can relax and enjoy the benefits of a truly intimate relationship.

In addition to the effects of growing intimacy and security on the quality of sex, another important role is played by the expectations mates have. As is always the case, when the norms created at the start of a relationship are very high (as they were for Ellen and Anthony), sex is likely to fall short of them. Conversely, when the norms are low (as they were for Bill and Mimi), sex is likely to surpass them. In spite of the simplicity of this observation, it is rarely taken into account by couples.

The initial stage of a relationship, albeit of great importance, is only one of the factors shaping our expectations. Cultural myths also have a profound effect. In our culture, the expectations of sex in a romantic relationship are very high indeed. Simply stated, the expectation is that sex will remain forever exciting, just as exciting as it was during infatuation. Couples who internalize these unrealistic expectations uncritically respond to the inevitable decrease in the intensity of their lovemaking with feelings of disappointment, guilt for their part, and blame for their partner's. Some readers would probably take issue with my choice of the word *inevitable* to describe the decreased intensity of sex in marriage, and would use Mimi as a case in point. In response to such an objection I would argue that Mimi did not describe increased intensity in her sex life with time, but rather increased comfort, security, and ease that for her were translated into increased sexual enjoyment.

The effect of myths on the quality of sex was confirmed by some of my research findings. In the study of romantic truisms (which was described in Chapter 1) I found that the more mates believed that "love is like a good wine, it improves with time," the worse was their sex life. (If the expectation is that things will get better with time, then finding out that not only don't they get better, but they actually get worse, must be quite devastating.) On the other hand, the more mates believed in myths like "a match made in heaven," the better was their sex life. (Feeling that one chose a unique and special mate gives sex its emotional significance.)[12]

## WHAT AFFECTS THE QUALITY OF SEX IN A MARRIAGE?

How would you describe the quality of sex in your relationship? When I analyzed the responses that one hundred married couples gave to this question, I found that the quality of sex tended to deteriorate with time.[13] (This was true even of couples who described themselves as very loving of each other.) One possible reason for this finding is that sex is more of a physiological drive than love. Infrequent sex, like hunger or thirst, is unpleasant. When one is not involved in an exciting love relationship, on the other hand, one may wish one were, but the wish is not likely to cause the same degree of physical discomfort. And as with food, the same dish all the time—even if that dish includes desired items such as caviar and champagne—eventually gets boring.

Another possible explanation has to do with the natural process of aging rather than with processes indigenous to long-term relationships. For males the highest point of sexuality occurs around the age of eighteen; for women it occurs later, at around the age of thirty. For the majority of people, following that peak, the intensity of the sexual drive gradually decreases. Indeed, the data revealed that the younger the couple, the better the quality of the sex life.[14]

Whatever the explanation, if the conclusion it forces us to reach is that the quality of sex inevitably deteriorates with time, then the outlook for love relationships in which sex is an important component is very grim indeed. The possible variations on sex are, after all, limited, and the sexual act is repeated at least once a week for most married couples, according to a recent survey. After ten years of marriage—and approximately five hundred sexual encounters with the same person—it is inevitable that boredom will set in, no?

Not necessarily. Because sex is not merely a physiological drive, boredom is not inevitable. In my research I found that the quality of a couple's sex life had almost as much to do with their emotional and intellectual attraction to each other as it had to do with their physical attraction.[15] Physical attraction, which originates in our internalized romantic image, is, of course, a major ingredient of good sex. (Who of us would not wish that we and our lovers still had the bodies we had as twenty-year-olds?) But physical attraction cannot, in and of itself, sustain a long-term relationship. In casual sexual encounters with no emotional or mental bond, once passion is over it is often replaced by boredom or even disgust. Mark, who is thirty-eight, described his life as a swinging single:

> I would find myself, after sex, wondering what in the hell I was doing there. I would try to find the best excuse I could to get out of there as soon as possible. Sometimes I was so desperate to get away I wouldn't even look for an excuse. I would just say "I have to go" and I would leave.

Those sexual encounters in which the physical attraction is combined with an emotional and an intellectual attraction are the encounters that transform sex into the magic of making love. Joel Block writes:

> Without the intimate exchange of thoughts, feelings, and desires even the most fiery of sexual relationships will soon dry up. . . . Sexual satisfaction often corresponds to the degree of nonsexual satisfaction within the relationship.[16]

In my research, mates who described each other as "the biggest love of my life" reported better sex than those who did not. Similarly, those mates who described each other as "best friend" had better sex than those mates for whom that was not the case.[17] Sadly, it seems that such friendships are the exception. Joel Block, in a study on friendship that involved over two thousand people, reported that scarcely more than one-third of the married respondents regarded their mates as friends. Couples living together fared no better.[18]

Good sex affects and is affected by the emotional bond between lovers. It also affects and is affected by the general quality of a relationship—good sex helps make a relationship good, and a good relationship helps make sex good.[19] In rare cases a couple may say that they have no emotional connection to speak of, and yet describe sex as good. ("We have nothing left to talk about, and yet I must say that sex is still good. It is definitely not as fantastic as it used to be . . . but it still is better than with anyone else.") In bad relationships sex was seen most often (especially by women) as an unwelcome invasion or as a cold exercise of marital privilege. Based on all these findings there can be two approaches to improving the quality of sex in relationships: One is to improve the sex, the other is to improve the relationship.

Sex therapists believe that improved technical skills of lovers can improve the quality of their sex life, and as a result improve the whole relationship. The problem is (as Dave and Lillian showed us) that in the absence of emotional arousal the effects of improved technique are likely to be temporary.[20] The alternative approach is to improve the relationship, assuming that once the relationship is good, sex is bound to be good as well. Let's take Ruth as an example. Ruth's anger at her husband destroyed her sexual feelings toward him:

> I get so mad at him sometimes that I see red. Every time I run out of gas because he used the car the night before and "forgot" to fill it, every time a check bounces because he "forgot" to mention to me a check he wrote, every time I have no milk for the children in the morning because he developed all of a sudden an irresistible thirst for milk in the middle of the night, I feel like screaming. I can no longer look at each incident in isolation. There have been far too many incidents like that during our twenty-two years together. Every annoying thing he does provides a further demonstration of his narcissism, inconsideration, and total self-centeredness. But I can never express any of those feelings directly because he goes wild at the slightest criticism. . . . I get so furious that even if I had some sexual feelings—simply because it has been such a long time since we had sex—my anger and resentment cure me real quick. I once considered myself a sexual person; by now I have learned the easiest road to celibacy—a bad marriage.

If Ruth and her husband were to go to a sex therapist, her husband would most likely complain that Ruth is not sexual. He has a "normal healthy sexual appetite" and is frustrated by Ruth's disinterest in sex. Ruth, on her part, is unable to express the extent of her anger and resentment. ("How can I tell him that my rage is such that even seeing his body in the mirror is enough to make me sick?") So what is the solution?

The answer is open, nondefensive, and direct *communication.* Sounds like an old and tired cliché, doesn't it? When communication between husband and wife is good, however, the data show that the sex and the relationship are also good. Conversely (as both Lillian and Ruth demonstrated), when communication is bad, sex is bad.[21] If a couple can talk openly and freely about sex, there is a much greater chance they will continue to get what they want in bed than if one or both of them is too embarrassed to talk about it. Communication is not limited to sex. It includes the permission to express anger, frustration, and irritation openly—something many couples have a great deal of difficulty doing with each other. When mates talk like best friends, there is little chance that small resentments will accumulate to the point of interfering with sex. Such openness also enables mates to be inappropriate sometimes and contradict whatever image they have of themselves, or try to project. Even if you are a "sexy person" it is possible that at times you will not feel sexy. Even if you are a "terrific lover" it is possible that sometimes you wouldn't feel like making the effort. If you are able to talk to each other honestly and openly, you'll be able to say that you're not interested in sex *tonight* without making your mate feel that you aren't interested in sex *ever,* or that you aren't interested sexually in your mate. Breaking such images and old patterns of behavior can be very exciting.

Open communication, as Dave and Lillian demonstrated, can help sustain the emotional and sexual intensity of a relationship because it enables mates to discuss emotionally loaded taboo subjects. The emotional intensity enhances the general level of arousal, which heightens sexual arousal, which makes sex more exciting. There are other things, however, that enhance the general level of arousal and thus can increase sexual arousal. One such thing, which was mentioned in this context before, is *variety.* Variety is indeed the spice of a sexual life. Data show that the more variety there is in a marriage, the better the couple describe their sex life. On the flip side, the more boredom, the poorer the quality of sex.[22]

Is it possible to have sexual variety with one person? The

answer, it turns out, depends on one's definition of sex. If it is defined as genital sex—intercourse—the answer is no. The number of possible permutations in genital sex is, as we know, finite, and the number of those sex positions practiced by most couples is even more limited than that.

If sex is defined as a total body experience, however, then the answer is yes. The number of possible permutations in touching, kissing, stroking, petting, necking, mutual masturbation, massage, dirty talk—to mention just a few of the possible activities—is virtually infinite. In addition, sex that involves the whole body can be fast or slow, intense or relaxed, and most important, it can, but does not have to, end in orgasm.

People for whom sex is mostly genital tend to burn out fast in relationships. Typically, an attractive new person is the most arousing sexual stimulus for them. The nervousness and mystery before the first sexual encounter are the most exciting aspects of the experience. Everything else pales by comparison. The excitement makes them feel alive, and makes life seem worth living—which is why they seek it so desperately. After such a person becomes familiar with the other person's body and sexual response, the novelty wears off, and with it the sexual arousal. Boredom sets in, and the search for a new partner begins. These people almost never develop close intimate relations with their sexual partners. Their "best friend" is usually someone with whom they have not been sexually involved. This separation between sexuality and intimacy is very deep-seated, and even when they are aware of its emotional cost they find it difficult to change.

For other people the intimacy in a relationship is its most rewarding aspect, while getting involved with a new person generates emotional arousal of the wrong kind—such as feelings of insecurity, embarrassment, and anxiety. Because of their emphasis on intimacy, their need for variety in the sexual act itself tends to be limited. Nora Ephron describes it in her book *Heartburn*:

> I have never been big on invention in [the sex] department. Why kid around? Every so often I browse through books full of tasteful line drawings of supplementary positions—how to do it standing, and in the swimming pool and on the floor! Why would anyone want to do it on the floor when a bed was available? I'll tell you the truth: even sex on the beach seems to me to be going too far.[23]

When we talk about "people for whom sex is mostly genital" or about "people for whom intimacy is the most important part of a sexual relationship," we are making a dispositional attribution about these people ("that's the way they are"). But even such dispositions can change under the appropriate circumstances. An example may help clarify this point. Earlier I quoted Mark, a thirty-eight-year-old man who talked about his frequent urge to get away after sex. It may be worth noting that in addition to being a very successful attorney, Mark is also good-looking, sure of himself, extremely flirtatious, and very successful with women. Mark described himself as someone who could maintain an interest in a sexual relationship for a maximum of four months. After that he would get bored and start pursuing other women. A less charitable acquaintance described him as "a vagina tourist." Mark specialized in short affairs, often with several women at once.

Then, one evening, Mark met the woman of his dreams at a party. He had never felt as strong an attraction, and pursued her with passionate determination. He wanted to marry her. He wanted her to have his children. He wanted to spend the rest of his life with her. Sex was no longer a physical need that he sought to satisfy with the least possible hassle. With her it became a magical expression of love and intimacy. He had no interest in other women and didn't want her to see other men. His excitement about her did not diminish after four months or four years of marriage.

People who had known Mark for years and had only seen him wild and reckless, chasing women and disposing of them shortly thereafter, were amazed at the transformation. Several of them, who also had a chance to meet Mark's parents, noted the incredible similarity between Mark's mother and the woman he finally managed to convince to marry him (but only after months of persistent pursuing). "It is almost as if his wife were a younger version of his mother," one said. Both women were very beautiful, with petite and well-proportioned bodies, short blond hair, green eyes, and strong, vivacious personalities. The similarity went even beyond appearance and personality to a seeming replay of a childhood trauma. Mark's mother was an alcoholic. When she was sober, she was very loving and nurturing. When she was drunk she was cold and rejecting. The woman Mark fell in love with was involved with another man when they first met. When she was with Mark she was warm and loving. When she was with the other man she was out of his reach. In short, Mark's lady love fitted his romantic image in every possible way.

The circumstances were also ripe for Mark to fall in love. He had just finished a law apprenticeship and was leaving town to join a distinguished law firm on the East Coast. The emotional arousal generated by this big change in his life made it more likely that he would interpret meeting someone who fitted his romantic image as love. The love gave sex a significance it never had before for him.

Variety in sex, like in other things, is in the eyes of the beholder. As we have seen, variety in sexual partners, which may be the prerequisite for sexual arousal for one person, may be totally unnecessary to another. Similarly, variety in sexual positions that is wildly exciting to one person may seem utterly ridiculous to another. The difference between couples who have a good sex life and those who don't does not lie in the particular expression of variety, but rather in the acknowledgment of its importance.

The techniques for bringing variety into a sexual relationship are as different as people are. One couple, with five teenage children, posted on their bedroom door a sign saying "NO!" and proceeded to spend a whole afternoon giving each other a sensuous massage. Another couple likes to make a date for sex so they can look forward to it, make the practical arrangements, and begin getting in the mood well in advance. For a busy dual-career couple, a luxurious breakfast-in-bed ceremony as the backdrop for slow and lingering foreplay provides welcome relief from the quick and hurried sex they usually engage in during the week. A couple with four young children hires a live-in babysitter one weekend a month so they can get away to some nice hotel in the city where they can have "wild sex." Creating a special time for sex requires planning ahead and scheduling. Such planning may take away from the spontaneity of the sexual experience, but according to the couples, it does not reduce its intensity.

Some couples, in order to increase the level of arousal in their sex life, watch erotic movies or read pornographic books and magazines together. Other, more daring couples, used to go to sex clubs or swingers' parties (nowadays these practices are almost nonexistent because of the danger of AIDS). There are couples who smoke marijuana, wear erotic clothes, or use sex "toys." In all cases the specific techniques are aimed at making certain sexual encounters special and different. A gay man says:

We have a sort of routine form of sex that we have regularly . . . that is, without the special kind of intimacy and the production number. A production number would be a more full, complete, intimate expression. It takes longer, is more involved, more passionate. We don't do it too often, maybe once a week, or once every two weeks, so when we do it's a treat. There is a red light somewhere, music playing at the beginning . . . the works . . .

Joel Block, in *The Magic of Lasting Love,* suggests yet another way to introduce variety, and through it emotional arousal, into sex. His recommendation focuses on changing the sex roles played by mates (masculine is rough and tough; feminine, soft and sweet). Breaking those sex roles (especially for couples who are boxed into them) increases the mates' range of sexual satisfaction. One way to do that is by reversing roles:

If you are a male and conceive of a woman as being gentle and seductive, cuddly or passive, sexually be that way yourself. If you are female and view men as aggressive, initiatory, active, you may be that way. Be true to form in coming "out of role" in your sex play. For instance, if the female partner usually lies on her back and is mounted by the male, reverse this; if the male partner usually fondles his lover's nipples, she is to fondle his.[24]

Barbara, a San Francisco businesswoman, committed to keeping the spark alive in her twenty-year-old marriage and to helping other couples bring it back to their marriages, developed a board game called An Enchanted Evening. The instructions for playing the game include creating a special time, place, and atmosphere: the time—without children, telephone calls, and other possible interruptions; the place—comfortable and pleasant; the atmosphere—romantic, preferably with candlelight, soft music, pleasant area to lie on, sensuous lounging clothes, tantalizing edibles, and good wine. At the beginning of the game each player takes a blank "wish card" and writes down a secret wish that the player wants fulfilled by or with his/her partner. The wish has to be one that can be completed the same night. Then, without disclosing the wish, they place the cards in a special "wish box." The goal of the game is to be the first to reach that box. The "loser" is obliged to make the partner's wish come true.

During the game, players in alternating turns role a die and respond to cards corresponding to the design on which they landed. Some cards include questions such as: "In what way is your partner supportive of you?" Other cards include instructions such as: "Gently fondle something your partner has a pair of" or "The scene is a theater balcony, back row; give your partner a 'matinee' kiss." The game, which is recommended by some sex therapists, is valuable because it provides a break from the routine, a way to be totally focused on each other in a relaxed, sensuous, and entertaining way.

*Security,* according to my research findings, is yet another important component for a good sex life.[25] A sixty-two-year-old Catholic woman, married for thirty-six years, says she has never had such good sex in her life. With five children in the house she and her husband had to make an effort to be quiet during lovemaking. She was always nervous that the sounds they made might be heard through the thin wall separating the children's bedrooms from their own. Not believing in the use of contraceptives, she was also nervous about the possibility of getting pregnant. The rhythm and withdrawal methods they used to prevent pregnancy never seemed safe enough to enable either of them to relax completely. Now that all the children have finally left home and she has gone through menopause, they can, for the first time in their lives, really relax and enjoy sex. So they do it all over the house. Their favorite place is the floor in front of the fireplace. They do it any time they feel like it, day or night. And they make as much noise as they like.

The security that comes from living with another person for many years provides for some people (such as Mimi and Bill, whom I quoted earlier) a relief from the burdensome pressure to perform sexually. The security gives them the freedom to enjoy their bodies unbashfully. Because of this welcome relief from the pressures and awkwardness, which sometimes hamper the early stages of a sexual relationship, for them sex tends to get better with time.

In order to feel secure in their sexuality, it is important for mates to know themselves and each other. It is important for them to be comfortable with their bodies and be able to express openly (which is to say, without fear, guilt, or embarrassment) likes and dislikes, "turn-ons" and "turn-offs." Yet it is knowing themselves and each other and feeling comfortable with their own and their partner's bodies that is going to make them feel more secure. How does one break the cycle?

The answer is, it doesn't really matter. Open communication about such things as sexual fantasies and erogenous zones, for example, can help mates know each other's sexual preferences. Talk about such subjects is not only sexually arousing in itself, but it also increases the bond of trust between mates. Reading sex-education literature can also increase knowledge and, with it, a sense of security.[26] Reading such literature together can be not only educational, but also sexually exciting when it gives partners the permission to experiment with their bodies in ways they did not know about or had not considered before.

The same experiences, however, can be anxiety-provoking rather than security-enhancing when they are used for establishing new norms for sexual performance. "Sensate focus" is a technique that can be sexually arousing without being threatening. In it mates take turns touching each other nonsexually for five minutes or more, without making demands that the caressing lead to sexual performance.

## WHEN THE SEXUAL SPARK IS DEAD

Having said all that I have said about keeping the sexual spark alive, I should emphasize that being overanxious about the sexual spark is one of the best ways to kill it. In every couple's life there are times when one or both is either uninterested in sex or unable to perform sexually. In those relationships in which too much is made of that, sex usually deteriorates rapidly. A couple married twenty-five years provides an example. For twenty-three of their years together sex had been a very satisfying aspect of the relationship, one that compensated for many annoyances. Then one night the husband couldn't perform sexually, which the wife took as a personal insult. Her shocked response made their next attempt at lovemaking a nerve-wracking experience. The performance anxiety made the husband's next "sexual failure" a near certainty. Thus, an incident that should have been taken very lightly (especially in light of their long history of good sex) ended up destroying their sex life altogether.

This brings me to the question: What do you do when the sexual spark is dead? Unfortunately, when the spark is gone completely, in my experience, there is no way to revive it. Sometimes that means the end of the relationship, but not always. People differ in their sex drive and the importance they give to it. This chapter has been written mainly for couples who value passionate sex, who still have at least a spark of it left, and who would like to protect it in a "slow and steady fire."

# CHAPTER 7

## Is Burnout Inevitable?

The only way to conquer love is to run away from it.

Napoleon Bonaparte

## PREVENTING BURNOUT BY
## FORSAKING ROMANTIC LOVE

Among the people I interviewed, two groups had an important thing in common: They did not experience any marriage burnout whatsoever. Both groups assured me that they never burned out and could not imagine ever burning out in their future intimate relationships. The first group were Orthodox Jews living in one of the most religious neighborhoods in Jerusalem. The second group were the members of a very unorthodox commune I mentioned once before—Kerista Village.[1]

One Orthodox Jewish wife I interviewed said:

I simply don't understand the concept of marriage burnout. When I was introduced to my husband I didn't fall madly in love with him. But I knew right away that he was someone I could share my life with, someone who had the same values and world view that I did. I don't expect either one of us to change our basic value system, so what is there that could possibly burn out?

This woman was saying, in effect, that since her religion gave her life its sense of meaning, she did not expect her marriage to do that. Consequently, she was not going to be disappointed in the marriage.[2] I would wager that I might find similar ideas about marriage in Amish communities, in Mormon communities, among evangelistic Christians, and among the devoutly religious all over

181

the world. People who are deeply religious seek a connection with something larger than themselves in God. Thus, they are far less likely than nonreligious people to idealize romantic love and use it as the most important element in the selection of a mate. (Instead, they are likely to seek someone who shares their religious beliefs.)

In other conversations I had with Orthodox Jewish couples I was told that an additional reason they are not likely to burn out is that they are better prepared for marriage than non-Orthodox people. Schooling in the holy Scriptures includes discussions of the proper relationship between husband and wife and the prescribed behavior for both. Secular schooling does not provide such (much-needed) preparation for marriage.

As different as members of Kerista Village are from the Orthodox Jews in their life-style, the reason they give to explain why they could never burn out is very similar. The eight men and eleven women of the commune call their relationship "polyfidelity"—a coined word describing "a group of best friends living together with sexual intimacy occurring equally between all members of the opposite sex, no sexual involvement outside the group, a current intention of lifetime involvement, and an intention to raise children together with multiple parenting."[3] Kerista Village resembles a traditional marriage in that members do not become sexually involved with each other until they make the mutual commitment to lifetime involvement and, once the commitment is made, they are faithful to each other. It differs markedly from a traditional family in the assumption that a long-term relationship doesn't need to be limited to two people, and that a person is capable of loving many people simultaneously and equally. Sexual relationships within the commune are supposed to be nonpreferential (everyone loves everyone else equally) and happen within a rotating sleeping cycle.

The commune started over fifteen years ago as an alternative life-style with both personal and global goals (such as overcoming sexual jealousy, and working toward world peace). Jud, one of the founding members of the commune, explains: "Working on a vision together provides a basis for nonpreferential love in a group. In our group people don't draw security from each other. They draw it from their shared ideals."

All members of the commune describe themselves as having been drawn to the group because of its ideals and life-style. They, like the Orthodox Jews, don't believe in romantic love as the most important basis for mate selection. They consider such love flimsy and short-lived because it is based on the shallow foundation of physical attraction. Since they don't believe in romantic love, and they didn't make the commitment to the group marriage because of it, they argue, there is no chance they will ever burn out.

In their recent book *Habits of the Heart,* sociologist Robert Bellah and his coauthors contrast two images of love: "Love as a spontaneous inner freedom, a deeply personal, but necessarily somewhat arbitrary, choice" and "love as a firmly planted, permanent commitment, embodying obligations that transcend the immediate feelings or wishes of the partners in a love relationship."[4] The authors find that the second view of love is held most strongly among certain evangelical Christians for whom "emotion alone is too unstable a base on which to build a permanent relationship," who "must subordinate or tame their feelings so they follow the mind's guidance."[5]

Howard Crossland, a scientist from a rural background and an active member of an evangelical Christian church, is presented as an example. Although Crossland and his wife of twelve years had a fairly good marriage, according to his own testimony, without the Christian faith he "probably would have been divorced by now."[6]

Only in the Christian faith it is "logical" to say "till death do us part," claims Crossland. Otherwise, "if the relationship is giving you trouble, perhaps it is easier to simply dissolve the thing legally, and go your way, than it is to maybe spend five years trying to work out a problem to make a lasting relationship." In any relationship there will be crises. The Christian faith allows you to "weather the storm until the calm comes back. If you can logically think through and kind of push the emotions to the back, I guess the love is always there. Sometimes it's blotted out." Not surprisingly, Crossland's definition of love—"when another's needs are greater than your own"—is not very romantic.[7]

Like the Orthodox Jews and the polifidelitous Keristans, the evangelical Christians reject romantic love as the most important form of love, and as the best basis for the foundation of a permanent relationship. These three examples, as different as they are, draw our attention to the importance of shared ideals: ideals you can identify with, ideals you can get excited about, ideals that enable you to make a connection with something larger than yourself, something that makes your life matter in the larger scheme of things. Unfortunately, ideals are in pitifully short supply in the pragmatic and materialistic culture of the United States. (Making money and acquiring things don't quite make it as ideals.) In the absence of other ideals and ideologies, interpersonal relationships acquire a great value, and too much is expected of them if they are to give meaning to life.

Shared ideals have the same positive effect on relationships based on romantic love that they have on relationships based on a shared religious or political belief. The shared ideology provides roots of a deep emotional bond and a strong commitment, together with wings of joint opportunities for spiritual growth. In a life devoted to a religion, to working for world peace, or working for political change, where two people also love each other passionately, love is only one of the things that bind them, rather than being the only one. When love wanes temporarily—as it almost always does—the bond of their shared ideal keeps them together. In addition, the emotional arousal they both feel from working toward their ideal helps keep their romantic spark alive.

Walter and Betty are both in their fifties and even after three decades of marriage are still very happy together. They have a satisfying sex life and a strong emotional and spiritual bond. In their youth both of them were active members of a socialist group. They were excited about the ideals of socialism and believed that socialist politics would make the world a better place. It was wonderful to be in love and share such ideals. Several times they were arrested together. The arrests did not weaken their emotional bond; like the ideological commitment they shared, they brought them closer together, and kept their relationship alive. Walter and Betty didn't get married because of their socialist ideology. They got married because they were "in love." They expected their marriage as well as their ideology to give their life meaning.

The Orthodox Jews and the Keristans get their sense of "cosmic significance" from their respective ideologies, and not from love (therefore, when they burn out it is on those ideologies, not on love). Still they can tell us a lot about the different ways people try to protect their intimate relationships and make them work. No matter how secure we feel in a relationship, and how good things are, there is never a guarantee that things will continue being good. Yet it is impossible to operate with the conscious awareness of just how insecure and unstable love is (just as it is impossible to operate with the conscious awareness of the inevitability of death). The focus on ideologies enables people to feel that they have control over their relationships. The need for control explains why romantic attraction is dismissed as a basis for mate selection (low level of control), and why ideology is emphasized (high level of control).

While relationships that are based on a shared religion or a shared ideology can be very satisfying, the couples in them are not struggling with the challenge to keep a romantic spark alive, since that spark wasn't important to them to begin with. Like Napoleon, they conquer love by running away from it. For those unwilling to forsake the ideal of romantic love, the knowledge that rejecting it can guarantee against burnout is not much of a comfort. Furthermore, even if we can conclude with certainty that burnout does not happen in relationships *not* based on romantic love, that doesn't tell us whether it is inevitable in relationships that *are based* on love.

## IS BURNOUT INEVITABLE?
## SOME THEORETICAL ANSWERS

Throughout this book I have argued that people who believe in romantic love expect it to give their life a sense of meaning. Otto Rank describes modern man as fixing on his beloved his "urge to cosmic heroism."[8] The love partner becomes the divine ideal within which to fulfill one's life. Ernest Becker, a great admirer of Rank, expanded on his ideas:

> As we know from our own experience this method gives great and real benefits. Is one oppressed by the burden of his life? Then he can lay it at his divine partner's feet. Is self-consciousness too painful, the sense of being a separate individual, trying to make some kind of meaning out of who one is, what life is, and the like? Then one can wipe it away in the emotional yielding to the partner, forget oneself in the delirium of sex, and still be marvellously quickened in the experience. . . . But we also know from experience that things don't work so smoothly or unambiguously. The reason is not far to seek: it is right at the heart of the paradox of the creature. Sex is of the body, and the body is of death.[9]

The fact that romantic love has an erotic component, which is related to the sexual function of the mortal body, is according to Rank and Becker "central to the failure of romantic love as a solution to human problems, and is so much a part of modern man's frustration."[10] The procreative function of sex assures the continuation of the species, but not the continuation of the unique individual. This is why sex is a "disappointing answer to life's riddle," and why the sexual partner does not and cannot represent a complete and lasting solution to the human dilemma.[11]

The romantic solution, according to Rank and Becker, may be ingenious and creative, but because it is still an attempt to deny the mortal body by spiritualizing it, it is a lie that must fail. The failure of romantic love to give meaning to people's lives explains, according to Becker, its "historical bankruptcy." "It is impossible to get blood from a stone, to get spirituality from a physical being." No human being can be "everything" to another. No human relationship can bear this burden "and the attempt has to take its toll in some way on both parties."[12] However much we may idealize and idolize our beloved, he can never be perfect because he is human and real. If he is "all" to us, then any shortcoming in him becomes a major personal threat to us. Like Augustine and Kierkegaard, Rank and Becker believe that since man cannot fashion an absolute from within his human and mortal condition, "cosmic heroism" must transcend human relationships, and come from a belief in God.

Scott Peck, author of *The Road Less Traveled,* is also sure that love must fail, but for a different reason. Peck defines love as "the will to extend one's self for the purpose of nurturing one's own and another's spiritual growth." Love, to him, is an effortful act of will. According to this definition, points out Peck, falling in love is not real love. It is not an act of will, and it is effortless. The best proof for that is the annoying observation that "lazy and undisciplined individuals are as likely to fall in love as energetic and dedicated ones."[13]

Peck has to remove falling in love from his definition of love for two reasons: First, "the experience of falling in love is specifically a sex-linked erotic experience." Second, "the experience of falling in love is invariably temporary."[14]

No matter whom we fall in love with, we sooner or later fall out of love if the relationship continues long enough. This is not to say that we invariably cease loving the person with whom we fell in love. But it is to say that the feeling of ecstatic lovingness that characterizes the experience of falling in love always passes. The honeymoon always ends. The bloom of romance always fades.[15]

To understand the nature of the phenomenon of falling in love and the inevitability of its ending, according to Peck, it is necessary to understand the nature of "ego boundaries"—the internalized images of our physical and psychological self that define our individual identity as separate from the rest of the world. According to Peck, the essence of falling in love is

> a sudden collapse of a section of an individual's ego boundaries, permitting one to merge his or her identity with that of another person. The sudden release of oneself from oneself, the explosive pouring out of oneself into the beloved, and the dramatic surcease of loneliness accompanying this collapse of ego boundaries is experienced by most of us as ecstatic. We and our beloved are one! Loneliness is no more![16]

The collapse of ego boundaries is always temporary and partial:

> Sooner or later, in response to the problems of daily living . . . reality intrudes upon the fantastic unity of the couple who have fallen in love . . . both of them, in the privacy of their hearts begin to come to the sickening realization that they are not one with the beloved, that the beloved has and will continue to have his or her desires, tastes, prejudices and timing different from the other's. One by one, gradually or suddenly, the ego boundaries snap back into place; gradually or suddenly, they fall out of love. Once again they are two separate individuals.[17]

By excluding falling in love from his definition of love, Peck has an easy time arguing that with will and discipline love can remain in relationships indefinitely—but only in those relationships based on what he calls "real love," which is to say, a spiritual rather than a physical love. Unfortunately, by excluding falling in love from his definition, he manages to exclude what is for many people the most intense and significant emotional experience in life.

Social psychologist Elliot Aronson has another explanation for why people fall out of love. In *The Social Animal* he writes:

> In the words of the well-known ballad, "You always hurt the one you love." That is, once we have grown certain of the rewarding behavior of a person, that person may become less potent as a source of rewards than a stranger.[18]

Because we have learned to expect love, favors, and praise from a mate, after a while we start taking these for granted. Things can't get any better than unqualified praise and adoration; but they can get worse. Therefore, with the passage of time, mates increase their power to hurt, but lose power to reward. An example Aronson presents helps clarify this point:

> After fifteen years of marriage, a doting husband and his wife are getting dressed to attend a formal dinner party. He compliments her on her appearance—"Gee, honey, you look great." She hears his words, but they do not fill her with delight. She already knows that her husband thinks she's attractive; she will not turn cartwheels at hearing about it for the thousandth time. On the other hand, if the doting husband (who in the past was always full of compliments) were to tell his wife that he had decided that she was losing her good looks and that he found her quite unattractive, this would cause her a great deal of pain, because it represents a distinct loss.[19]

The longer the history of love, esteem, and reward, the easier it is to get used to them, and the more devastating is their withdrawal. Thus, with time, couples lose their ability to make each other truly happy. A vivid description of this process appeared in Marilyn French's novel, *The Women's Room:*

> Marriage accustomed one to the good things, so one came to take them for granted, but magnified the bad things, so they came to feel as painful as a grain in one's eye. An opened window, a forgotten quart of milk, a TV left blaring, socks on the bathroom floor, could become occasions for incredible rage.[20]

Nathaniel Branden also describes the painful process of disillusionment in love in *The Psychology of Romantic Love:*

Many persons begin a relationship genuinely in love and with good will and high hopes for the future, and then, across time, tragically, painfully, and with a good deal of bewilderment, watch the relationship deteriorate and ultimately collapse. They think back to the time when they were deeply in love, when so much seemed right and good and rewarding, and they are tortured by not knowing how and why they lost what they had. If *that* love could die, they find themselves feeling, can *any* love last? Is romantic love possible for me at all? Or for anyone?[21]

Otto Rank, Ernest Becker, Scott Peck, Elliot Aronson, Marilyn French, and Nathaniel Branden all seem to be telling us the same thing: Romantic love ends and burnout is inevitable. Depressing, isn't it? Couples in love are almost universal in their desire to hear that burnout is not inevitable. Their response to the skepticism that holds that all romantic relationships burn out eventually is to insist that their love is one of the rare exceptions.

## IS BURNOUT INEVITABLE?
## RESEARCH EVIDENCE

If burnout is inevitable, and a function of the time a couple has lived together, then it can be expected that the longer a relationship has lasted, the more burned out it will be. To find out if that is true, I conducted two studies. For one study I tried to select people who varied as much as possible in terms of relationship length and style. The one hundred men and women who participated in the study included married, cohabiting, and living-separately-but-seriously-involved couples, in various traditional and nontraditional arrangements. The length of relationships varied from 4 months to 41 years, with an average of 7 years and 7 months. By contrast, the second study included as homogenous and traditional a bunch of married couples as I could find. For all but six of the one hundred couples who participated in the study, this was the first marriage. Most couples had two or three children still living at home. The average length of the marriages—15.1 years—was almost twice the average of the first study, and ranged from one to over 34 years.

Analysis of the data in both studies indicated that *there was no correlation at all between the length of the relationship and burnout!* If the mere passage of time produces burnout, there should be a strong correlation between the two. This, most definitely, was not the case. The correlation between time and burnout was virtually zero in both studies.[22]

Apparently, a long-term relationship has as good a probability of being alive as a short-term one does of being dead. Sometimes marriages that survived the test of time consisted of couples who had discovered how to stay not only married but in love. Other times long-term marriages consisted of couples who could barely stand the sight of each other but who stayed together for economic reasons (this was particularly true for women), for the sake of the children, or for lack of a better alternative. A man in his forties explained why he was staying in his burned-out marriage of fifteen years:

> I don't expect anything from my marriage anymore, which suits me just fine. I don't get anything, but I also don't give anything, and I can invest myself in my work, where I feel I can make a significant contribution that will be recognized and appreciated. To get a divorce at this stage of the game would be too much of a hassle. I simply can't afford the waste of time and energy.

These data seem to violate common sense, and disconfirm many people's personal experiences. Indeed, it is hard to accept that time, together with the mundane problems of living, does not facilitate disillusionment, boredom, and taking the other for granted. The unequivocal nature of the findings, however, forces us to search for a different explanation for burnout than the passage of time. Even if most people will agree that the marriages that defy burnout and remain vital and alive over many years are the exceptions that need analysis and understanding, we need to look for something other than time to explain their rarity.

The study of these "deviant" marriages was one of the most fascinating and significant parts of my research. The fact that some couples stay married for years, for decades, without falling out of love helps explain why burnout is not correlated with time. It also suggests, contrary to all the theoretical arguments presented earlier, that burnout is not inevitable.

In many of the books and articles that have appeared in the last few years on staying together in an age of divorce, the focus has not been on these deviant couples, but rather on the far larger group of couples who merely remain married for twenty, thirty, forty, fifty years, and more. The main question researchers addressed in their studies of these long-term marriages has been, Why do some couples stay married? The far more interesting question, in my opinion, is, Why do some couples stay in love?

Many times people stay married not out of love, but out of fear of the unknown, and would have left if they had dared to. The truly interesting couples are those rare cases that seem to violate all the theoretical explanations for the inevitability of burnout. These couples continue to find "cosmic significance" in their romantic relationships, even though it is with another mortal who is aging in front of their very eyes. They describe their sex life as exciting and satisfying even though the arousal of the infatuation stage is long gone. And they have a strong sense of bonding and togetherness even though their ego boundaries are snapped securely into place.

## COUPLES IN LOVE

All couples would like to remain in love forever, but they go about preserving their love in very different ways. One of those ways was described by Robert Johnson in his book *We: Understanding the Psychology of Romantic Love.* It involves transforming the emotional arousal of falling in love into "stirring-the-oatmeal love," which according to Johnson

> symbolizes a relatedness that brings love down to earth . . . [and] represents a willingness to share ordinary human life, to find meaning in the simple, unromantic tasks. . . . To "stir the oatmeal" means to find the relatedness, the value, even the beauty, in simple and ordinary things, not to eternally demand a cosmic drama, an entertainment, or an extraordinary intensity in everything. . . . It represents the discovery of the sacred in the midst of the humble and ordinary. . . .
>
> The real relatedness between two people is experienced in the small tasks they do together: the quiet conversation when the day's upheavals are at rest, the soft word of understanding, the daily

companionship, the encouragement offered in a difficult moment, the small gift when least expected, the spontaneous gesture of love. When a couple are genuinely related to each other, they are willing to enter the whole spectrum of human life together. They transform even the unexciting, difficult, and mundane things into a joyful and fulfilling component of life.[23]

In a stirring-the-oatmeal love, people find meaning in the little joys of day-to-day living with an intimate partner. For some people, however, leading a "down-to-earth" existence pales in comparison with the thrill and ecstasy of falling in love with a new person. For them, falling in love is the most fulfilling part of the relationship. It is the quality of this experience, rather than the quality of the particular relationship, that they want to preserve.

Such people tend to see themselves as pawns in a "cosmic drama," and love as a magical experience that they have no control over. They want to be open to the possibility that love will "strike" them at any moment, because it is the most significant experience in life and the highest "high." So they stay in a relationship only as long as the intensity and the passion are there. They leave when the intensity and passion wane and hope to be struck by love again, with another person. Alan Watts describes this "divine madness" and says that "making it the basis for marriage is an extraordinarily dangerous thing to do":[24]

> Falling in love is a thing that strikes like lightning and is, therefore, extremely analogous to the mystical vision. . . . We do not really know how people obtain [them], and there is not as yet a very clear rationale as to why it happens. If you should be so fortunate as to encounter either of these experiences, it seems to me to be a total denial of life to refuse it.[25]

It is interesting that Alan Watts describes as a "denial of life" the same experience that Ernest Becker describes as "a denial of death." Since both authors see the denial as motivated by fear, they seem to suggest that the fear of life and the fear of death are flip sides of the same experience. Both Becker and Watts note that one person who "in the eyes of everyone else is a perfectly plain and ordinary person, can appear to be a god or goddess incarnate" to someone smitten with love. For both writers, the deification of the beloved shows that romantic love gives ordinary people a vehicle for cosmic heroism.

The "stirring-the-oatmeal love" described by Robert Johnson emphasizes the roots of a relationship. The "divine madness" described by Alan Watts emphasizes its wings. The third kind of love relationship involves, of course, both roots and wings. People enter the three kinds of relationships with different expectations, face in each one different dangers, and when their expectations are not met, they are disappointed differently. In a divine-madness love, they expect an ecstatic bonding with a beloved who represents the whole world. There are two dangers in this kind of love, both related to the collapse of ego boundaries characterizing it. One danger is that one would be totally lost in the love, and never be able to regain one's sense of self. The other danger is that with successive series of such temporary mystical experiences, there will be no ego growth. When they are in the midst of such an experience, people can't avoid hoping that it will last. Hence, when it's over, because such a state can't continue indefinitely, they feel disappointed and betrayed.

In a stirring-the-oatmeal relationship people expect permanence, security, stability, and understanding. Love is reduced to what can be controlled by acts of will, and the ego boundaries are all in place. There are two dangers in that kind of a relationship as well. One danger is that the love will die because of the lack of emotional intensity. The other danger is that in spite of the commitment, one mate will still fall in love with someone else and leave. In both cases, the disappointment and betrayal are related to the failure of security to give meaning to life.

In a relationship with roots and wings, the expectations are highest, and seemingly contradictory, namely, to get the relatedness, the permanence, and the security of the oatmeal with the emotional, physical, and spiritual intensity of the divine madness. In such a relationship mates' ego boundaries are partially collapsed permanently. The two dangers are a combination of the dangers involved in the two previous relationships. On the one hand a danger of losing one's sense of identity in the relationship, and on the other hand a danger of the betrayal of the lover and the loss of the security provided by the permanence of the relationship. In relationships with roots and wings mates are trying to live a contradiction: lose their ego in the unification with each other, and at the same time strengthen their ego and sense of self by growing roots. In spite of the difficulty involved in balancing these contradictory expectations, some couples succeed in achieving the balance, and thus assure that their relationship will remain exciting and still provide the gentle comfort of security.

Since the romantic solution can't solve the existential dilemma, every version of that solution is going to fail in some way. The question is what can couples live with. While relationships with roots and wings are just one such solution, and can't but fail to completely fulfill the romantic ideal, some people are able to live with that particular compromise quite happily looking at their relationship as a creative challenge. The intensity of such a relationship does not derive from the hope that it will give meaning to life, but from the realization that it actually does, and that one's mate is indeed "the one." Instead of the promise of a relationship, it reflects the joy of having the promise come true. Instead of fears about the future there are now certainties based on years of life together. This point was articulated by the Italian sociologist Francesco Alberoni in his book *Falling in Love:*

> Falling in love, when all goes well, ends in love; the movement, when it succeeds, produces an institution. But the relationship between falling in love and love itself, between nascent state and institution, is comparable to that between taking off or flying and landing, between being in the sky above the clouds and firmly setting foot on the ground again. Consider another image, that of the flower and the fruit. The fruit issues from the flower, but they are two different things. When there is fruit, there is no longer any flower. And there is really no point in asking if the flower is better than the fruit or vice versa. By the same token, there is no point in asking whether the nascent state is better than the institution. One does not exist without the other. Life is made up of both. Still, there is no point in confusing them, because they are distinct.[26]

Falling in love is unique and special: It involves the romantic images we have before we are confronted with the realities of daily life, the images that draw us to our mates. Those who dismiss falling in love as not "the real thing" miss out on dreams, on important information that affects couple's expectations for the future. For people who believe in romantic love—and who do not have a shared religious or political belief—making those dreams come true can become the shared ideal.

## IS BURNOUT INEVITABLE?
## THE ROMANTIC ANSWER

When Rank and Becker argue that sex, which is a bodily function, can't possibly give spiritual significance to life, they are right. Yet the conclusion they reach—that as a result, the burnout of love is inevitable—is not. Because sex is only the basis on which we impose our ideology of romantic love. That ideology itself is spiritual, and as such capable of giving meaning to life. The ecstasy generated by the fulfillment of a romantic ideal can replace sexual arousal, which diminishes with time.

Rollo May discusses in his book *Love and Will* the difference between sex and love (eros) and argues that in our society, some people use sex as a way to avoid involvement with eros. He writes:

> Eros is the drive toward union with what we belong to—union with our own possibilities, union with significant other persons in our world in relation to whom we discover our own self fulfillment. Eros is the yearning in man which leads him to dedicate himself to seek arate, the noble and good life.
>
> Sex . . . is the mode of relating characterized by tumescence of the organs (for which we seek the pleasurable relief) and filled gonads (for which we seek satisfying release). But eros is the mode of relating in which we do not seek release but rather to cultivate, procreate, and form the world. In eros, we seek increase of stimulation. Sex is a need, but eros is a desire.
>
> . . . The ancients made Eros a "god," or more specifically a daimon. This is a symbolic way of communicating a basic truth of human experience, that eros always drives us to transcend ourselves. . . . The ancients, taking sex for granted simply as a natural bodily function saw no need to make it into a god.[27]

What about the argument that burnout is inevitable because our beloveds are mortal human beings, and as such incapable of giving indefinitely a sense of cosmic significance to our lives? The best answer is those couples who continue to get a sense of meaning from their relationships in spite of their beloveds' humanness. Possibly, for these people, romantic love is a more appealing answer to the existential dilemma than any religious belief. Other people—who feel that they don't have any control over romantic love, who do not feel that romantic love would answer the central question in their lives, or who for whatever reason cannot make the "leap of faith" required of them to make a commitment to one person—will instead commit themselves to God, or to our modern God, work. People who are willing to make this leap of faith, on the other hand, see themselves as having control over their love. These people seek romantic love and some of them find it.

For such people, a certain part of the ego boundaries is permanently collapsed. There is a sense of "we," a shared identity that coexists along with their individual identities. Such people do not become "as one" in everything. Simply, a certain part of themselves has blended with their mate, even after the stage of falling in love is over. The sense of "we-ness," the bonding, the togetherness, are associated with feelings of safety and security. But as we know by now, a sense of security can be stifling if it is not counterbalanced by openness to growth.

The reader may recall Aronson's example of Mr. and Mrs. Doting who have, with the passage of time, growing power to hurt each other, but diminished power to provide each other with meaningful rewards. This pessimistic future can be avoided, but only when mates are willing to take responsibility for creating an open, honest, and authentic relationship, in which they are able to share their true feelings with each other and to grow:

> Although Mr. Doting has great power to hurt his wife (by telling her that she is losing her looks), Mrs. Doting is apt to be very responsive to such criticism and will likely strive to gain his interest. It goes without saying that the reverse is also true: If Mrs. Doting suddenly was to change her high opinion of Mr. Doting, he could—and chances are that he would—take action to regain her approval. A relationship becomes truly creative and continues to grow when both partners strive to grow and change in creative ways—and in all of this "authenticity" assumes great importance. Carrying this reasoning a step further, the more honest and authentic a relationship, the less the possibility of reaching the kind of dull and deadening plateau on which the Dotings appear to be stuck.[28]

The creativity and the striving to grow and change are the wings of the relationship. They also increase a couple's ability to reward each other. In a closed relationship, mates are the least likely to change, or improve, or reward each other:

> In a closed relationship, people tend to suppress their annoyances and to keep their negative feelings to themselves. This results in a fragile plateau that appears stable and positive but that can be devastated by a sudden shift in sentiment. Unfortunately, this may be a common kind of relationship in this country.
>
> In an open, honest, authentic relationship, one in which people are able to share their true feelings and impressions (even their negative ones), no such plateau is reached. Rather, there is a continuous zigzagging of sentiment around a point of relatively high esteem.[29]

When mates suppress their negative feelings, there is no way for them to deal directly with those feelings, and no way to grow as individuals and as a couple. Honesty, of course, is not always motivated by a desire for communication and for growth. Sometimes people use honesty as a weapon against each other. This kind of honesty can be cruel and damaging. Its use is one of the ways in which couples increase their power to punish each other. The nondefensive, aimed-at-self-growth exploration of negative feelings and taboo subjects (which was discussed in Chapter 6 as a way to ensure mutual growth and an optimal level of emotional arousal) also characterizes what Aronson terms "open, honest and authentic relationships."

So all a couple needs to make a love relationship work is to "strive to grow and change in creative ways"? That seems rather simple, doesn't it? And if it is so simple, why do so many couples who get married because of love, who desperately want the marriage to work, end up trapped in dead relationships? For the answer we can look, once again, at the environment. If the events that a couple has to face for a long time are extremely negative, it is reasonable to assume that such events will take their toll on the relationship. Yet the experience of couples who survived wars and natural disasters, and whose relationships were not weakened but actually strengthened by the experience suggests that this is not always the case.

Burnout is not inevitable even in the most stressful of situations because it depends on the way the stress is perceived by people. One of the happiest couples I interviewed had been married for forty-six years, had escaped Nazi Germany, and had gone through the long and hard years of the war together. This stress did not break their spirit or their marriage. On the contrary, it made them stronger, more appreciative of each other, and more committed to each other. Both of them felt that having the other was the only thing that kept them going—even when hungry, sick, and exhausted. Together, they felt united in a struggle against a cruel and hostile world.

What is it that makes some people stronger and others weaker as a result of the same stress? One answer, according to personality psychologists Susan Kobasa and Salvador Maddi, is "hardiness."[30] Hardiness defines a particular personality structure that is resistant to illness even in situations of great stress. One of the important dimensions in this personality structure is a sense of control over the environment. In their research, Kobasa and Maddi looked at two groups that were as similar as possible in terms of background as well as work and life stresses, yet were different in terms of vulnerability to illness. Under the same conditions of extreme stress one group got sick, while the other one, which they later termed "hardy," did not. The researchers discovered three things that differentiated the hardy group from the nonhardy group:

- Involvement—as opposed to alienation—and curiosity about their environment, which they considered interesting and significant.

- Control—as opposed to helplessness—and belief in their ability to influence their environment with ideas, words, and actions.

- Challenge—as opposed to indifference—and an assumption that change is natural, necessary, and important for growth.

People in the hardy group were interested in and cared about everything around them, whether it involved their work, their family life, or their outside activities. Whenever they were involved in an activity, they were all-absorbed by it. They felt they were leading rich and meaningful lives. Most important, they felt in control of their environment, and believed that they had a significant impact on it. They took responsibility for creating the kind of lives they wanted to live. When things did not work out for some reason, they confronted obstacles directly and actively, and saw them as a challenge. They loved change and always looked for it in their work and in their intimate relationships.

People in the nonhardy group were far less interested in their environment. They tended to see it as boring, insignificant, or threatening. They felt alienated from the people around them, and helpless against what they saw as hostile, all-powerful forces. They disliked change and were fearful of it; they believed that life is best when not threatened by change, and did not consider growth possible or important. They were passive and pessimistic, always expecting the worst, and because of that only willing to give the least of themselves.

Maddi and Kobasa came to a not very startling conclusion: It is better to be hardy than it is to be nonhardy. This kind of statement may be nice for the naturally hardy person to hear, but it is not of much value for the nonhardy person. It is possible, however, to see hardiness not as an inborn attribute but as a way of interacting with the environment that can be learned. From this perspective, the hardy person can be seen as more likely to make situational attributions in dealing with the world; the nonhardy person as more likely to make dispositional attributions. When we transfer the concept of hardiness from the individual to the couple, we can see that its three components—emotional involvement, sense of control, and love of challenge—can be as important for the couple's life as they are for the individual's. While hardy couples see a certain stress as an exciting challenge that is within their control and that provides an excellent opportunity for growth, the nonhardy couples are likely to feel alienated, threatened, and powerless, thus enhancing their burnout.

Shifting from the dispositional attribution of hardiness as a personality structure to hardiness as a set of attitudes that is learned, and thus can be unlearned and relearned, leaves some hope even for those people unlucky enough to have been born nonhardy, or to have entered a nonhardy relationship. How does a couple learn to be hardy? Culture, it turns out, has a lot to do with it. Different cultures socialize people to perceive the world around them differently, and cope with it differently. In some cultures (such as that in

Israel), there is an emphasis on direct and active coping style; in others (such as that in Japan), indirect coping is valued more. These cultural differences have a big influence on the likelihood of burn-out, above and beyond the effect that cultures have on people's expectations from their intimate relationships and from their life in general. The comparison between Israelis and Americans is an example.

As anyone who has spent time in both countries knows, life in Israel is considerably more stressful than life in America. There are tensions between groups of different cultural origins, different religious beliefs, and different political affiliations; there are the physical and the emotional stresses of constant warfare and a com-pulsory military service (which for young men is three years and for men on reserve duty is one month a year) and there are severe economic stresses. One might expect that burnout would be higher in Israel than in America. The data, however, show that Israelis report less burnout in their marriages than do Americans.[31] It is noteworthy that the same results were found in all the studies in which samples from the two countries were compared. These stud-ies, which involved comparable groups in terms of sex, age, and profession, investigated burnout on the job and at home. Their data confirmed the same unexpected result—Israelis report less burnout than Americans.[32] I can think of several reasons why this might be so:

> Israelis expect, more than Americans, that their marriages will last forever, and have a stronger commitment to them than Americans.
>
> Israelis expect less of life and of marriage because the Israeli culture does not build as many unrealistic expectations as the Ameri-can culture does and, therefore, couples are less likely to be disap-pointed.
>
> Israelis' way of coping with stress, which tends to be more confrontational (active and direct) than Americans' (while Ameri-cans' way of coping with stress tends to be more avoidance-seeking than Israelis', and more dependent on drugs and alcohol), is better because it is more likely to produce changes.[33]
>
> The problems of existence in Israel, on the personal and the national level, are so immense that one's marital problems seem trivial by comparison. Americans, on the other hand, live in a fairly benign culture, where one's marital problems loom large.

The social structure in Israel provides more support for couples, and Israelis' social support networks are more stable and protect them better from stress.

The one-month-a-year military service gives the Israeli couple an important yearly vacation from each other, a vacation that helps reaffirm the significance of their marriage and reestablish their commitment to each other.

There are stronger social norms against admitting the existence of personal or marital problems among Israelis. Because of such cultural sanctions Israelis are less likely than Americans to report burnout, even if they experience it to the same or even a higher degree.

Israelis report, and experience, less burnout than Americans, not *in spite of* their greater stress, but *because* of it. When an American fails, either on the job or in marriage, the focus of the blame is most often dispositional ("How could I be so dumb!"). When an Israeli fails, on the other hand, the blame is assigned most often to the situation or the system ("those stupid bureaucrats," "the lousy government," "the unreasonable time demanded for army duty," or "the crazy economy"). Israelis, both as individuals and as couples, are least likely to blame themselves for failure. Their networks of family and friends also tend to reinforce that outward-directed focus of blame.

There is no reason to think that Israelis are constitutionally different from Americans. We can say, therefore, that Israeli couples, either because of their situation or because of the way they have learned to deal with problems, have learned how to cope with burnout better.

The comparison between Israelis and Americans, together with the discussion of the individual differences mediating between the effects of the environment and the experience of burnout, leads to the familiar conclusion that burnout depends on the interaction between people and their subjective environment, and thus is not inevitable. This ought to be good news not only for married couples who are struggling with burnout in their relationships but also for people who have shunned serious relationships because they fear that "there is no hope, every marriage ends unhappily, why bother?"

The implication from the conclusion that burnout is not inevitable is not always eagerly drawn or accepted, because it implies that couples have more power to influence the quality of their relationship than some care to admit. The power results from the fact that couples are actually providing part of the "subjective environment" for each other. In other words, each mate is part of the environment of the other. Couples are not only affected by the atmosphere in which they live; they also influence and affect it. A science fiction story I read many years ago demonstrates that effect.

> Two scientists wish to discover the origin of an ancient god symbolized by a winged lightning bolt. According to legend, the mysterious god visited earth and then vanished. Using a special time machine, the scientists go back in time and experience many thrilling adventures. At the end of their last adventure, they are pursued by a group of angry warriors and barely make it back to the time machine to escape the past and return to their own time. Once safely back home again, the scientists recount their adventures, noting that they have failed to find the origin of the winged-snake god. Suddenly they notice that there is a sign of lightning on their safety helmets. They realize that they themselves, visiting the ancient people and later disappearing in their time machine amid clouds of smoke and fire, must have been the origin of the legend.

Like the scientists back in time, we all play an active part in creating our relationships. And like those scientists, we often don't notice our own impact. Yet our influence is very powerful. It is derived in part from the power of self-fulfilling prophecies. That power was demonstrated in an experiment by social psychologist Mark Snyder and his colleagues at the University of Minnesota.[34] In the experiment, pairs of unacquainted male and female students participated in what they thought was an investigation of the processes by which people become acquainted with each other. All they were told was that they would engage in a telephone conversation with a person of the opposite sex. The male subjects received a snapshot of what they believed was the female they were about to talk to. Actually, the snapshots were not of the female subjects but were pictures chosen previously for receiving either very high or very low attractiveness ratings. The decision whether a man would get a picture of a very attractive or a very unattractive woman was made randomly. Female subjects did not get snapshots and knew nothing about them being given to the men.

Each twosome then engaged in ten minutes of unstructured conversation by means of microphones and headphones. A tape recorder recorded each participant's voice on a separate channel of the tape. Raters, who knew neither the subjects nor the true purpose of the study, listened *only* to the track of the tape containing the women's voices. They rated those recordings on dimensions such as animation, flirtatiousness, enthusiasm, intimacy, and friendliness. The results revealed that those women who (unbeknown to them) were perceived by the men they were talking to as very attractive actually came to behave in a flirtatious, friendly, and likable manner. Those women who spoke with men who thought them unattractive, on the other hand, were more cool and aloof.

Similarly in intimate relationships, people who perceive their mates as unattractive behave toward them in a way that helps bring out their mates' more unattractive qualities and thus fulfills their negative prophecy. Such people are surprised to discover that their mates can be much more attractive—flirtatious, friendly, and warm—in another social encounter. This surprise is most painful and disturbing when it happens after a divorce that was initiated because of the mate's supposed unattractiveness. A man who divorced his wife because he perceived her as homely, unattractive, and asexual is shocked to discover that after the divorce his wife has again blossomed into the sexy, elegant, and interesting woman she was when they first met and fell in love, the kind of woman he is now looking for.

The same person, depending on the situation, can be sexual or asexual, flirtatious or not flirtatious, warm or cold, exciting or boring. Being treated as a physically attractive person by your mate is likely to bring out more of your physically attractive behavior. That behavior, in turn, will reinforce your mate's positive perception of you. You have the power to influence the quality of your relationship. It isn't all up to fate. Your situation didn't just happen to you. It happened to you for a reason, and you can deal with that reason. Your ability to avoid marriage burnout depends, in large measure, on your willingness to take (at least some) responsibility for what happens in your relationships. Some people avoid taking this kind of responsibility because they are socialized by romantic myths to expect the romantic spark to remain in the relationship by itself—effortlessly, spontaneously, by magic.

This socialization to passivity in love is akin to a training toward nonhardiness, of people whose approach to the world in everything else can be active and direct. The negative effects of such training for passivity are compounded by the effects of socially sanctioned unrealistic expectations that are bound to disappoint, and the erosive effects of everyday living.

There is another reason people avoid taking action—fear. Rollo May, in his introduction to *Love and Will,* describes that fear:

> The old myths and symbols by which we oriented ourselves are gone, anxiety is rampant; . . . we do not will because we are afraid that if we choose one thing or one person we'll lose the other, and we are too insecure to take the chance. The bottom then drops out of the conjunctive emotions and processes—of which love and will are the two foremost examples.[35]

Earnest awareness of the dangers of burnout is not enough. In order to avoid burnout one needs to take action. Couples who do that don't need awareness of what they are doing right to have a vital relationship. Still, awareness is a good first step. As with any problem, it is important to be aware of and to desire change, but much more direct action is needed to reverse a problem once it has already happened.

Burnout is not inevitable. While it is definitely true that the person we fall in love with is human and thus incapable of fulfilling all of our needs, some couples manage to live with this sad reality quite successfully. That is not to say that they never have problems in their marriages or disagreements or disappointments. But it is to say that they choose to take responsibility for those problems, disagreements, and disappointments.

In part their success can be attributed to an environment that is supportive, challenging, and relatively free of hassles and stresses. In part their success can be attributed to positive childhood experiences that enabled them to develop compatible positive romantic images, and a romantic ideal that is both achievable and growth enhancing. Another important part is a cluster of attitudes that includes:

- A high degree of commitment to the relationship. (A couple that feels "if it works out, fine; if not I can take it or leave it" has little hope of making love last.)
- A sense of control over the relationship. (If either the husband or the wife feels that "it doesn't matter what I do" they are not likely to invest themselves in the marriage.)
- A love of challenge. (What is the notion of spending the rest of your life with one person except one of the greatest challenges most of us will ever face?)

Armed with this set of attitudes these couples channel their creative energy into creating a love relationship that satisfies their most important physical, emotional, and spiritual needs. Having committed themselves to what Erich Fromm calls "the art of loving,"[36] they build their relationships with the energy and creativity that an artist puts into building an important work of art.

# CHAPTER 8

# Burned-out Couples
and Couples in Love

**To be loved, be loveable.**

Ovid,
*The Art of Love*

Ovid, the Roman poet, in his counsel for lovers seeking romantic success, suggested that love be seen as an art to be mastered. A similar suggestion was made nineteen centuries later by Erich Fromm in *The Art of Loving:*

> There is hardly any activity, any enterprise, which starts with such tremendous hopes and expectations, and yet, which fails so regularly, as love. If this were the case with any other activity, people would be eager to know the reasons for the failure, and learn how one could do better—or they would give up the activity. . . . The first step to take is to become aware that love is an art; if we want to learn how to love we must proceed in the same way we have to proceed if we want to learn any other art. . . . The process of learning an art can be divided conveniently into two parts: one, mastery of the theory; the other, the mastery of the practice. . . . But, aside from learning the theory and practice, there is a third factor necessary to becoming a master in any art—the mastery of the art must be a matter of ultimate concern.[1]

How does one master the art of love? Does mastering the art guarantee no burnout? One way to answer these questions is to look at couples who did burn out and couples who did not. Which is just what I did. In examining the descriptions couples I worked with gave about their relationships, I tried to identify what differentiated between those who burned out from those who, after the same number of years, had relationships that were vital and passionate. I also examined couples' responses to a structured questionnaire.

In one study involving 100 couples, I compared the 17 percent who had the highest scores on the Burnout Test (see p. 257) with the 17 percent who had the lowest burnout scores.[2] The two groups were similar in terms of age, the number of children they had, and the length of marriage. In analyzing the data I found ten variables that best accounted for the difference in burnout between them. The ten variables are discussed in this chapter in order of their significance. Each one of these variables touches, in one way or another, on issues discussed throughout the book. In that sense, this chapter represents a summary as well as a translation of the abstract ideas expressed in the book into the actual life experiences of couples. While the variables will be presented separately it is important to emphasize that they never operate in isolation. They are all dynamically interrelated, affecting each other and being affected by each other in all relationships and at all times.

Because it can be cumbersome and confusing to describe the way these variables operate in the lives of different men as compared with women in the high- as compared with the low-burnout groups, I decided to use two couples as examples. Both couples have been mentioned several times throughout the book. One couple—Dona and Andrew—is my yardstick for burnout; the other one—Ellen and Anthony—is happily married.

## LOOKING POSITIVELY AT THE RELATIONSHIP AS A WHOLE

The biggest difference between the high- and the low-burnout groups was in the ability, or lack of ability, to look positively at the relationship as a whole.[3] Ellen, in the low-burnout group, explains:

> I am careful about money, and Anthony is casual, even wasteful. I like to plan what I'm going to do with our money, and to spend money on things that we both value, and he just lets it run through his fingers without even knowing what he spent it on. I often look on his attitude toward money with complete bewilderment. . . .
>
> There is something else. He burns pots. Not just once, or twice, or three times. He burns pots about once a month. He puts

the kettle on the stove, or puts on a pot of soup, and then he starts reading and the next thing you know the whole house is full of smoke.

But every time I get furious with him, I stop short of saying "That's it, I've had it" because I remember what a good thing we have going between us; how lucky I feel to have a husband who is my best friend, with whom I can talk about anything, who is loving and supportive even after all these years.

Ellen can keep her composure over little things—like scorched pots—and big things—like money—because she knows that Anthony is the right husband for her, her best friend. What about a guy who burns pots and also can't or won't communicate with his wife, a guy who isn't her best friend? Dona, in the high-burnout group, explains how her husband's annoying habits make her feel toward him and toward their marriage:

What really gets me are the things he does repeatedly, things that seem to be motivated by nothing else but a desire to drive me crazy. . . .

. . . like putting bottles of soft drink in the freezer and leaving them there till they explode. And each time this happens and I tell him he is going to forget to take the bottles out in time, he insists he knows what he is doing. . . . Or like his habit of not paying parking tickets till they've tripled the fine . . . or not giving me my telephone messages. . . . But the one thing that is most likely to drive me out of this marriage is his habit of eating in bed. When I feel those crumbs in the sheets, I just want to bite his head off.

Andrew expresses similar feelings:

I am not a very organized person. One could even say that I am messy and forgetful. But I have my own priorities about things I value. I am very careful about things I consider important, and I like to have my things in the order I left them, even if for someone else my order may appear as disorder. When I can't find an important document, because it has been put under some neat pile of papers, I am ready to explode. At that moment I can't think of anything positive about either Dona or our marriage.

When people are able to look positively at the relationship as a whole, burned pots, crumbs, and tidying up can be seen in context. But when love has gone out of a marriage, little annoyances can become the focus of incredible rage. Anger out of proportion to the crime is perhaps the clearest sign of the disappointment in love. On the other hand, if your relationship continues to give a sense of meaning to your life, you will be able to turn aside anger and remember how much joy the relationship gives you, and you are less likely to be burned out.

Of course it is not clear whether burnout causes one to focus on the little irritations of marriage, or whether focusing on the little irritations causes burnout. One thing is clear: The two are closely related. Dona, who is burned out in her marriage, has even kept track of these irritations:

A lot of things took place on symbolic occasions, which made them easy to remember. One of the things that actually cemented my decision to get a divorce was my birthday. I got a phone call at six o'clock in the morning from Europe, from a cousin, wishing me a happy birthday. Here was someone far away, taking the trouble. And Andrew just sat there listening. He didn't even say "Happy birthday!"

I'd given him a lot of opportunities to get me a present because it is also symbolic. And I said I'd like a book, maybe a book certificate. And here's what he said to me when I got home from work that night: "I went to look for a book, but then I decided that a book or a book certificate wasn't a good idea. Why don't you just go to the bookstore and pick out what book you want?" Which I haven't done, obviously. I suddenly realized that here are all these people who love me, and here is my husband who doesn't even appreciate me. He doesn't value me. He doesn't love me. If he did he wouldn't treat me the way he did. He would want to do something special for me.

I kept a hate book all these years. Whenever I've been depressed or upset I've written it down. I've got it in this book . . . fourteen years worth . . .

Keeping the hate book helped Dona focus on the negative and remember all the bad times she had experienced in her fourteen years with Andrew. We can assume that if she had kept a love book instead, she might have been able to remember the good times. Whenever something happened that bothered her, she could have looked in her love book and remembered what was good about her marriage. Ellen describes keeping track of the good:

I don't like to carry grudges. I don't like harping on things that I can't do anything about, or things that have already happened. I imagine myself sometimes standing on a bridge, and throwing whatever troubles me down into the water, visualizing it as going with the "water under the bridge." I remember, for example, getting very upset with Anthony on my birthday. My family and friends gave me a big party, which was very touching, and made me feel loved and cared for. The only one who did not give me a present was Anthony. I was very surprised and hurt by this.

After everyone else was gone, and after some hesitation, I asked him why he hadn't bothered to get me a present. He said he was obsessing about it for weeks, knowing how important such things were for me. But as hard as he tried, he couldn't come up with something that he felt sure would make me happy. By the day of the birthday he said he was in a real panic. He finally decided just to wait and ask me what I wanted to get from him.

I can't say it really made it all right. Birthdays, anniversaries, New Year's Eve—all those occasions are very important to me. I wished he had given me something . . . anything . . . I told him that, just as I tell him all my feelings. And as I was doing that I was thinking how lucky I am to be able to tell him I am upset. It was something I had never been able to do with my first husband. Anthony and I talked for quite a while about the birthday and at the end I just sent the rest of my bad feelings with the water under the bridge.

Jeannette and Robert Lauer interviewed three hundred couples in marriages lasting at least fifteen years. Their goal was to identify the characteristics of long-lasting, happy marriages.[4] They found that:

Couples in a happy marriage genuinely like and respect each other. Husband and wife consider their spouse to be their best friend and generally would rather be in their company than anyone else's.

Happy couples had their major conflicts over the years, but always kept in mind that "the relationship was more important than any issue that came up." Happy couples argue by focusing on the issue rather than the person.

Happy couples spend most of their leisure time together.

Happy couples realize that marriage is rarely a 50–50 proposition. They seem to know that sometimes you have to give 80 percent and get only 20 percent and realize that over time it tends to balance out.

All four of these characteristics are, in one way or another, reflections of the ability (willingness?) to look positively at the relationship as a whole. When your mate is your best friend, annoyances are kept in perspective. When your best times are spent together, bad times are seen within that positive context. When you can avoid attacking your partner and instead tackle the problem, when you can keep your relationship foremost in your mind, minor conflicts are not likely to become major destructive fights. When you are willing to give more than your "fair share," your positive attitude is likely to be reciprocated and become the norm.

## QUALITY AND QUANTITY OF COMMUNICATION

How much time do you and your spouse spend daily in direct communication with each other? (This does not include time spent together doing things that do not require talking, or time spent together talking to other people.) How satisfied are you with the quality of your communication with your spouse? How many taboo subjects do the two of you have—subjects that affect the relationship but are never talked about, such as attraction to other people or feelings toward inlaws?

The second highest difference between the low- and the high-burnout groups was the difference in quality and quantity of communication.[5] Mates whose relationships were vital and satisfying described themselves as talking to each other "all the time," and as being able to talk "about absolutely everything." Couples who were burned out described great difficulty in talking to each other, even about trivial issues. Their communication tended to be curt, mechanical, and kept to the bare minimum.

Ellen, who burned out in her first marriage after ten years and who has been happily married to Anthony for thirteen, says that much of the success of her second marriage is due to "the magic of passionate words." Ellen describes the difference between her two marriages:

> With my first husband I felt we were not *really* honest with each other. There were so many subjects that were taboo. Toward the end of our marriage all we ever talked about were things like who would pick the kids up from piano lesson. We never talked, for example, about being attracted to someone else. That was simply unacceptable. But, of course, in the ten years of our marriage it did happen. So we had to deny it, which made us lie to ourselves and to each other. After doing it for so long I didn't know whether it was even possible to untangle this gigantic tangle of lies, half truths, and things unspoken.
>
> This is why I value so much my relationship with Anthony. We share everything with each other. And it is such a relief not to have to worry about what can be said and what cannot be said. To be able to share every thought and every feeling. Of course part of it also means feeling a pang of jealousy when he tells me another woman looks sexy. But experiences like that also add spice to life.

As part of my research on marriage burnout, I asked people what were the major stresses in their marriages, and how they coped with them. I presented couples with a list of twelve coping techniques (which were discovered as the primary ones in previous research).[6] The techniques included: I try to change the source of the stress; I ignore the source of stress (or my spouse); I talk about it with a supportive friend; I drink, take a tranquilizer, or a drug; I confront my spouse directly; I avoid the source of stress (or my spouse); I try to find the positive aspects in the situation; and so forth. To my great surprise I discovered that "talking to a supportive friend" was highly correlated with burnout. In other words, the more you speak to your best friend about the problems with your spouse, the more burned out you are likely to be in your marriage.[7]

I must admit that when I first saw these results I went back to my computer printouts, sure there was an error. There wasn't. Looking further I discovered that, as expected, confronting one's spouse directly had the opposite effect—the more direct confrontation, the less burnout.[8] Furthermore, I found that talking directly to one's spouse had far greater power to prevent burnout than talking to one's best friend had power to cause it. What these findings are telling us is that the best person to talk to about a problem in your marriage is your spouse. Not your best friend. Your best friend is on *your* side. He or she will take your perspective, and this one-sided support is not very likely to help you understand your *mate's* side. And it is understanding the other side that makes it possible to change. (Needless to say, talking to a best friend doesn't help your mate understand what's troubling you either.)

It is important to remember, however, that like all generalizations, this one is not true in all cases. Talking to a good and trusted friend can help rather than hurt a marriage if the friend is familiar with the problem and can help you understand your mate's point of view. This, by the way, is what should happen with a good therapist. It is also possible that people start confiding in a best friend not before but only after communication has broken down within the relationship. They turn to the friend because they feel lonely and have no emotional or verbal contact with their mates. The function the best friend serves then is to provide emotional support, to help clarify messy and confused feelings, and, most important of all, to help affirm one's view of reality. A friend's horrified response to a battered woman's story, for example, can give the woman the courage to leave a destructive relationship.

Many books have been written in recent years detailing for couples the "how to" of communication. For example: How to express your feelings without hurting your mate, and making him or her defensive. (A general rule of thumb is to imagine yourself hearing the same statement. How could your mate say the very same thing you are about to say, without hurting *your* feelings?) How to fight fair in a way that will enable you to vent frustrations but not close off channels of communication. The best advice for couples interested in improving their communication is to spend more time talking. A couple told me that their communication improved tremendously when they got a dog. Their nightly walks with the dog increased significantly the amount of time they spent talking to each other. Whether it's going for long drives in the country—just the two of you—or playing a couple of hands of gin rummy, if you spend time together, chances are you will start talking.

Having more time to talk (quantity) means that it is more likely that something of real importance (quality) will be discussed. Discussing issues of conflict or of potential conflict increases couples' ability to look positively at the relationship as a whole. Ellen explains how working on a communication problem in her marriage affected her feelings about the marriage as a whole.

In Anthony's family, both the parents and the four siblings are all very verbal, very opinionated, and very very loud. In order to be heard you need to scream louder than everyone else, and be persistent, so they'll quiet down long enough to let you speak. In my family, on the other hand, people rarely raise their voices. This difference presented a real problem for me at the beginning of our relationship. Whenever there was a disagreement between us, Anthony would start screaming, which would make me withdraw as fast and as far away as possible. Several times I even considered breaking up with him because of it.

But there were enough good things about the relationship even at the very beginning to make us both want to solve this problem. I made myself stay in conversations even when the urge to withdraw was overwhelming. And I explained to him each time that the volume of his voice made me feel intimidated. Tony tried to suppress his urge to raise his voice, knowing that if he did we will be dealing with the volume of his voice, rather than with the content of what he was trying to say. The fact that we were able to overcome this major hurdle made us feel good about the whole relationship and gave us a lot of faith in it.

For simplicity, I will discuss the last eight variables in three clusters of related variables, since things like physical attraction, sex, and variety have so much influence on each other. I will discuss at some length the interaction between the variables in each cluster, but will only hint at the interaction between the clusters.

## PHYSICAL ATTRACTION, SEX, AND VARIETY

The degree of physical attraction mates experienced and expressed toward each other was the third highest difference between the high- and the low-burnout groups.[9] Burned-out couples talked about feeling anything from little attraction, through no attraction at all, to absolute revulsion toward each other. Dona describes her feelings:

> When we were first married I used to look at Andrew's body, like on the beach, with something akin to admiration. He is tall, and at that time was trim, in great physical shape. Now I look at him sometimes and I feel sick to my stomach. The sight of his back is enough to make my skin crawl. . . . He is overweight. His face pudgy. It is my physical reaction to him that tells me, against all my intellectual protestations, how burned out I really am in this marriage.

Andrew describes similar feelings:

> There is absolutely nothing left of the physical interest that was there at the beginning of our marriage. The only thing I feel when I look at her is deep, deep boredom. I don't believe anything can be done to change that. I stay in the marriage because of the children. Because it is convenient. And because I can get the physical excitement I need elsewhere.

Ellen, in the low-burnout group, feels quite different:

> When I look at Anthony sometimes, after all these years together, I still find him exquisitely beautiful. Even when I get mad at him, I can't stay mad for long because there he is with those gorgeous eyes, and hair, and lips that I love. . . . My anger just melts away.

Anthony sounds similar when he talks about Ellen:

> I never believed physical attraction could last. But even after more than a decade I still find Ellen one of the sexiest women I know. Her sexual energy, her body, the touch of her skin, are even more exciting to me today than they were when we first met.

Which comes first: burnout or finding your mate no longer physically appealing? Which comes first: feeling in love or thinking your mate is sexy? I don't know if the answer to that question is as important as what we can learn from it: If you change one, you can change the other.[10] Even if you are aware of how much physical

attraction means in a relationship, you may defeat yourself by saying: "We both look older, we're never going to be teenagers again,
what's the use? What's gone is gone." This is simply not so. It is
easy to "let yourself go" around the house, to let your stomach stick
out, to run around the house in an old housedress, an old pair of
shorts, with dirty hair and dirty fingernails. You take your mate for
granted and so you stop making an effort. But if there is any
message in this chapter it is that you have to make the effort and
break the downward spiral; otherwise burnout is just around the
corner.

And what if, you say, you simply don't *feel* attracted to your
mate? William James, the father of American psychology, said that
the best way to get out of a bad mood is to whistle a happy tune.
By whistling, you are "behaving as if" you are in a good mood. The
whistling makes you change your posture, which changes your
mood. This trick will work in a relationship too. If you act *as if* you
are attracted to your mate, you will not only find yourself more
attracted, you will most likely also increase your mate's attractiveness and attraction to you. And when you feel more attractive, you
are more attractive. What that means depends on each couple.
Fortunately, you have a pretty good idea where to start if you
simply remember how you behaved when you first fell in love. You
may think it is artificial, silly, and even impossible to pull off, to
pretend to be attracted to your mate when you are not, but what
do you have to lose? What is more silly, pretending you have the
hots for your spouse, or living in a cold and unrewarding relationship?

Behaving toward your mate as if he or she were physically
attractive is likely to bring out your mate's more attractive qualities
in the same way that a positive self-fulfilling prophecy does. This
happens most clearly when the two of you are in love. Similarly, if
you think that with time and domesticity your mate has become
unattractive, and you behave in accordance with that perception,
your behavior will bring out your mate's most unattractive qualities
in the same way that a negative prophecy does. This happens most
clearly when a relationship burns out. In both cases, your behavior
helps reaffirm preconceived notions about your mate. In my interviews I discovered that couples in the low-burnout group were far
more likely to behave as if their mates were fulfilling all their needs,
and as if the relationship provided a full answer to their quest for

cosmic significance. Needless to say, couples in the high-burnout group acted as if their partners and the relationship didn't fulfill any of their needs, thus helping to ensure that they also never will.

SEX LIFE

It should come as no surprise that couples in the low-burnout group reported significantly better sex lives than couples in the high-burnout group.[11] The quality of sex affected the physical attraction between mates, and was affected by it.[12] Dona describes the downside of sex:

> Most of the time either I would go to bed early and he would stay up late or, if he went to bed early, I would stay up late—so the issue of sex often didn't come up at all. I really didn't want to make love to him. I didn't even want to kiss him. When we had sex I just wanted to get it over and done with. He was actually much better at it than I was. In fact, he gave more to me sexually these last few years than I gave to him. I had already tightened up inside, and wasn't able to give. He lost all physical attraction to me.

Ellen, on the other hand, describes sex life that is exciting and enriching:

> Sex colors everything pink. It is so good that at times I feel like all the cells in my body are vibrating for hours after we make love. A part of me keeps being surprised that things can be so intense even after doing basically the same thing so many times. . . . Every time we make love a part of me expects to be ever so slightly disappointed. But it never happens. I wonder sometimes whether it is not blinding me from seeing problems in the relationship. But you know what? I don't care. This is what being alive is all about.

The relationship between poor sex and burnout[13] can mean two things: It can mean that burnout causes sex to deteriorate ("There was no spark left between us so how could sex be good?"). It can also mean that when sex gets boring, it facilitates the process of burnout. ("When I would rather read a book than make love I know that the end of the relationship is inevitable, and close by.")

Sex is clearly important. Yet, it came only fifth in the list of variables that separate the high- and low-burnout groups. This probably tells us that—even after we have studied all the sex books, learned new positions, turned the lights low, and had a glass of wine—if we no longer love the person we are going to bed with, sooner or later sex cannot help but become disappointing. Sex manuals and how-to books have their value, especially in providing information. They are less helpful for those couples who know all the positions, all the erogenous zones, and the various ways to stimulate each zone, but who are nonetheless bored with their sexual partner. Rollo May talks about the disappointment with technique in the introduction to his book *Love and Will*:

> Sex, as rooted in man's inescapable biology, seems always dependable to give at least a facsimile of love. But sex, too, has become Western man's test and burden more than his salvation. The books which roll off the presses on technique in love and sex, while still best-sellers for a few weeks, have a hollow ring: for most people seem to be aware on some scarcely articulated level that the frantic quality with which we pursue technique as our way to salvation is in direct proportion to the degree to which we have lost the salvation we are seeking.[14]

Good sex is a by-product of the emotional arousal of love. While the intensity of sex may go down with time, the overlay love imposes on the biological drive makes it possible for sex to remain exciting and fulfilling. This is especially true in those relationships in which mates continue to grow and get from their love a sense of meaning. Variety is one of the ways these couples continue to grow.

### VARIETY

After eighteen months in solitary confinement as a suspected spy in France, Christopher Burney wrote, "I soon learned that variety is not the spice; it is the very stuff of life."[15] Earlier in the book I noted that variety buffers against burnout. Boredom, on the other hand, fosters burnout, especially in men. Thus it should not be surprising to discover that variety made the top ten.[16]

A prerequisite for variety is change, what the behaviorist Joel Block calls, in *The Magic of Lasting Love,* "the deliberate breaking out from accustomed patterns, in other words, changing one's own behavior." Block notes that

> change requires a kind of flirting with inadequacy, the courage to fumble, a willingness to open ourselves to a degree of pain in the present in the hope that greater satisfaction will be delivered in the long run. . . . This, of course, is not easy.[17]

Dr. Richard Stuart, a behavioral therapist, describes in *Helping Couples Change* "the Fear-of-Change Principle."[18]
Joel Block elaborates:

> Although we may want to change our responses and behaviors, we do not necessarily welcome the change. In most areas of our lives, we put a premium on security and resist change even if the novel behavior is toward the relief of pain and the promise of pleasure.[19]

Block believes that there are three common obstacles to change in long-term relationships: pride, inertia, and fear:

> Both partners typically decide to withhold positive changes on the basis of pride; they feel that "giving in" implies they have been wrong all along. In essence, they adopt a "change-second" rather than a "change first" attitude, which results in a hopeless deadlock.
>
> Just as false pride makes progress more difficult, inertia comes into play. This is the tendency for an established pattern to remain unaltered. In order for us to move forward, an extra push is needed. Once the initial energy is exerted and change is well under way, less effort will be required. But it is often onerous to exert this extra energy.
>
> It is fear, though that exerts the most powerful influence in the change process. Fear is the feeling that engulfs us when we seriously consider altering a pattern that is well established, even if it is dysfunctional.

In order to overcome these obstacles one needs to be gradual, to persist, to expect resistance, and to remain positive—all at the same time. Each couple needs to decide where variety is needed in their lives, but the simple rule of thumb is—whatever you do, at times do it differently. The sexual arena is where for many couples boredom sets in fastest. Here you can change not only what you do, but when you do it and where and how. For example, a couple who always makes love in the missionary position, in their bedroom, with both mates naked, after the children are asleep, can wake up very early and make love in the guest room, partially clothed, with both mates facing each other sideways.

These and similar recommendations are based on the assumption that people want their need for variety fulfilled within their marriages, which is not always true. As we know, some people believe that the most essential element in sexual variety is the sexual partners. In order to get that kind of variety they go outside their marriages. They get security from marriage and variety from the affairs.

One group, the reader probably remembers, tries to get both variety and security from the relationship—Kerista Village. Lil, one of the members of the commune, explains:

> Asking one person to satisfy all of our needs for sexual, emotional, intellectual, and spiritual fulfillment is, after all, a tall order. Polifidelity is an attempt to find a way out of this quagmire without sacrificing the depth of intimacy. It combines the best features of monogamy with the best features of the open life-style. Since intimacy is shared, and since the base of security is broadened, no one feels pressured by an expectation to be all things to each person. People look to different partners to share different things. Since variety gives each person plenty of exciting nooks and crannies to explore in each partner, relationships refuse to get dull.

For the Keristans, variety increases the quality of sex. For Andrew, lack of variety ruins sex:

> From the beginning of our relationship Dona was very reserved sexually and quite conservative in her sexual tastes. Sex got boring for me very soon. Now I still initiate it once in a long while, when I get horny enough, but our sex life is as boring as it can get. I stopped looking at Dona as a sexual person a long time time ago. I don't find her physically attractive.

Andrew could not see a way out. Since he did not find Dona physically attractive, he did not know what could possibly improve their sex life. He was most probably right, since there was no sexual spark left in the marriage. In those cases where there is some spark left, however, variety is one of the surest ways to intensify it. Variety makes lovemaking more exciting, which improves the quality of sex, which makes couples more physically attractive to one another. Physical attraction, sex, and variety represent the wings of a relationship. The next three items represent its roots.

## APPRECIATION, SECURITY, AND SUPPORT

People in the low-burnout group felt more appreciated than people in the high-burnout group did.[20] Andrew knows Dona doesn't appreciate him:

> She always put down my work. She said it was pedestrian, not artistic like her work. . . . I have never been in love with accounting, but I still don't like having her put it down. Her ankle-biting derogatory references to accounting got pretty repetitive . . . kinda old. It was like chipping at a stone.

Dona feels both unappreciated and unappreciating:

> I began to find myself feeling hopeless, feeling locked in a situation I could do nothing with. I thought it was obvious that neither of us could change and that, in fact, we would both be better off if we found someone who liked us for who we were and appreciated the good qualities we both have. Andrew really does have some lovely qualities. . . . I feel like I'm a special kind of person—someone with enthusiasm, exuberance, joy of people—and Andrew doesn't care about that at all. He doesn't like any of that in me.

Ellen, on the other hand, knows she is appreciated:

> I guess that in part it's because my ex-husband was so critical of me that Anthony's appreciation is so important. To my ex-husband everyone in the humanities was a "soft head," and anything they had to say was by definition trivial. He once read a paper I wrote, muttering all the while to himself, "What nonsense." He was also critical of me as a mother and as a woman. Anthony, on other hand, appreciates me both as a professional and as a woman. I know he respects my mind, likes my personality, and loves my looks. And let

me tell you something, it feels wonderful. My self-concept has improved tremendously as a result of being with him.

Isn't it a shame that people who realize full well how important it is to show appreciation at work completely forget how important it is to show appreciation at home? The more appreciation, respect, and recognition you receive from your spouse, the data show, the less likely you are to burn out.[21]

Many people give these positive rewards generously and easily to all other people in their life, yet have great difficulty giving them to their mates. While speaking to a casual aquaintance they may feign attentiveness, sympathy and respect. When speaking to their mates, however, whom they supposedly love, they are often rude, impatient, or openly critical. Their assumption, conscious or unconscious, is that since they "have" their mates, they don't need to exert effort. The strong relationship between feeling unappreciated and burnout shows just how short-sighted some people can be.

It is important to note that there are some people who could stay for many years in relationships with people who put them down and give them little or no appreciation. Psychoanalysts believe that these people secretly harbor low self-esteem. They cannot admit this low self-esteem even to themselves. By being with someone who constantly criticizes them, someone who puts them down, they can externalize the source of their unhappiness—it is not themselves that they dislike but rather the critical mate who is making them unhappy, and it is easier to deal with the outer critic than with the inner critic. The only solution for this problem, according to the psychoanalytic approach, is for these people to develop a more positive self-concept. This can be achieved most effectively in the context of long-term therapy. For the rest of us, a little bit of kindness and appreciation might go a long way toward guaranteeing that we will not burn out.

Focusing on the pathology of the individual is not the only way to understand or treat a relationship where mates are caught in a negative cycle in which neither one gives nor receives the rewards possible in a love relationship. An alternative approach suggests that with the routine of marital life, the "romantic schema" that operated when a couple fell in love has changed to a far less romantic "marital schema." "Schemata" are frames of reference for

understanding the social world that are built through experience.
They are scaffolds within our minds that help provide order, structure, and organization for incoming information. We rarely receive
information in a totally passive manner. Instead, input is usually
filtered, organized, and interpreted through those existing frames
of reference, or cognitive structures.[22]

Romantic relationships start out with both partners sharing the
romantic role schema of "lover." With time, the far less romantic
role schemata of "husband and wife," "father and mother," or
"housewife and breadwinner" replace that of lover. In order to
reinstate the lover schema, the behaviors and atmosphere associated with it need to be recreated. When responding to something nice your mate has just done or said, think how much
appreciation you would have expressed if this very thing was said
or done not by your husband or wife of twenty years, but by your
lover. Positive action is reinforcing. If your mate does something
you appreciate, even if it is only bringing in the morning paper, if
you recognize it with a smile and thanks, it is much more likely to
happen again.

### SECURITY

It is not surprising to find that burned-out couples describe
themselves as having little or no security in their relationships. For
couples who are not burned out, security provides a very positive
and important reward.[23] Ellen, a professional woman, describes it:

> In my work I am always "on." I have to be on top of things, always
> with perfect control and a perfect smile. When I come home I can
> take off my shield and all my masks. I am completely myself. And
> I feel loved and accepted. My marriage is my foundation. From here
> I can go anywhere and do anything—knowing I will always be
> supported.

Anthony says that he and Ellen are one of the few couples he
knows who are truly happy:

> If you were to ask me how we have stayed happily married, I would
> have to say that it has to do with making the commitment to stay
> together and letting each other develop as individuals. To me this
> commitment and the security that derives from it provide the oppor-
> tunity to experience life to the fullest.

Knowing that security helps prevent burnout doesn't tell us how to make our own marriages more secure. Besides, what makes one person feel secure may make another feel stifled. Unfortunately, one of the most threatening topics of conversation for a couple is the things that make either the husband or the wife feel insecure. In addition, the people who feel most insecure in their marriage are the ones least likely to talk about it. In short, while threats to security are the topic most couples are least likely to talk about, it is possibly the topic couples should talk about most.

Security is what gives a relationship its roots, its depth, and its strength. For some of the people I interviewed, security was the most positive aspect of a long-term relationship, and one that more than compensated for the loss of excitement and the rush of expectations in new love. For others, however, too much security was stifling. Security implied stagnation, and boredom, lack of challenge. Andrew has this negative notion about emotional and financial security:

> She always talks about security. Security, security, security. It became oppressive. I mean, I'm only just now beginning to think about security. I've still got lots of time. And I have lots of confidence in my ability to earn money and provide for that. It's just a question of when. But with her it is the overriding concern—and that was very oppressive to me.

Women tend to perceive security as more important than do men. Jeanne H. Block, a developmental psychologist, argues that in our society we encourage boys to develop only wings, and girls to develop only roots—to the detriment of both.[24]

## SUPPORT

Sidney Cobb, M.D., defines social support as the knowledge that you are cared for, loved, esteemed, and valued, and that you belong to a network of people who share communication and mutual obligation. Cobb reviews an extensive literature showing that social support protects against the health consequences of life stress: from arthritis through tuberculosis to depression, alcoholism, and emotional breakdown.[25] In my own work, I found that social support provides a buffer against burnout.[26] The comparison between the high- and the low-burnout groups showed that burned-out individuals feel significantly less supported by their mates than do individuals in happy marriages.[27] Elliot Aronson and I discovered that support serves a multitude of functions that are essential to our psychological well-being. These can be condensed into six basic functions: listening, professional appreciation, professional challenge, emotional support, emotional challenge, and the sharing of social reality.[28]

We all need someone who will listen to us, especially in times of crisis. We especially appreciate someone who will listen actively, without immediately giving us advice ("Here's what you need to do") or making judgments ("How could you have been so dumb?"). We want someone who will share both our pain and frustration and our joy and pride, someone with whom we can share major conflicts as well as trivial incidents.

At work, we need professional appreciation from someone who is an expert in our field, and who is also someone whose integrity we trust. In other words, we want professional support from someone who is expert enough to understand the job we do, and who is courageous enough to give us honest feedback. If we are not challenged in our work, we run the risk of stagnation and boredom. A good boss—or a talented colleague—can keep us from growing stale. A good critic can challenge our way of thinking and encourage us to stretch ourselves.

All of us, when we are in a difficult situation, need to have someone on our side, even if he or she is not in total agreement with what we are doing. At least on occasion we need to have someone who is unconditionally supportive ("My friend, right or wrong"). This can be vital in stressful situations. When we are under stress, we need someone who will support us "come hell or high water." This person does not have to be an expert in our field, only a friend. An emotional challenge can stretch us psychologically by forcing us to question if we are really doing our best to fulfill our goals and overcome obstacles. Most of us can easily delude ourselves into thinking we are doing our best when we are not. It is comforting to convince ourselves that all avenues have been explored when they have not. Occasionally, it is easy to blame someone else rather than take responsibility for problems or crises. At that point an emotional challenge can help by forcing us to question our excuses. It is easier to temper our natural resistance to this kind of prodding if we trust that the challenge is done in our best interest.

Having someone who shares our social reality, who understands the world the way we do, and who has a similar value system is especially important when we think we are losing the ability to assess accurately what is happening around us. In a room full of people who are all agreeing with something that to us sounds like utter nonsense, it is enough to exchange understanding looks with this one person to know that we are not crazy after all.

A moment's reflection makes it clear that a spouse cannot fulfill all six of these functions. For example, the functions of professional appreciation and challenge are best provided by a co-worker or a superior familiar with the intricacies of our work. To be disappointed in our mate for not supplying every kind of support we need (and the kind of support that cannot reasonably be expected from him or her) is not only self-destructive, but also terribly unfair. We *can* expect our mates to listen and to give us unconditional support, at least occasionally. (Even if your mate told you not to do it, but you went ahead and did it anyway and now you're sorry, you want to know that your mate still loves you, and is on your side.) The third form of support you can expect from a mate is emotional challenge. Mates can encourage each other to examine defense mechanisms, question excuses, and explore seemingly impassable roadblocks. You can also expect your mate to share your social reality. Mates can help affirm each other's world view and perspective on reality.

Unfortunately, many people, especially when they are under stress at work, do not make the effort to discriminate between the various forms of support. They want their mates to be all things to them and then are disappointed when they can't or won't. Frequently, this disappointment is not verbalized, but becomes associated with home life. The atmosphere of regret and disappointment begins to erode the marriage; the result is burnout at work that spills over to burnout in the marriage.

Support, security, and appreciation interact with each other at all times, and the results of their dynamic interaction influence the likelihood of burnout in a relationship. Feeling listened to and supported unconditionally increases the sense of security in the relationship. Feeling secure and appreciated makes it easier to be challenged emotionally and grow. Sharing social reality increases security and mutual appreciation. Conversely, when these support functions are not available in a relationship, their combined negative impact is multiplied. Dona describes it:

> I get a lot of appreciation for my professional skills, my skills as a homemaker, and just the way I am in the world, from most of the people I come in contact with. But I never feel supported or appreciated in the same way by Andrew. It's as if he is afraid to pay me a compliment because it will take something away from him. Since I don't get support from him, I don't give it back either. Besides, I don't think he would appreciate my support anyway. He would rather get compliments and recognition from the people at work. Feeling unappreciated pushes all my insecurity and inferiority buttons. And I don't know anyone who can do that as well as Andrew can.

Since Dona feels insecure, unappreciated, and unsupported, she is unwilling to provide Andrew with any kind of support. Andrew feels similarly insecure, unsupported, and unappreciated, and consequently is unwilling to provide Dona with the support he knows she needs. Thus both of them are stuck in a negative cycle where neither one gets what he wants. Since they aren't communicating there is no way to break this negative cycle, which affects the way they both are feeling about their whole marriage.

## SELF-ACTUALIZATION AND INTELLECTUAL ATTRACTION

Self-actualization, the highest need in the human hierarchy of needs according to Abraham Maslow,[29] and intellectual excitement give relationships their spiritual wings. Self-actualization, growth, and reaching one's potential are important not only for each mate as an individual, but are important and enriching for the relationship as well. The more people are able to actualize themselves in the marriage the less burned out they are.[30]

If self-actualization is so good, why does it cause so much stress in some relationships, and end others? Andrew explains:

> When Dona went back to school we started developing in different directions. She was spending more and more time with her school

friends. She had new subjects she was interested in that I knew nothing about—and frankly they were subjects I didn't want to know anything about. She preferred to spend her free time in ways that did not include me. So I also started developing interests and friends that did not include her. Eventually we had nothing left in common. We had no shared interests, no mutual friends, nothing of any significance we enjoyed talking about together, or doing together. We were two strangers sharing a household.

Why did Andrew have such a different experience from that described by Anthony, who attributes the success of his marriage to the fact that he and his wife have continued to grow:

While we have a very strong bond between us, we still let each other grow and develop as separate and independent individuals. We both have our own professional interests, as well as outside interests that we don't always share. So I go to football games and I play golf with my friends, and she goes folk dancing and attends lectures I am not interested in with her friends. And that's okay because we share so many other things. I think we are both self-actualized individuals.

The difference, of course, has to do with the balance between roots and wings. Couples who grow wings when the relationship has no roots (which is to say, achieve individual self-actualization without their mate's involvement and support, and without the security of a deep commitment to the relationship) end up flying away from each other, because there is nothing to root them and hold them together. On the other hand, couples who grow only roots (of deep commitment and security) without developing wings (of self-actualization and growth) end up locked in a stifling relationship, feeling trapped, hopeless, and helpless—in other words, burned out. In order to keep the spark alive in a romantic relationship, couples have to grow both roots and wings, which is to say develop as individuals and strive to reach self-actualization without sacrificing their commitment to the relationship and without losing the foundation of trust and security. It is important that mates take at least some interest in their partners' other activities, because any activity that involves other people can ultimately represent a threat to the relationship.

The first step in achieving self-actualization is finding out such essentials as what is it that gives, or could give meaning to one's life, and how it can (if it can) be achieved within the marriage. Try the following exercise: Imagine meeting a good fairy who can grant only one wish. What would your wish be? Can it be achieved without the help of a magic wand?

## INTELLECTUAL ATTRACTION

Intellectual attraction to one's mate was the tenth variable differentiating between the high- and the low-burnout groups.[31] People in the high-burnout group often complain that they are intellectually bored with their mates, even when those mates seem an intellectual challenge to most other people. Dona, who is aware of the respect Andrew gets from others, says:

> I know he is a very bright man. He must be, to be as successful as he is in the work he does. But in terms of those things that matter to me he is anything but bright. He doesn't understand—and doesn't seem to care—about the areas that mean the most to me: aesthetics, human emotions. . . . Actually, in these areas, with all his vast knowledge, he is simply dumb.

Mates in the low-burnout group, on the other hand, describe intellectual attraction as a very important and stimulating part of their relationship. Ellen says:

> In all my years with Anthony, I have never been bored with him, not for one moment. I love talking to him about books, movies, people, and everything else. I love to hear his analysis of events, it always seems so profound. I am challenged by his intelligence. And it is a very important component of the relationship for me.

Intellectual attraction, like self-actualization, is part of the wings of the relationship. Individuals who have independent minds and interests are better able to challenge their mates and to maintain an intellectual spark in the relationship. Such personal interests, when brought back to the relationship, enhance growth. They enable both mates to be their best selves, and enable the relationship to be the best that it can be.

## SHARING CHORES

There were other things that differentiated between the burned-out group and the happily married group,[32] but the ten presented in this chapter differentiated between the two groups best. It is interesting to note, in this regard, a variable that in spite of all expectations to the contrary did not keep couples from burnout—sharing chores. It appears that when couples are able to look positively at their relationship as a whole, when they feel heard and cared for, and when the relationship gives their lives a sense of meaning, the exact sharing of chores is seen as trivial in comparison. Ellen, in talking about her first marriage, describes the diminishing value of her husband's help with household chores:

> Only when things were getting really bad, and I began to consider getting a divorce, did he start helping me around the house. After a dinner party for his business colleagues, he started helping me do the dishes. But it was too late. I was so furious at the idea of laboring over this dinner party for hours that I was no longer able to appreciate his help as much as I would have been if he had pitched in earlier in our marriage. At the beginning of our marriage he did absolutely nothing around the house.

In spite of the development of labor-saving devices, there is more housework today than there was fifty years ago. (Yes, we have electric washers and driers, but we also have more clothes that need to be washed separately and higher standards of cleanliness.) In spite of the couple-speak that praises the idea of sharing chores, women still carry most of the burden of the household. Ellen explains:

> It's not that he doesn't want to help. He simply doesn't notice that things need to be done, obvious things that I couldn't ignore if I wanted to. We're both trying to cope with the problem and to change. He tries to pay attention to the things I point out, such as the dirty kitchen counter left after he's supposedly "finished" washing the dishes. And in exchange, I try to ignore such things as dirt on the carpet until the cleaning lady comes once every two weeks. But it is an effort for both of us, and a constant source of conflict.

A recent national survey concluded that wives most often complain about their husbands' messiness and husbands most often complain about their wives' nagging about their messiness. Yet in all the studies on marriage burnout in which I looked at household chores, they never came out significantly correlated with burnout.[33]

Most women I worked with reported carrying significantly more of the burden of household work than the husbands. Most husbands reported feeling unappreciated for what they did do around the house and for the effort they were making. In both cases it was not housework that made or broke the relationships. Complaining about housework served as a barometer of other stresses in the relationship. When other things—especially communication and sex—were good, housework was considered unimportant and often became the focus of jokes. When communication—either physical or emotional—was problematic, household chores at times became a major stress in the relationship. All this shows that in spite of the big issue made of this particular aspect of living together, sharing chores is but one of the many elements interacting dynamically and affecting the overall quality of a marriage.

## A DYNAMIC SYSTEM

All ten of the variables I have discussed (and many others I did not mention because of space limitations) interact with one another. This means that, in addition to their own individual effects, they also influence each other, thus multiplying their combined impact. In this way, for example, improved communication improves sex life, which improves physical attraction, which improves the ability to look positively at the relationship as a whole, which improves communication, and so forth and so on. Because all the variables interact dynamically with each other, making a positive move in any one area tends to start an upward spiral, while making a negative move tends to start a downward spiral whose final stage is burnout.

This "domino effect"[34] makes the task of changing a burned-out relationship into one with roots and wings seem very simple. All you need to do is adopt a positive attitude toward your relationship, or perhaps improve the quality and quantity of communication in it. Yet we all know that this kind of advice is easier to give than to execute. Most people already know what they *should* do; their problem is that they can't make the "shoulds" happen.

Psychoanalysts believe that unconscious motives compel us to destroy our relationships. Because of traumatic experiences in childhood, we (or some of us) don't believe that love can last, so we actively destroy it to make our fears come true. While it is true that such unconscious destructive forces operate in some relationships, they are not what destroys most. Hassles, stresses, habit, and routine erode love and passion. Couples don't need to destroy their relationships actively; all they need to do is watch passively as they slip away from them. Once this process of love's erosion starts operating, it is very difficult to stop, and even harder to reverse. Change is never easy. The greatest block against it is inertia, and it is primarily because of inertia that people cannot make the "shoulds" happen in their lives.

Energizing a relationship that has lost its spark is not an easy task. It requires commitment and the combined effort of both mates. When only one mate decides to change things, and the other mate does not respond in the "right" way, the first can throw his or her hands up and say, "See! I tried, but nothing works." Yet people can change their lives in important ways when both mates are committed to the change. Another reason why people can't make the shoulds happen in their relationships is that those shoulds involve changing themselves or their partners—for example: "I should be more patient"; "He should be more open about his feelings"; "She should be less demanding." Change is much easier when it involves changing the environment, not people. When a couple is spending a romantic evening together, chances are that it will be easier for him to be more open about his feelings and for her to be less demanding.

Many of the recommendations I have presented in this chapter were mentioned during discussions elsewhere in the book. I tried to make the recommendations as general as possible. In my experience, most couples are able to translate such generalizations into specific recommendations that are best suited to their particular circumstances. In order to do this translation it is helpful for couples to know that their problems, most likely, are not pathological; that much of what they are experiencing is a result of unrealistic expectations and situational stresses; that they have power to change things, and that this is easier than trying to change either themselves or their mates. They also need the desire, the time, and the energy to apply these recommendations. The most difficult task, in most cases, is the first step—breaking the negative cycle. After that, once a positive cycle is started and is set in motion, all the next steps are smaller and easier.

It is always easy to put off making changes by telling ourselves "it won't work," or even if it does work, "I can't do it," or even if it works and you believe you can do it "the time isn't right." The anticipation of change almost always produces some anxiety. Yet, if a certain change is an important one to make, it is unlikely that there will be a better time than now. As Rabbi Hillel said in *Wisdom of Our Fathers,* "If I am not for myself, who will be for me? If I am only for myself, what am I? And if not now, when?"[35]

# Notes

# CHAPTER 1

1. Elaine Walster and W.G. Walster, *A New Look at Love* (Reading, Mass.: Addison Wesley, 1978), p. 9. There are different kinds of love. Erich Fromm discussed love between parent and child, brotherly love, motherly love, erotic love, self-love, and love of God (*The Art of Loving: An Enquiry into the Nature of Love* [New York: Harper & Row, 1956]). Others talked about love of a mate, love of a friend, love of ideals, love of freedom, love of nature, love of beauty, and love of humanity. Greek philosophers and modern scholars talked about different styles of love: storge (best friends), agape (unselfish), mania (possessive), pragma (practical), lodus (playful), and eros (romantic) (M. Lasswell and N. Lobsenz, *Styles of Loving: Why You Love the Way You Do* [New York: Ballantine Books, 1980]). My own assumption is that while there may be differences between people in their styles of love, these are only differences in emphasis, and that all lovers would like to have all the positive aspects of love combined in their own relationship.

2. Erving Goffman, "On Cooling the Mark Out: Some Aspects of Adaptation to Failure," *Psychiatry* 15 (1952): 451–463.

3. It is important to note that since the mid-eighties, divorce rates in the United States have been declining. According to the National Center for Health Statistics, after rising sharply between 1970 and 1980, the divorce rate has leveled off and even begun to decline. In 1986 it was 4.8 per 1,000 people, .2 percent below 1985, and the lowest since 1975. At the same time, the median length of marriage has been increasing—from 6.5 years in 1976 to slightly more than 7 years in 1986.

4. Ingrid Bengis, *Combat in the Erogenous Zone* (New York: Alfred A. Knopf, 1972).

5. Otto Rank, *Will Therapy and Truth and Reality* (New York: Knopf, 1936).

6. I.D. Yalom, *Existential Psychotherapy* (New York: Basic Books, 1980).

7. Søren Kierkegaard, *The Concept of Dread* (1988, Princeton: Princeton University Press edition, 1957, translated by Walter Lowrie) p. 39.

8.    Erich Fromm, *The Art of Loving: An Enquiry into the Nature of Love* (New York: Harper & Row, 1956).

9.    Ernest Becker, *The Denial of Death* (New York: Free Press, 1973) p. 160.

10.    I found, for example, that the more people believed that "true love is forever," the less burned out they were. On the other hand, the more they believed that "marriage kills love," the more burned out they were. But since a correlation between two variables does not tell us which variable caused which, the same findings can be interpreted as indicating that the more burned out people are, the more they believe that marriage kills love; and conversely, the less burned out they are, the more they believe in true love. I am indebted to Dr. Ofra Nevo of Haifa University in Israel for her contribution to the ten romantic truisms.

11.    In the U.S. Bureau of the Census, Current Population Report (1981) there were 2,422,000 marriages and 1,213,000 divorces, which constitutes slightly over 50 percent. "Marital dissolution in the United States is at an all-time high," wrote Oliver Moles and George Levinger in their introduction to the *Journal of Social Issues* special issue on divorce and separation (1976, p. 1). Similarly, James and Janice Prochaska, in their 1978 introduction to *Marriage and Marital Therapy,* (ed. T. Paulino and McCrady [New York: Buner/Mazel, 1978]) note that "the United States now has the highest rate of divorce in the world. While divorce rates leveled off and even began to decline in the mid eighties, the same fact is quoted again in an August 24, 1987 article published in *Newsweek.* Trends between the seventies and the eighties also indicated that the divorce rate was higher than ever before in history and for a whole decade was climbing at an unprecedented pace" (p. 3). In P. Blumstein and P. Schwartz, *American Couples* (New York: William Morrow, 1983), demographers are quoted as projecting that half of all first marriages would end in divorce and that 41 percent of all American adults will at some time in their life experience a divorce.

12.    Nathaniel Branden, *The Psychology of Romantic Love* (New York: Bantam Books, 1983), pp. 5–6.

13.    Denis de Rougemont, *Love in the Western World* (New York: Pantheon Books, 1940, 1983), pp. 291–92.

14.    Troubled marital relationships have been identified by several investigators as frequent precipitants of suicide attempts. See, for example, N. Kessel, "Self Poisoning," *British Medical Journal* 2 (1965): 1265–1340.

15.    D. Everett Dyer, *Courtship, Marriage, and Family: American Style* (Homewood, Ill.: The Dorsey Press, 1983).

16.    R.N. Bellah, R. Madsen, W.M. Sullivan, A. Swidler, and S.M. Tipton, *Habits of the Heart: Individualism and Commitment in American Life* (Berkeley: University of California Press, 1985).

17.    James L. Framo, "The Integration of Marital Therapy with Sessions with Family of Origin," in *Handbook of Family Therapy* (New York: Bruner/Mazel, 1981), pp. 131–158. Framo also quotes marriage counselors Whitaker and Keith: "Marriages end up driving some people mad, pushing others into homicidal and suicidal acts, producing hateful demons out of perfectly nice people" (p. 133). (C. Whitaker and D.V. Keith, "Counseling the Dissolving Marriage," in *Klemer's Counseling: Marital and Sexual Problems,* ed. R.F. Stahmann and W.J. Hiebert [Baltimore: William and Wilkins, 1977], p. 69).

**18.** A. J. Norton and P. C. Glick, "Marital Instability Past and Future," *Journal of Social Issues* 32, (1976): p. 12.

**19.** James Prochaska and Janice Prochaska, Introduction to Paulino and McCrady, *Marriage and Marital Therapy,* p. 3.

**20.** Philip Blumstein and Pepper Schwartz, *American Couples* (New York: William Morrow, 1983) p. 309.

**21.** Barbara Ehrenreich, *The Hearts of Men: American Dreams and the Flight from Commitment* (Garden City, N.Y.: Anchor Press, 1983) pp. 12–13.

**22.** Han Suyin, *A Many Splendoured Thing* (New York: Penguin, 1960) preface.

## CHAPTER 2

**1.** Elaine Walster and Ellen Berscheid, "Adrenalin Makes the Heart Grow Fonder," *Psychology Today* (June 1971), pp. 47–62; idem, *Interpersonal Attraction* (Menlo Park, Calif.: Addison-Wesley, 1969).

**2.** Ibid.

**3.** Marilyn French, *The Women's Room* (New York: JOVE/HBJ, 1977), pp. 365–66.

**4.** J. H. S. Bossard, "Residential Propinquity as a Factor in Mate Selection," *American Journal of Sociology* 38 (1932), pp. 219–24.

**5.** E. W. Burgess and P. Wallin, *Engagement and Marriage* (Philadelphia: Lippincott, 1953).

**6.** Elaine Walster and Ellen Berscheid, *Interpersonal Attraction* (Menlo Park, Calif.: Addison-Wesley, 1969).

**7.** Theodore Reik, *The Need to Be Loved* (New York: Bantam, 1964).

**8.** Robert Winch, *Mate Selection: A Study of Complementary Needs* (New York: Harper, 1958).

**9.** Bernard Murstein, *Who Will Marry Whom?* (New York: Springer, 1976).

**10.** A. Kerkoff and K. Davis, "Value Concensus and Need Complementarity in Mate Selection," *American Sociological Review* 17 (1962): 295–303.

**11.** Personal communication with Gerald Kaplan.

**12.** The research involved asking people to describe various aspects of their relationships and correlating those descriptions with their responses to the burnout measure (see Research Appendix). Since the results were consistent in the different samples studied, it seems sufficient to present here only those generated by one of these studies. The study involved one hundred couples. The average length of their marriage was fifteen years, ranging all the way from several months to thirty-four years.

  It should be noted that all the participants were asked openly and directly to describe their relationships and their feelings about those relationships. All the data presented are based on self-reports and consequently may be influenced by such factors as the honesty of the respondents or the respondents' desire to say things in order to put themselves in a more favorable light. My best guess is that these factors account for only a small part of the findings. This "best guess" is an informed judgment based on corroborating evidence from in-depth interviews with a subsample of the subjects.

13.  In the study of one hundred couples the correlation between overload and marriage burnout was r=.54 p<.0001.

14.  In the same study, the correlation between conflicting demands and marriage burnout was r=.49 p<.0001.

15.  The correlation between the pressure of family commitments and burnout in marriage was r=.48 p<.0001.

16.  The correlation between variety and burnout in marriage was r=−.44 p<.0001.

17.  E. Duffy, *Activation and Behavior* (New York: Wiley, 1962).

18.  The correlation between boredom and burnout was r=.35 p<.0001.

19.  The correlation between appreciation and burnout was r=−.43 p<.0001.

20.  The correlation with self-actualization was r=−.39 p<.0001.

21.  Abraham Maslow, *Toward a Psychology of Being* (New York: Van Nostrand, 1962), p.35.

22.  Carl Rogers, *On Becoming a Person* (Boston: Houghton Mifflin, 1961).

23.  Richard Lazarus, *Psychological Stress and the Coping Process* (New York: McGraw-Hill, 1966); and *idem* and Susan Folkman, *Stress, Appraisal, and Coping* (New York: Springer, 1984) pp. 31–32.

24.  The Love and Burnout Model (see p. 242) has several key points:

- People who believe in romantic love expect it to give life a sense of meaning.
- There is a direct relationship between romantic love and burnout. Falling in love is the initial stage in and the prerequisite for the burnout process.
- In spite of the magical uniqueness of the experience of falling in love, the "how" and the "why" of the experience are universal.
- There is a dynamic interaction between couples and the environment in which they live. It is not the obnoxious characteristics of one's mate that cause burnout, but rather the destruction of one's romantic ideals by situational stresses that are erroneously attributed to the mate.
- The environment is not a totally objective external reality. It is a perceived subjective representation of the world the way each one of us sees it.
- Expectations about romantic love result from learned cultural values as well as from personal experiences and always exist as part of people's belief systems. They are activated when people fall in love and are in full force when a commitment is made, whether the commitment is formal or not. Expectations have a powerful effect on love relationships, even when unconscious and not openly verbalized, because they are associated with what is perceived as the essence of life.
- Frustrated romantic expectations cause bitter disappointment and with it the erosion of love and commitment. Fulfilled expectations, however, are not a guarantee against burnout. Romantic ideals can be frustrated by not being

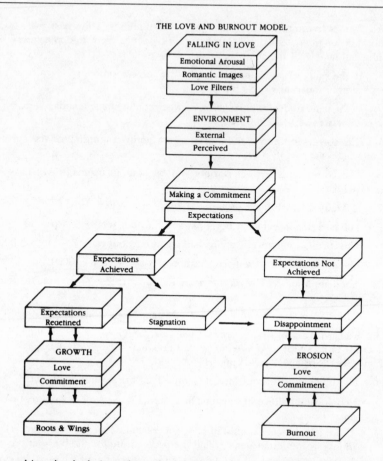

THE LOVE AND BURNOUT MODEL

achieved or by being achieved yet failing to give life the sense of significance they were expected to provide.

• The outcome of the ongoing interaction between a couple and their perceived environment can be positive or negative for their love relationship. In the best possible case the outcome is "roots and wings," an ideal balance between security and growth. In relationships with roots and wings, love is enhanced with time and continues to provide a sense of meaning to life. In the worst possible case, the outcome is burnout, the death of love.

## CHAPTER 3

1.   Ephraim Kishon, *It Was the Lark* (in Hebrew, *Ho, Lo Julia,* Tel Aviv: Sifriyat Maariv, 1974) p. 36.

2.   Rollo May, *Love and Will* (New York: Dell, 1969), p. 20.

3.   Benjamin Wolman, *Dictionary of Behavioral Science* (New York: Van Nostrand, 1973), pp. 298 and 41.

4.   In a study involving lengthy interviews with several hundred couples, 80 percent of the participants indicated that they had seriously considered divorce at

one time or another. Many said that the primary factors that kept them from divorce were economics and concern for their children. The researchers concluded that marriage is in a state of calamity. (See W. Lederer and D. Jackson, *The Mirages of Marriage* [New York: Norton, 1968].)

5. See Thomas Paolino and Barbara McCrady, *Marriage and Marital Therapy: Psychoanalytic, Behavioral and Systems Therapy Perspectives* (New York: Brunner/ Mazel, 1978): and R. Taylor Segraves, *Marital Therapy: A Combined Psychodynamic-Behavioral Approach* (New York: Plenum Medical Book Company, 1982).

6. Benjamin Wolman, *Dictionary of Behavioral Science*, pp. 294–295.

7. See William Meissner, "The Conceptualization of Marriage and Family Dynamics from a Psychoanalytic Perspective," pp. 25–88 and C. Cooperman Nadelson, "Marital Therapy from a Psychoanalytic Perspective," in Paolino and McCrady, pp. 89–164.

8. See Taylor Segraves, *Marital Therapy*.

9. Richard B. Stuart, "Operant-interpersonal Treatment for Marital Discord," *Journal of Consulting and Clinical Psychology* 33 (1969): 675–82.

10. See Daniel O'Leary and Hillary Turkewitz, "Marital Therapy from a Behavioral Perspective," in Paolino and McCrady, *Marriage and Marital Therapy*, pp. 240–297.

11. Carlos Sluzki, "Marital Therapy from a Systems Theory Perspective," in Paolino and McCrady, *Marriage and Marital Therapy*, pp. 366–394; Jay Haley, *Problem Solving Therapy: New Strategies for Effective Family Therapy* (San Francisco: Jossey-Bass, 1977); and Salvador Minuchin, *Families and Family Therapy* (Cambridge: Harvard University Press, 1974).

12. Victor E. Frankl, *Man's Search for Meaning: An Introduction to Logotherapy* (New York: Washington Square Press, 1966), pp. 153–155.

13. Ibid., p.163.

14. I.D. Yalom, *Existential Psychotherapy* (New York: Basic Books, 1980).

15. Benjamin Wolman, *Dictionary of Behavioral Science*, p. 300.

16. For a further discussion of this point as related to jealousy, see Ayala Pines and Elliot Aronson, "The Antecedents, Correlates, and Consequences of Sexual Jealousy," *Journal of Personality* 51 (1), (1983), pp. 108–136.

17. Philip Zimbardo, C. Haney, W.C. Banks, and D.A. Jaffe, "Pirandellian Prison: The Mind Is a Formidable Jailer," *New York Times Magazine*, April 8, 1973, pp.38–60.

18. I am indebted to Professor Arie Kruglanski of Tel Aviv University for his contribution to the conceptual development of this part of the research. As for the study's results, the hardworking Joe and his wife Judith received an average of 5.3 in one study (N=200) and 5.1 in the second study (n=100). Tina, with her four young children, and her husband Tom received an average of 5.1 in one study and 5.0 in the second. The newlyweds Gary and Gina received the lowest burnout scores: 1.6 in one study and 2.0 in the second. The compatible Mark and Mary were seen as less burned out—averaging 2.3 in one study and 2.7 in the other—than the incompatible David and Dalia, who averaged 3.7 in one study and 3.6 in the other. The effect of the difference in compatibility was much smaller than the effect of the difference in the quality of the environment—2.3 vs. 3.7 as

compared with 5.3 vs. 1.6 in the one study and 2.7 vs. 3.6 as compared with 5.1 vs. 2.0.

19. This integrated approach is described in Ayala Pines, "Marriage Burnout: A New Conceptual Framework for Working With Couples," *Psychology in Private Practice* 5, no. 20, (1987), pp. 31–44.

## CHAPTER 4

1. For example, in one study involving 384 subjects, when asked what was their favorite day, 29 percent said Saturday, 26 percent said Friday, and 17 percent said Sunday.

2. The three studies, in which the stresses in work and at home were compared, were presented in D. Kafry and A. Pines, "The Experience of Tedium in Life and Work," *Human Relations* 33, no. 7 (1980): 477–503.

3. In study 2 of the trilogy, for example, the average correlation between overall work satisfaction and burnout was r = −.38 as compared with an average of r = −.52 for life satisfaction.

4. See, for example, A.H. Cantril and C.W. Roll, Jr., *Hopes and Fears of the American People* (New York: Universe Books, 1971). The similarity between the process of job and marriage burnout was discussed in the paper "Job Burnout and Marriage Burnout, Two Responses to Failure: The Existential Quest for Meaning," American Psychological Association, New York, August 7, 1987.

5. The motivational model of job burnout is presented in great detail in A. Pines, "Who Is to Blame for a Helper's Burnout?" in *Self Care for Health-Care Providers,* ed. C. Scott (New York: William Morrow, 1985) and in A. Pines and E. Aronson,

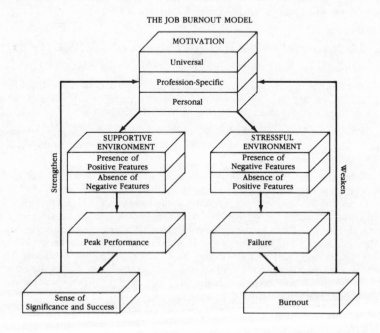

THE JOB BURNOUT MODEL

*Career Burnout* (New York: Free Press, 1988). The initial motivation to work includes universal expectations, those shared by everyone who works (e.g., to do something interesting that will pay well). It also includes profession-specific expectations. (For people in the human services, for example, this includes helping people and making the world a better place in which to be). And it includes some personal expectation based on an internalized image of an important person or event. Combined, these motivations form an expectation that the job will make one's life matter in the larger scheme of things.

The universal, profession-specific, and personal components of the initial work motivation are presented in great detail in A. Pines, "Helper's Motivation and the Burnout Syndrome," in *Basic Processes in Helping Relationships*, ed. T.A. Wills (New York: Academic Press, 1982).

When in a supportive work environment, highly motivated workers can reach peak performance. Experiencing peak performance increases such workers' sense of significance and success, which, in turn, increases their original motivation.

When the same highly motivated workers enter a stressful work environment where they can't get the resources, support, challenge, and sense of significance they need, burnout is almost inevitable. For highly motivated individuals whose egos are tied to their performance at work, failure is a powerful cause of burnout.

Job burnout impacts most those who start out idealistic and highly motivated, expecting the work to give meaning to their lives. Burnout on the job is the result of a dynamic interaction between people and their perceived environment. The interplay between the original ideas and expectations an individual has when starting a job and the work environment as it is experienced by that individual determines whether a highly motivated worker will burn out or will reach peak performance.

The effects of a supportive vs. a stressful environment are presented in great detail in A. Pines, "Changing Organizations: Is a Work Environment without Burnout an Impossible Goal?" in *Job Stress and Burnout*, ed. W.S. Paine (Beverly Hills, Calif.: Sage, 1982).

6. Wayne E. Oates, *Confessions of a Workaholic* (Nashville: Abingdon Press, 1971).

7. Lillian Rubin, *Intimate Strangers* (New York: Harper & Row, 1983), p. 162.

8. William Bridges, *The Seasons of Our Lives* (San Francisco, Calif.: The Wayfarer Press, 1977).

9. For details of the study, see A. Pines and D. Kafry, "Tedium in the Life and Work of Professional Women as Compared with Men," *Sex Roles* 7, no. 10 (1981): 963–977.

10. In the Pines and Kafry study involving 191 professionals, the mean burnout score for men was $M\bar{x} = 3.1$; for women it was $W\bar{x} = 3.3$. In the study involving 205 professionals, the mean burnout score for men was $M\bar{x} = 3.1$; for women it was $W\bar{x} = 3.3$. In the study involving 220 professionals, the mean burnout score for men was $M\bar{x} = 3.5$; for women it was $W\bar{x} = 3.8$. In the study involving 118 human service workers, the mean burnout score for men was $M\bar{x} = 3.0$; for women, $W\bar{x} = 3.3$. In the study involving 89 teachers, the mean burnout score for men was $M\bar{x} = 2.7$; for women, $W\bar{x} = 3.2$. In the study involving 66 Israeli managers men's mean burnout score was $M\bar{x} = 2.8$; women's, $W\bar{x} = 3.1$. See A.

Pines and E. Aronson, *Career Burnout: Causes and Cures,* (New York: Free Press, 1988).

11.   For a review, see Susan A. Basow, *Gender Stereotypes,* (Monterey, Calif.: Brooks/Cole, 1986) pp. 234–260.

12.   Margaret Hennig and Anne Jardim, *The Managerial Woman* (New York: Doubleday, 1976).

13.   Delia Etzion, "Burning Out in Management: A Comparison of Women and Men in Matched Organizational Positions," (Paper Presented at the Second International Interdisciplinary Congress on Women, Groningen, Holland, April 17–19, 1984).

14.   Ibid.

15.   Pines and Kafry study.

16.   A. Pines, "The Influence of Goals on People's Perceptions of a Competent Woman," *Sex Roles* 5, no. 1 (1979): 71–76.

17.   Rhona Rapoport and Robert Rapoport, "The Dual Career Family," *Human Relations* 22 (1969): 3–30.

18.   A review of these studies, in which dual-career couples were compared with couples in which the wife didn't work, is included in Fran Pepitone-Rockwell's *Dual-career Couples* (Beverly Hills, Calif.: Sage, 1980).

19.   T.W. Martin, K.J. Berry, and R.B. Jacobsen, "The Impact of Dual-career Marriages on Female Professional Careers," (Paper presented at the annual meeting of the National Council on Family Relations, Salt Lake City, August 1975).

20.   R. Bryson, et al., "The Professional Pair: Husband and Wife Psychologists," *American Psychologist* 31 (1976): 10–16.

21.   Cynthia Fuchs Epstein, "Law Partners and Marital Partners: Strains and Solutions in the Dual Career Family Enterprise," *Human Relations* 24 (1971): 549–63.

22.   Ivan Nye and Lois Hoffman, eds., *The Employed Mother in America,* (Chicago: Rand McNally, 1963).

23.   Carol C. Nadelson and Theodore Nadelson, "Dual-career Marriages: Benefits and Costs," in Pepitone-Rockwell, *Dual-career Couples.*

24.   Ernest Becker, *The Denial of Death* (New York: Free Press, 1973).

## CHAPTER 5

1.   Warren Farrell, *Why Men Are the Way They Are: The Male–Female Dynamic,* (New York: McGraw Hill, 1986).

2.   Walter Gove, "The Relationship Between Sex Roles, Marital Status, and Mental Illness," *Social Forces* 51, no. 1 (1972): 34–44.

3.   Jessie Bernard, *The Future of Marriage* (New York: Bantam, 1983) pp. 16–27.

4.   Susan Basow, *Gender Stereotypes,* (Monterey, Calif.: Brooks/Cole, 1986), p. 217.

5.   Jessie Bernard, *The Future of Marriage,* pp. 28–58.

6.   James Prochaska and Janice Prochaska, "Twentieth Century Trends in Marriage and Marital Therapy" in *Marriage and Marital Therapy,* ed. T.J. Paulino and B.S. McCrady (New York: Brunner/Mazel, 1978).

7. Philip Blumstein and Pepper Schwartz, *American Couples* (New York: William Morrow, 1983), p. 309.

8. Barbara Ehrenreich, *The Hearts of Men: American Dreams and the Flight From Commitment,* (Garden City, N.Y.: Anchor/Doubleday, 1983) pp. 10–11.

9. R. Liem and P. Rayman, "Health and Social Costs of Unemployment: Research and Policy Considerations," *American Psychologist* 37, 1116–23.

10. S. V. Kasl and S. Cobb, "Blood Pressure Changes in Men Undergoing Job Loss," *Psychosomatic Medicine* 6 (1970): 95–106.

11. Barbara Ehrenreich, *The Hearts of Men,* pp. 10–11, 70–71.

12. The studies are described in A. Pines, "Sex Differences in Marriage Burnout," in *Israel Social Science Research,* 1988, in press.

13. Women reported feeling more often depressed about the relationship ($M\bar{x} = 3.3$, $W\bar{x} = 3.7$), more often emotionally exhausted ($M\bar{x} = 3.3$, $W\bar{x} = 3.7$), wiped out, nothing left to give ($M\bar{x} = 2.7$, $W\bar{x} = 3.1$), and rejecting ($M\bar{x} = 3.0$, $W\bar{x} = 3.4$). Out of the twenty-one burnout symptoms, women experienced sixteen more than men in the negative direction, while men experienced only three more than women, the three being feeling trapped ($M\bar{x} = 3.8$, $W\bar{x} = 3.5$), optimistic ($M\bar{x} = 3.2$, $W\bar{x} = 3.1$), and anxious ($M\bar{x} = 4.3$, $W\bar{x} = 4.0$). Three symptoms were reported with equal frequency by both men and women. Using the binomial test, three out of sixteen is significant at $p < .002$.

14. Israeli women were more burned out in their marriages than their husbands, and significantly so ($M\bar{x} = 2.6$, $W\bar{x} = 3.0$; $t = 4.1$, $p < .0001$). Out of the twenty-one burnout symptoms, women experienced nineteen more than men in the negative direction; eleven of those were statistically significant differences: Women felt more often depressed ($M\bar{x} = 2.5$, $W\bar{x} = 3.2$; $t = 4.7$, $p < .0001$), emotionally exhausted ($M\bar{x} = 2.8$, $W\bar{x} = 3.5$; $t = 4.1$, $p < .0001$), unhappy ($M\bar{x} = 1.8$, $W\bar{x} = 2.4$; $t = 3.9$, $p < .0001$), physically exhausted ($M\bar{x} = 3.1$, $W\bar{x} = 3.7$; $t = 3.8$, $p < .0002$), weak ($M\bar{x} = 1.6$, $W\bar{x} = 2.2$; $t = 3.5$ $p < .0006$), and anxious ($M\bar{x} = 2.5$, $W\bar{x} = 3.3$; $t = 4.4$, $p < .0001$). Using the binomial test this difference is significant at $p < .001$. Men had only one symptom more than women; they were less often optimistic, but the difference was not statistically significant. Only one item (energetic) was reported with equal frequency by both men and women.

15. Israeli women reported more anxiety than did Israeli men ($M\bar{x} = 2.5$, $W\bar{x} = 3.3$; $t = 4.4$, $p < .0001$), while American women reported less anxiety than did American men ($M\bar{x} = 4.3$, $W\bar{x} = 4.0$; this difference was not statistically significant).

16. John Nicholson, *Men and Women: How Different Are They?* (Oxford, England: Oxford University Press, 1984).

17. These data are also discussed in A. Pines, "Sex Differences in Marriage Burnout," *Israel Social Science Research,* 1988, in press.

18. The correlation between burnout and home/work conflict for men was: $r = -.02$ (n.s.); for women it was: $r = .29$ ($p < .005$). When asked what was more important to them, home or work, women indicated that home was more important significantly more than men ($M\bar{x} = 5.4$, $W\bar{x} = 5.9$; $t = 2.8$, $p < .006$). Women described their marriages as more significant to them than men did ($M\bar{x}$

$= 5.6$, W$\bar{x} = 6.1$; $t = 2.5$, $p < .01$), and women "expressed themselves" in their marriages more than men did (M$\bar{x} = 5.0$, W$\bar{x} = 5.5$; $t = 2.7$, $p < .009$). Men felt trapped in the marriage more than women (M$\bar{x} = 3.8$, W$\bar{x} = 3.5$).

19. Responses to the question "How important are the various aspects of romantic love to you personally?" generated the following sex differences:

Security: W$\bar{x} = 6.3$ vs. M$\bar{x} = 5.5$; $t = 3.9$, $p < .0001$

Understanding: W$\bar{x} = 6.8$ vs. M$\bar{x} = 6.4$; $t = 4.9$, $p < .0001$

Intellectual interest: W$\bar{x} = 6.1$ vs. M$\bar{x} = 5.4$; $t = 4.2$, $p < .0001$

Trust: W$\bar{x} = 6.8$ vs. M$\bar{x} = 6.5$; $t = 3.3$, $p < .0009$

Friendship: W$\bar{x} = 6.5$ vs. M$\bar{x} = 6.0$; $t = 3.2$, $p < .001$

Shared life: W$\bar{x} = 5.7$ vs. M$\bar{x} = 5.0$; $t = 3.0$, $p < .003$

Emotional attraction: W$\bar{x} = 6.4$ vs. M$\bar{x} = 6.0$; $t = 3.0$, $p < .003$

It should be noted that in spite of the sex differences in the importance given to the various aspects of romantic ideology, in many cases the rank ordering of these aspects was rather similar. Thus, for example, for both sexes, trust, understanding, and friendship ranked highest (for women both trust and understanding: W$\bar{x} = 6.8$; friendship $= 6.5$; for men: M$\bar{x}$ trust $= 6.5$, understanding $= 6.4$, and friendship $= 6.0$).

20. Robert N. Bellah, et al., *Habits of the Heart* (Berkeley, Calif.: University of California Press, 1985). pp. 88–89.

21. Lillian B. Rubin, *Intimate Strangers: Men and Women Together* (New York: Harper & Row, 1983); Dorothy Dinnerstein, *The Mermaid and the Minotaur: Sexual Arrangements and Human Malaise* (New York: Harper & Row, 1976); Nancy Chodorow, *The Reproduction of Mothering: Psychoanalysis and the Sociology of Gender* (Berkeley, Calif.: University of California Press, 1978).

22. Rubin, *Intimate Strangers,* p. 50.

23. Ibid., p. 103.

24. The correlation between the quality of sex life and burnout for men was $r = -.49$; for women it was $r = -.40$ ($p < .0001$). That between physical attraction and burnout for men was $r = -.44$; for women $r = -.40$ ($p < .0001$). That between burnout and boredom for men was $r = .48$; for women it was $r = .23$ ($p < .0001$).

25. See Table IV in the Appendix. The table presents the rank order of Pearson correlation coefficients between burnout and marriage descriptors for men and the corresponding rank order for women. No distinction was made between positive and negative terms in this analysis. The rank order is only in terms of the size (not the direction) of their correlation with burnout.

26. All these findings are repeated in Table IV.

27. In the study, which was done in collaboration with Ditsa Kafry, the correlation between children's impulsivity and mother's burnout was $r = .49$, $p < .001$.

28. In the study, which was done in collaboration with Teresa Ramirez, at that time a University of California Berkeley student, the average burnout score of the abusive parents was 4.4 while the average burnout score of 30 other samples totaling 3,659 people was 3.3.

29. In the Haifa study the correlation between number of children and burnout in marriage was r = −.11, p = .11 (not significant). The correlation between burnout in marriage and number of children at home was r = −.13, p = .07 (not significant).

30. This point is elaborated in A. Pines, "Marriage Burnout from Women's Perspective" in *Everywoman's Emotional Well Being,* ed. Carol Tavris (New York: Doubleday, 1986).

31. The correlation between burnout and overload for men was r = .51, p < .0001; for women it was r = .48, p < .0001. The mean overload reported by men was M$\bar{x}$ = 2.9; by women, W$\bar{x}$ = 3.7, t = 4.3, p < .0001, which is to say, while the actual overload reported by women was higher than that reported by men, it ranked first for men and third for women.

32. Ehrenreich, *The Hearts of Men.*

33. The correlation between burnout and boredom for men was r = .48, p < .0001; for women it was r = .23, p < .02.

34. Bernard, *Future of Marriage,* p. 5.

35. Men described the communication as better than did women (M$\bar{x}$ = 4.8, W$\bar{x}$ = 4.2); men described more sharing of chores (M$\bar{x}$ = 5.0, W$\bar{x}$ = 4.6), sex life as better (M$\bar{x}$ = 4.6, W$\bar{x}$ = 4.9), and themselves as more desirable sexual partners (M$\bar{x}$ = 5.2, W$\bar{x}$ = 4.9) than did women. Women had only four relationship features more positive than men, including intellectual attraction (M$\bar{x}$ = 5.1, W$\bar{x}$ = 5.6), variety, things in common, and overall relationship evaluation. Only two relationship descriptors were evaluated equally by men and women: security ($\bar{x}$ = 4.9) and goal similarity ($\bar{x}$ = 4.4). Using the binomial test, four out of sixteen is significant at p < .04.

36. For example, in the Haifa study, women reported being significantly more burdened by housework than men did (M$\bar{x}$ = 3.6, W$\bar{x}$ = 5.8, p < .0001). Women also experienced overload significantly more than men did (M$\bar{x}$ = 2.9, W$\bar{x}$ = 3.7; t = 4.3, p < .0001), as well as a significantly heavier burden of family commitments (M$\bar{x}$ = 3.3, W$\bar{x}$ = 4.0; t = 3.2, p < .002). In addition, as noted earlier, women described their marriages as more significant to them than men did (M$\bar{x}$ = 5.6, W$\bar{x}$ = 6.1; t = 2.5, p < .01), and women "expressed themselves" in their marriages more than men did (M$\bar{x}$ = 5.0, W$\bar{x}$ = 5.15; t = 2.7, p < .009).

37. See, for example, E. Donelson, "Social Influences on the Development of Sex-typed Behavior," in *Women: A Psychological Perspective,* ed. E. Donelson and J. Gullahorn (New York: Wiley, 1977), pp. 140–153.

38. M. Scarf, "The More Sorrowful Sex," *Psychology Today* 12, no. 11 (1979): 44–52.

39. This point was elaborated in a paper Ayala Pines presented at the American Psychological Association entitled "Marital Burnout: Love Gone Wrong," New York, August 1987.

40. Fran Pepitone-Rockwell, *Dual-Career Couples* (Beverly Hills, Calif.: Sage, 1980).

41. A. Pines, "On Burnout and the Buffering Effects of Social Support," in *Stress and Burnout in the Human Service Professions,* ed. B. Farber (New York: Pergamon, 1982).

42. In the study involving 220 professionals it was found that men confronted the source of their job stress more frequently than women—$M\bar{x} = 4.3$, $W\bar{x} = 4.1$—and ignored it more frequently than women—$M\bar{x} = 3.7$, $W\bar{x} = 3.1$. Women, on the other hand, used talking to a supporting other as a coping strategy more often than men: $M\bar{x} = 4.7$, $W\bar{x} = 5.3$. The study was described in A. Pines and D. Kafry, "Coping with Burnout," in *The Burnout Syndrome,* ed. by J. Jones, (Park Ridge, Ill.: London House Press, 1981), pp. 139–150.

43. In the Haifa study it was found that men used more frequently the direct and inactive strategies of ignoring the stress—$M\bar{x} = 3.3$, $W\bar{x} = 2.9$—and of avoiding the stress—$M\bar{x} = 3.0$, $W\bar{x} = 2.4$; $t = 2.9$, $p < .004$. Women, on the other hand, used more frequently: confrontation $M\bar{x} = 4.3$, $W\bar{x} = 4.8$; $t = 2.0$, $p < .05$, and talking to a friend: $M\bar{x} = 2.4$, $W\bar{x} = 4.0$; $t = 6.2$, $p < .0001$.

44. Sex differences in confrontation as a coping strategy for dealing with job stress: $M\bar{x} = 4.3$, $W\bar{x} = 4.1$; sex differences in confrontation as a coping strategy for dealing with marital stress: $M\bar{x} = 4.3$, $W\bar{x} = 4.8$. Even though these data come from two different studies, it is interesting to note that men's frequency of using confrontation was identical at work and at home ($M\bar{x} = 4.3$). For women, confrontation in marriage was much more frequent than it was on the job (4.8 vs. 4.1).

45. Guttman's findings were reported at the 1984 meeting of the American Psychological Association.

46. The average frequency of women's talking to a supportive other as a way to cope with marital stress was $W\bar{x} = 4.0$; for men it was $M\bar{x} = 2.4$. The correlation between the frequency of using this coping technique and burnout was $r = .28$, $p < .02$.

## CHAPTER 6

1. The commune is described in detail in Ayala Pines and Elliott Aronson, "Polyfidelity: An Alternative Lifestyle Without Jealousy," *Alternative Lifestyles* 4, no. 3 (1981): 323–392.

2. Ernest Becker, *The Denial of Death* (New York: Free Press, 1973).

3. M. Scott Peck, *The Road Less Traveled* (New York: Simon & Schuster, 1978).

4. Jordan Paul and Margaret Paul, *Do I Have to Give Up Being Me to Be Loved by You?* (Minn.: Compcare, 1983).

5. Ibid, p. 119.

6. Ibid, p. 122–23.

7. Ayala Pines and Elliot Aronson, "Antecedents, Correlates, and Consequences of Sexual Jealousy," *Journal of Personality* 54 (1983): 108–35.

8. Ayala Pines, *Sexual Jealousy as a Cause of Violence,* (Paper presented at the annual convention of the American Psychological Association, Anaheim, California, 1983).

9. The correlation between burnout and jealousy was $r = .51$, $p < .0001$.

10. For example, there was no correlation between the length of the relationship and jealousy, and there was no correlation between age and jealousy. On the other

hand, there was a very high correlation between jealousy and a desire to leave the relationship. The correlation between jealousy and length of the relationship was r = .0007 (p = .967). The correlation between jealousy and age was r = .107 (p = .664). The correlation between jealousy and a desire to leave the relationship was r = .41 (p = .002).

11.   Stanley Kelleman, *Emotional Anatomy* (Berkeley: Center Press, 1985).

12.   The correlations between the quality of sex life and believing that "love is like a good wine, it gets better with time" was r = −.36, p < .0001; "living happily ever after": r = .25, p < .0005; "matches made in heaven": r = .20, p < .006.

13.   The study, in which one hundred married couples took part, was described at length in previous chapters. The correlation between length of relationship and sex was r = −.25, p < .0003.

14.   The correlation between age and the quality of sex life was r = −.24, p < .0009.

15.   The correlation between the quality of sex life and physical attraction was r = .66; sex and emotional attraction: r = .49; sex and intellectual attraction: r = .46. All p values < .0001. The correlation between quality of sex life and an overall positive evaluation of the marriage was r = .58; sex and relationship with mate: r = .58; as compared to the correlation between sex and the length of the relationship: r = −.25.

16.   Joel Block, *The Magic of Lasting Love* (New York: Cornerstone Library, 1982), p. 86.

17.   The correlation between the quality of sex life and describing one's mate as the biggest love of one's life was r = .49; between sex and describing one's mate as one's best friend was r = .38. Both p levels < .00001.

18.   Joel Block, *Friendship* (New York: Macmillan, 1980).

19.   The correlation between quality of sex life and physical attraction was r = .66; sex and emotional attraction: r = .49; sex and intellectual attraction: r = .46. All p levels < .0001.

The correlation between quality of sex life and an overall positive evaluation of the marriage was r = .58, p < .0001.

The correlation between the quality of sex and the general feeling toward the mate was r = .57; between sex and the relationship with the mate: r = .58 (not surprisingly the correlation with relationships with both friends and colleagues was zero); between sex and the mate's feelings about the respondent: r = .51. All p values < .0001.

The correlation between the quality of sex and burnout was r = −.41; sex and partner's burnout: r = −.40. Both p values < .0001.

In both cases of physical attraction and overall evaluation of the relationship the correlation with quality of sex was r = .66, which is the highest correlation obtained with sex.

20.   All this is not meant as a criticism of the behavioral approaches to sex therapy. Many of the behavioral techniques used by sex therapists are extremely effective. Yet few people will be surprised to discover that those techniques are more effective with couples who have good communication than with those who don't.

21.   The correlation between communication and the quality of sex life was r = .56, p < .0001.

22.   The correlation between variety and the quality of sex was also r = .56; between sex life and boredom it was r = −.37.

23.   Nora Ephron, *Heartburn* (New York: Pocket Books, 1983).

24.   Joel Block, *The Magic of Lasting Love* (New York: Cornerstone Library, 1982).

25.   The correlation between the quality of sex life and security was r = .51, p < .0001.

26.   It may be worth mentioning two books—one about male sexuality, the other about female sexuality—that can be read by both men and women: Bernie Zilbergeld's *Male Sexuality* (Boston: Little Brown, 1978), and Lonne Barbach's *For Yourself: The Fulfillment of Female Sexuality,* (New York: Doubleday, 1976).

## CHAPTER 7

1.   For a more detailed description of Kerista Village, see Ayala Pines and Elliott Aronson, "Polyfidelity: An Alternative Lifestyle Without Jealousy?" in *Alternative Lifestyles* 4, no. 3 (August, 1981): 373–92.

2.   Growing rates of divorce among Orthodox couples suggest that even religious life does not shield a marriage completely from societal influences and environmental stresses. In one of the workshops I held in Israel, I was told, for example, that four of the graduates from one of the most famous yeshivas (religious graduate schools) in Jerusalem got divorced. While four out of a whole class may not sound like much, it represents an increase of 400 percent.

3.   Pines and Aronson, "Polyfidelity," p. 374.

4.   Robert N. Bellah, et. al., *Habits of the Heart: Individualism and Commitment in American Life* (Berkeley, Calif.: University of California Press, 1985), p. 93.

5.   Ibid, p. 95.

6.   Ibid, p. 95.

7.   Ibid, p. 95.

8.   Otto Rank, *Will Therapy and Truth Reality* (New York: Knopf, 1945) and *Psychology and the Soul* (New York: Perpetual Books Edition, 1961) ch. 4.

9.   Ernest Becker, *The Denial of Death* (New York: Free Press, 1973), pp. 159–70.

10.   Ibid, pp. 162–163.

11.   Ibid, pp. 164–165.

12.   Ibid, p. 166.

13.   M. Scott Peck, *The Road Less Traveled* (New York: Simon and Schuster, 1978), pp. 84–85.

14.   Ibid, pp. 84–85.

15.   Ibid, pp. 84–85.

16.   Ibid, p. 87.

17.  Ibid, p. 88.

18.  Elliot Aronson, "Attraction: Why Do People Like Each Other?" *The Social Animal* (San Francisco: Freeman, 1984), ch. 7, p. 313.

19.  Ibid, pp. 313–314.

20.  Marilyn French, *The Women's Room* (New York: JOVE/HBJ, 1977), p. 558.

21.  Nathaniel Branden, *The Psychology of Romantic Love* (New York: Bantam, 1983), p. 2.

22.  The findings were obtained in the two studies that were mentioned during the discussion of sex differences in marriage burnout.

   The first study involved one hundred men and women from the San Francisco Bay Area. The correlation between time and burnout was .05. While the zero correlation between time and burnout was statistically a very strong finding, it still left unanswered numerous questions. As noted earlier, one could wonder whether these results are unique to the San Francisco sample. This town is not conventional in its viewpoints regarding relationships or the freedom of its life-style, as the world well knows. Perhaps the data were skewed because people described different kinds of relationships, including traditional marriages, cohabitation, and open marriages. It was important to see whether there would be any difference in the results in a different sample.

   In order to address these questions, a second study was conducted in San Francisco's sister city, the Israeli port town of Haifa. The assumption was that if any finding can be replicated in two such different samples, they could be considered more reliable and trustworthy. Indeed, the Haifa sample was very different. Even in Israel, which is generally more conservative in sexual and social matters than the United States, Haifa is considered a quiet, conservative, family-oriented city. The Haifa sample included one hundred suburban married couples. For all but six of the couples this was their first marriage. Most couples had two or three children still living at home. The average length of the marriages was 15.1 years and ranged from one to over thirty-four years. When the data were analyzed, once more, there was no correlation whatsoever between time and burnout. The correlation between burnout and the length of the relationship in the Haifa study was $r = .10$ as compared with $r = .05$ in the San Francisco study.

23.  Robert Johnson, *We: Understanding the Psychology of Romantic Love* (New York: Harper & Row, 1983), pp. 195–196.

24.  Alan Watts, "Divine Madness" in *Challenge of the Heart*, ed. J. Welwood (Boston: Shambhala, 1985), p. 21.

25.  Ibid, p. 23.

26.  Francesco Alberoni, *Falling in Love* (New York: Random House, 1983).

27.  Rollo May, *Love and Will* (New York: Dell, 1969) pp. 72–73.

28.  Aronson, "Attraction," p. 315.

29.  Ibid, p. 316.

30.  Susan Kobasa and Salvador Maddi, "Personality and Constitution as Mediators in the Stress-Illness Relationship," *Journal of Health and Social Behavior* 22 (1981): 368–78.

31.   The mean burnout score was 3.4 for the American sample and 2.8 for the Israeli. This difference was discussed in A. Pines, "Sex Differences in Marriage Burnout," *Israel Social Science Research,* 1988, in press.

32.   Ayala Pines, D. Kafry, and D. Etzion, "Job Stress from a Cross Cultural Perspective," in *Burnout in the Helping Professions,* ed. K. Reed, (Kalamazoo, Mich.: Western Michigan University, 1980).

33.   D. Etzion, A. Pines, and D. Kafry, "Coping Strategies and the Experience of Tedium: A Cross-Cultural Comparison Between Israelies and Americans," *Journal of Psychology and Judaism* 8, no. 1 (1983): 41–51; and D. Etzion and A. Pines, "Sex and Culture in Burnout and Coping" *Journal of Cross Cultural Psychology* 17, no. 2 (1986): 191–209.

34.   Mark Snyder, E.D. Tanke, and E. Berscheid, "Social Perception and Inter-personal Behavior: On the Self-Fulfilling Nature of Social Stereotypes," *Journal of Personality and Social Psychology* 35 (1977): 656–66.

35.   Rollo May, *Love and Will.*

36.   Erich Fromm, *The Art of Loving* (New York, Harper & Row, 1956).

## CHAPTER 8

1.   Erich Fromm, *The Art of Loving* (New York: Harper & Row, 1956), pp. 4–5.

2.   The burnout scores of the low-burnout group (LBG) were lower than 2.0; the scores of the high burnout group (HBG) were higher than 3.4—representing one standard deviation below the mean and one standard deviation above the mean, respectively.

3.   The average score for looking positively at the relationship as a whole for the LBG was $\bar{x} = 5.94$; for the HBG it was $x = 4.20$ ($t = 6.38$, $p < .0001$).
      When the responses of all 200 of the subjects in the study were analyzed to discover the highest correlation of burnout, the highest correlation was between burnout in the relationship and the ability to look positively at the relationship as a whole. ($r = -.53$, $p < .0001$). In a further analysis it was discovered that half of the variations in burnout could be explained by this one variable.
      Results in the San Francisco study involving 100 subjects indicated similarly that the highest correlation was between burnout in the relationship and the ability to look positively at the relationship as a whole ($r = -.72$, $p < .0001$).

4.   Jeannette Lauer and Robert Lauer, "Marriages Made to Last," *Psychology Today* 19, no. 6 (June 1985): 22–26.

5.   The average communication score for the HBG was $\bar{x} = 4.0$; for the LBG it was $\bar{x} = 6.0$ ($t = 5.9$ $p < .0001$) The average time spent in direct conversation with spouse in the HBG was $\bar{x} = 39$; in the LBG the average was $\bar{x} = 60$ minutes with a maximum of 4 hours ($F = 2.0$ $p < .05$).
      The correlation between burnout and quality of communication in the Haifa study was $r = -.47$, $p < .0001$. In the San Francisco study the correlation was $r = -.64$, $p < .0001$.

6.   A. Pines and D. Kafry, "Coping with Burnout," in *The Burnout Syndrome* ed. J. Jones (Park Ridge, Ill.: London House Press, 1981) pp. 139–150.

7.   The correlation between talking to a good friend about the problem and burnout was $r = .25$, $p < .0001$.

8. The correlation between confronting one's mate directly when having a problem and burnout was r = −.53, p < .0001.

9. The average score for physical attraction to mate for the HBG was x̄ = 6.5; for the LBG it was x̄ = 4.9 (t = 6.0, p < .0001).

10. The correlation between physical attraction to mate and burnout was r = −.43 in the Haifa study, and r = −.41 in the San Francisco study.

11. The average evaluation of sex life in the HBG was x̄ = 4.3; in the LBG it was x̄ = 5.8 (t = 5.2, p < .0001).

12. The correlation between physical attraction to mate and quality of sex life was r = .66, p .0001.

13. The correlation between the quality of sex life and burnout in the San Francisco study was r = −.54; in the Haifa study it was r = −.41 (in both cases p < .0001).
   In the Haifa study sex came fifth in the list of variables differentiating between the high- and low-burnout groups, following the ability to look at the relationship positively overall, communication, physical attraction, and mutual appreciation. In the San Francisco study, the quality of sex life came eighth with security, self-actualization, and significance added to the previous list.

14. Rollo May, *Love and Will* (New York: Dell, 1969), p. 14.

15. Christopher Burney, *Solitary Confinement* (New York: Coward-McCann, 1952).

16. The average variety score in the HBG was x = 3.3; in the LBG it was x̄ = 4.8 (t = 4.6, p < .0001). On the other hand, the average boredom score for the HBG was x = 3.8; for the LBG the average boredom score was x = 2.5 (t = −4.6, p < .0001). It is interesting that both t values were equal.

17. Joel Block, *The Magic of Lasting Love* (New York: Cornerstone Library, 1982), p. 20.

18. Richard B. Stuart, *Helping Couples Change: A Social Learning Approach to Marital Therapy* (New York: Guilford Press, 1980), p. 370.

19. Block, *The Magic of Lasting Love,* p. 20.

20. The average appreciation score in the HBG was x̄ = 3.6; in the LBG it was x̄ = 5.5 (t = 5.9, p < .0001).

21. The correlation between feeling appreciated and respected and burnout was r = −.43, p < .0001.

22. R. A. Baron, and D. Byrne, *Social Psychology: Understanding Human Interaction,* (Boston: Allyn and Bacon, 1984), pp. 88–97.

23. The average security score of the HBG was x = 5.1; the average of the LBG was x̄ = 6.4 (t = 4.9, p < .0001).
   The correlation between security and burnout in the Haifa study was r = −.42, p < .0001. In the San Francisco study the correlation was r = −.59, p < .0001.

24. Jean Block presented this idea in a talk she gave at U.C. Berkeley in 1979.

25. S. Cobb, "Social Support as a Moderator of Life Stress," *Psychosomatic Medicine* 5, no. 38 (1976): 300–14.

26.   Ayala Pines, "On Burnout and the Buffering Effects of Social Support," in *Stress and Burnout in the Human Service Professions,* ed. B. Farber (New York: Pergamon Press, 1982).

27.   The average support score for the HBG was $\bar{x} = 4.3$; for the LBG it was $\bar{x} = 6.1$ (t = 4.4 p < .0001).

28.   Ayala Pines and Elliot Aronson, *Career Burnout: Causes and Cures* (New York: Free Press, 1988) ch. 8.

29.   Abraham Maslow, *Toward A Psychology of Being* (New York: Van Nostrand, 1962).

30.   The average score for self-actualization in the HBG was x = 4.0; in the LBG it was $\bar{x} = 5.9$ (t = 4.4 p < .0001). The correlation between burnout and self-actualization in the San Francisco study was r = −.57; in the Haifa study it was r = −.39 (both p levels < .0001).

31.   The average intellectual attraction in the HBG was x = 4.4; in the LBG it was $\bar{x} = 5.9$ (t = 4.4, p < .0001).

32.   The other variables included, in rank order: feedback from mate; sense of success in the marriage; similarity in goals and expectations from life; emotional attraction to mate; shared decision making; independence and self-expression.

33.   Even though chores are supposed to be an important correlate of burnout for women, in one study involving 100 women, for example, the correlation obtained between sharing housework chores and reported burnout was r = .03 (not significant).

34.   The "domino effect" refers to the effect of one act on the acts that follow, like the effect of pushing a single domino on a row of dominoes placed behind it, all falling down one following the other.

35.   Rabbi Hillel, *Wisdom of Our Fathers,* ch. 1, verse 14.

# How Burned Out Are You?
## The Burnout Test

Whether you are madly in love, totally burned out, or somewhere in between, you may be interested in finding out your burnout score. For that purpose you will find two forms of the Burnout Test, one for you and one for your mate, plus a section for each of you on background issues. A brief discussion of the scoring system at the bottom of the test will help you interpret your score. In addition, the Research Appendix includes a detailed discussion of this test and some data that were obtained using it.

The two parts of the questionnaire can not only serve as tools for self-diagnosis, but can offer you a chance to discuss your relationship with your mate. How do you both feel about the relationship? What are your expectations for each other and for your life together? What things do you find most stressful about your partner, about your relationship? What stresses outside the relationship do you deal with on a regular basis? How do you cope? Do you feel successful in your coping?

Responding to these questions can help sensitize you to the issues involved, give you some substantial issues to discuss with your mate, and will probably make reading this book a more valuable experience.

### BACKGROUND ISSUES FOR YOU
What attracted you to your mate when you first met?

_____

_____

_____

What were your hopes and expectations when you decided to make a commitment to this relationship?

_____

_____

_____

What is your image of the ideal relationship?

_____

_____

_____

What three things do you find most stressful about your partner or about the relationship?

1 _____

2 _____

3 _____

How do you usually cope with these stresses?

1 _____

2 _____

3 _____

How successful are you in your coping?

_____

_____

_____

If you found someone else you could be intimate with, would you leave your mate?

|      1       |   2   |   3   |  (4)  |   5   |   6   |      7       |
|--------------|-------|-------|-------|-------|-------|--------------|
| definitely not |     |       | not sure |    |       | definitely yes |

Please explain your response.

## THE BURNOUT TEST FOR YOU

You can compute your burnout score by completing the following questionnaire, as it relates to your marriage or intimate relationship.

How often do you have any of the following experiences? (Insert the number on this scale that most closely matches your experience.)

| 1 | 2 | 3 | 4 | 5 | 6 | 7 |
|---|---|---|---|---|---|---|
| Never | Once in a great while | Rarely | Sometimes | Often | Usually | Always |

_4_ 1. Being tired.

_1_ 2. Feeling depressed.

_4_ 3. Having a good day.

_4_ 4. Being physically exhausted.

_4_ 5. Being emotionally exhausted.

_3_ 6. Being happy.

_3_ 7. Being "wiped out," whole body hurts.

_2_ 8. Feeling like you "can't take it anymore."

_5_ 9. Feeling unhappy.

_5_ 10. Feeling run-down, susceptible to illness.

_4_ 11. Feeling trapped.

_4_ 12. Feeling worthless.

_4_ 13. Being weary, nothing left to give.

_5_ 14. Being troubled.

_4_ 15. Feeling disillusioned and resentful about mate.

_5_ 16. Feeling weak, having sleep problems.

_4_ 17. Feeling hopeless.

_5_ 18. Feeling rejecting of mate.

_3_ 19. Feeling optimistic.

_3_ 20. Feeling energetic.

_4_ 21. Feeling anxious.

How to figure out your score (get your calculator):

**Step 1.** Add up the numbers you wrote next to these items: 1, 2, 4, 5, 7, 8, 9, 10, 11, 12, 13, 14, 15, 16, 17, 18, 21 ___73

**Step 2.** Add up the numbers you wrote next to these items: 3, 6, 19, 20 ___

**Step 3.** Subtract the answer for Step 2 from 32:
32 – ___ = ___

**Step 4.** Add the number in Step 1 to the number in Step 3:
___ (Step 1) + ___ (Step 3) = ___ .

**Step 5.** Divide the answer in Step 4 by 21: ___ : 21 = ___ .

**This is your burnout score.**

## BACKGROUND ISSUES FOR YOUR MATE

What attracted you to your mate when you first met?

_____

_____

_____

What were your hopes and expectations when you decided to make a commitment to this relationship?

_____

_____

_____

What is your image of the ideal relationship?

_____

_____

_____

What three things do you find most stressful about your partner or about the relationship?

1 _____

2 _____

3 _____

How do you usually cope with these stresses?

1 _____

2 _____

3 _____

How successful are you in your coping?

_____

_____

_____

If you found someone else you could be intimate with, would you leave your mate?

| 1 | 2 | 3 | 4 | 5 | 6 | 7 |
|---|---|---|---|---|---|---|

definitely not          not sure          definitely yes

Please explain your response.

## THE BURNOUT TEST FOR YOUR MATE

You can compute your burnout score by completing the following questionnaire, as it relates to your marriage or intimate relationship.

How often do you have any of the following experiences: (Insert the number on this scale that most closely matches your experience.)

| 1 | 2 | 3 | 4 | 5 | 6 | 7 |
|---|---|---|---|---|---|---|
| Never | Once in a great while | Rarely | Sometimes | Often | Usually | Always |

____ 1. Being tired.

____ 2. Feeling depressed.

____ 3. Having a good day.

____ 4. Being physically exhausted.

____ 5. Being emotionally exhausted.

____ 6. Being happy.

____ 7. Being "wiped out," whole body hurts.

___ 8. Feeling like you "can't take it anymore."

___ 9. Feeling unhappy.

___ 10. Feeling run-down, susceptible to illness.

___ 11. Feeling trapped.

___ 12. Feeling worthless.

___ 13. Being weary, nothing left to give.

___ 14. Being troubled.

___ 15. Feeling disillusioned and resentful about mate.

___ 16. Feeling weak, having sleep problems.

___ 17. Feeling hopeless.

___ 18. Feeling rejecting of mate.

___ 19. Feeling optimistic.

___ 20. Feeling energetic.

___ 21. Feeling anxious.

How to figure out your score (get your calculator):

**Step 1.** Add up the numbers you wrote next to these items: 1, 2, 4, 5, 7, 8, 9, 10, 11, 12, 13, 14, 15, 16, 17, 18, 21 ___ .

**Step 2.** Add up the numbers you wrote next to these items: 3, 6, 19, 20 ___ .

**Step 3.** Subtract the answer for Step 2 from 32:
32 − ___ = ___ .

**Step 4.** Add the number in Step 1 to the number in Step 3:
___ (Step 1) + ___ (Step 3) = ___ .

**Step 5.** Divide the answer in Step 4 by 21: ___ : 21 = ___ .

**This is your burnout score.**

*How to evaluate your burnout score:*
   A score of 4 indicates a state of burnout. A score of 3 may be seen as a danger sign. A score of 5 defines a crisis. A score above 5 defines a need for immediate help. A score of 2 or below 2 means that your relationship is in very good shape.
   Your burnout score indicates whether you are burned out in your marriage or intimate relationship. The same test (with slight modifications) can be used to evaluate whether you are burned

out in your job, volunteer work, your role as a parent, or life in general.

In order to evaluate your level of burnout at work, for example, you will need to go back to the test and respond to it (preferably using different-colored ink) as it relates to your work and the people involved in your work (boss, employees, service recipients, etc.). After calculating your burnout score, you can compare your level of marriage burnout to the level of burnout in your work, or in any other area of your life.

Of course, the value of all these burnout scores depends totally on your honesty in responding to the test. If you were dishonest (either in trying to make things appear better or worse than they really are) your test scores will be of very little diagnostic value.

# Research Appendix

## THE BURNOUT MEASURE

Burnout is a state of physical, emotional, and mental exhaustion, which occurs as a result of long-term involvement in situations that are emotionally demanding. The emotional demands of the situations are typically caused by too great a discrepancy between expectations and reality. The primary expectation people have is to find something that will give meaning to their lives. When they look to find it in their marriage and fail, the result is marriage burnout.

In order to evaluate their levels of marriage burnout, people are asked to respond to a twenty-one-item questionnaire representing its three components: physical exhaustion (e.g., feeling tired, run-down, and having sleep problems; weak and susceptible to illness), emotional exhaustion (e.g., feeling depressed, trapped, hopeless), and mental exhaustion (e.g., feeling worthless, disillusioned, and resentful about mate). All items are responded to on seven-point frequency scales. Respondents are asked to indicate how often they have these experiences specifically with regard to their marriage or intimate relationship (with 1 = never, 4 = sometimes, and 7 = always). The burnout score is calculated by averaging the responses given to the individual items.

Test-retest reliability of the measure was found to be .89 for a one-month interval; .76 for a two-month interval; and .66 for a four-month interval. Internal consistency was assessed by the alpha coefficients for most samples studied; the values of the alpha coefficients ranged between .91 and .93. All correlations between the individual items and the composite score were statistically significant at the .001 level of significance in all the studies in which it was used. In a study involving one hundred men and women (the San Francisco study), for example, all the correlations between the individual items and the composite burnout score were statistically significant at .0001 level of significance; ranging from $r = .53$ (being physically exhausted) to $r = .86$ (feeling weary).

The measure's high face validity can be seen in the close correspondance between the items and the theoretical definition of burnout, as well as in respondents' positive reaction to it as defining their own level of marriage burnout.

A factor analysis done on the responses of two hundred men and women (the Haifa study) gave evidence supporting the notion that the questionnaire is primarily assessing a single meaningful construct. (The analysis was done using the Initial Factor Method with a Principal Axis). As can be seen in Table I, Factor 1 (the emotional exhaustion factor) accounted for most of the variance in the composite relationship burnout score. Factor 2

**TABLE I**
Factor Loadings in the Marriage Burnout Measure

| Item | Factor 1 | Factor 2 | Factor 3 |
|---|---|---|---|
| Emotionally exhausted | .82 | .00 | .13 |
| Unhappy | .80 | .13 | .19 |
| Can't take it | .75 | .07 | .22 |
| Depressed | .75 | .12 | .01 |
| Disappointed | .72 | .18 | .31 |
| Trapped | .71 | .05 | .20 |
| Happy | .71 | .51 | .01 |
| Troubled | .68 | .10 | .15 |
| Rejecting mate | .67 | .21 | .22 |
| Hopeless | .64 | .11 | .07 |
| Good day | .64 | .35 | .20 |
| Inferior | .62 | .06 | .10 |
| Tired | .60 | .04 | .34 |
| Nothing left to give | .56 | .05 | .38 |
| Optimistic | .52 | .30 | .02 |
| Physically exhausted | .52 | .39 | .49 |
| Sleep problems | .49 | .44 | .11 |
| Whole body hurts | .48 | .58 | .30 |
| Anxious | .45 | .38 | .13 |
| Energetic | .41 | .51 | .55 |
| Susceptible to illness | .27 | .60 | .03 |
| Variance explained: | 8.2 | 2.1 | 1.3 |

(the physical exhaustion factor) explained far less of the variance.

Construct validity of the measure was examined by correlational analyses with several other theoretically relevant variables. For example, in a study involving 58 men and women it was found that the correlation between burnout and desire to leave one's mate was: $r = .56$, $p < .0001$. In a study involving one hundred couples burnout was found to be significantly and negatively correlated to life satisfaction ($r = -.52$); satisfaction from the marriage ($r = -.53$); satisfaction from spouse ($r = -.49$); and satisfaction from self ($r = -.45$) (all r values smaller than .0001). Burnout was also found to be negatively correlated to one's emotional state ($r = -.41$, $p < .0001$); and to one's physical condition ($r = -.35$; $p < .0001$). Self-diagnosis of burnout was correlated ($r = .42$, $p < .0001$) with one's burnout level as seen by one's spouse. The significant correlation, in addition to demonstrating that one can recognize burnout in one's mate, also served as an instrument validation. It is interesting that marriage burnout was more highly correlated to one's emotional state than to one's physical state. This finding fits the burnout profile seen in the factor analysis in which emotional exhaustion symptoms contributed much more to the composite burnout score than did the physical exhaustion symptoms. This was definitely not the case with job burnout. For example, in one study in which the burnout profiles of teachers, nurses, and police officers were compared, the highest contributor to their burnout score was feeling tired. (See Pines 1982 for details.)

Table II presents the rank order of Pearson correlations between burnout and eighteen relationship features obtained in the San Francisco study ($N = 100$).

The eighteen relationship features were entered one by one into a stepwise multiple regression in order to isolate a subset of the predictor relationship features that would yield an optimal prediction equation of burnout with as few independent variables as possible. As can be seen in Table III, one relationship variable alone (namely, positive outlook) accounted for 50 percent of the variance in the dependent variable—relationship burnout ($R^2 = .50$; $F(1,92) = 90$; $p < .000$). The three top-ranking variables (i.e., positive outlook, communication, and partner's desirability) accounted for 60 percent of the variance in relationship burnout ($R^2 = .60$; $F(3,90) = 43.5$; $p < .000$). The highest level of explained variance (68 percent) was accomplished by including fourteen varia-

## TABLE II
Pearson Correlation Coefficients for Burnout and
18 Relationship Features

|  | r | p |
|---|---|---|
| Positive outlook | −.72 | .000 |
| Communication | −.64 | .000 |
| Security | −.59 | .000 |
| Self-actualization | −.57 | .000 |
| Significance | −.55 | .000 |
| Emotional attraction | −.54 | .000 |
| Sex life | −.54 | .000 |
| Growth | −.50 | .000 |
| Compatability | −.50 | .000 |
| Variety | −.49 | .000 |
| Partner's desirability | −.46 | .000 |
| Physical attraction | −.41 | .000 |
| Things in common | −.40 | .000 |
| Similar goals | −.40 | .000 |
| Own desirability | −.36 | .000 |
| Intellectual attraction | −.33 | .000 |
| Control | −.23 | .011 |
| Sharing chores | −.14 | .084 |

## TABLE III
Stepwise Regression Analysis of Burnout with Relationship
Descriptors

| Relationship Descriptions | Steps Entered | Multiple R | $R^2$ (all p < .001) | F |
|---|---|---|---|---|
| Positive outlook | 1 | .70 | .50 | 90.4 |
| Communication | 2 | .75 | .56 | 57.7 |
| Partner's desirability | 3 | .77 | .60 | 43.5 |
| Security | 4 | .79 | .62 | 36.4 |
| Sharing of chores | 5 | .79 | .63 | 29.9 |
| Emotional attraction | 6 | .80 | .64 | 25.4 |
| Things in common | 7 | .80 | .65 | 22.4 |
| Variety | 8 | .81 | .65 | 19.9 |
| Significance | 9 | .81 | .66 | 18.0 |
| Control | 10 | .81 | .66 | 16.2 |
| Own desirability | 11 | .82 | .67 | 14.8 |
| Sex life | 12 | .82 | .67 | 13.7 |
| Intellectual attraction | 13 | .82 | .67 | 12.7 |
| Compatability | 14 | .82 | .68 | 11.7 |
| Similarity in goals | 15 | .82 | .68 | 10.8 |
| Physical attraction | 16 | .82 | .68 | 10.0 |
| Self-actualization | 17 | .82 | .68 | 9.3 |

bles in the regression analysis, which is to say 68 percent of the variation in burnout can be explained by linear dependence on fourteen independent relationship variables, while 60 percent of it can be explained by dependence on only three relationship variables operating jointly.

Table IV describes the rank order of the correlations men and women had between various relationship features and burnout. The correlations were obtained in the Haifa study, in which two hundred men and women took part. Due to space limitations only the statistically significant correlations are presented. The most interesting finding in the table is the sex difference in the rank ordering of the relationship features as burnout correlates.

Tables V and VI present the rank ordering of positive and negative features as burnout correlates, for women only.

### TABLE IV
Pearson Correlation Coefficients for Burnout and Marriage Descriptors for Men and Women

|  | Men | | Women | | Rank order (for women) |
|---|---|---|---|---|---|
|  | r | p | r | p |  |
| Positive outlook | −.60 | .0001 | −.56 | .0001 | 1 |
| Communication | −.58 | .0001 | −.46 | .0001 | 4 |
| Appreciation | −.50 | .0001 | −.42 | .0001 | 8 |
| Sex life | −.49 | .0001 | −.41 | .0001 | 9 |
| Overload | .51 | .0001 | .48 | .0001 | 3 |
| Boredom | .48 | .0001 | .23 | .02 | 16 |
| Conflicting demands | .46 | .0001 | .56 | .0001 | 1 |
| Success | −.45 | .0001 | .38 | .0002 | 11 |
| Physical attraction | −.44 | .0001 | −.40 | .0001 | 10 |
| Variety | −.44 | .0001 | −.45 | .0001 | 5 |
| Security | −.43 | .0001 | −.42 | .0001 | 8 |
| Compatible personality | −.39 | .0001 | −.35 | .0001 | 12 |
| Support | −.37 | .0001 | −.33 | .002 | 13 |
| Guilt and anxiety | .37 | .0002 | .44 | .0001 | 6 |
| Commitments pressure | .37 | .0002 | .50 | .0001 | 2 |
| Things in common | −.36 | .0003 | −.25 | .01 | 15 |
| Self-actualization | −.35 | .0005 | −.42 | .0001 | 8 |
| Emotional attraction | −.34 | .0008 | −.33 | .0007 | 13 |
| Intellectual attraction | −.34 | .0008 | −.32 | .001 | 14 |
| Demand to prove self | .31 | .002 | .22 | .03 | 17 |
| Feedback | −.29 | .004 | −.43 | .0001 | 7 |
| Similar goals | −.25 | .01 | −.43 | .0001 | 7 |

## TABLE V
### Women's Correlations between Burnout and Positive Marriage Features
#### (N=100 Women)

|  | r | p |
|---|---|---|
| Positive outlook | −.56 | .0001 |
| Communication | −.46 | .0001 |
| Variety | −.45 | .0001 |
| Feedback | −.43 | .0001 |
| Similar goals | −.43 | .0001 |
| Appreciation | −.42 | .0001 |
| Security | −.42 | .0001 |
| Self-actualization | −.42 | .0001 |
| Good sex life | −.41 | .0001 |
| Physical attraction | −.40 | .0001 |
| Success | −.38 | .0001 |
| Compatible personality | −.35 | .0001 |
| Emotional attraction | −.33 | .0007 |
| Input into decisions | −.33 | .0008 |
| Support | −.33 | .002 |
| Intellectual attraction | −.32 | .001 |
| Independence | −.27 | .007 |
| Things in common | −.25 | .01 |
| Significance | −.25 | .01 |
| Self-expression | −.21 | .04 |

## TABLE VI
### Women's Correlations between Burnout and Negative Marriage Features
#### (N=100 women)

|  | r | p |
|---|---|---|
| Conflicting demands | .56 | .0001 |
| Commitments pressure | .50 | .0001 |
| Overload | .48 | .0001 |
| Guilt and anxiety | .44 | .0001 |
| Exploitation | .32 | .002 |
| Work-home conflict | .29 | .005 |
| Stressful environment | .24 | .02 |
| Boredom | .23 | .02 |
| Demand to prove self | .22 | .03 |
| Housework | .03 | NS |

**TABLE VII**

Correlations between Burnout and Various Social Relationships

|  | Spouse | Family | Friends | Co-workers | Supervisors | Subordinates |
|---|---|---|---|---|---|---|
| 205 Americans | −.32* | −.25* | −.28* | −.26* | −.23* | −.24* |
| 118 Canadians | −.25* | NS | −.22* | −.12* | −.23* | −.17* |
| 81 Israelis | −.32* | −.37 | −.18* | −.39* | −.25* | NS |

*P < .05.

Table VII presents the correlations between burnout and various social relationships at home and at work in an American, an Israeli, and a Canadian sample.

Table VIII presents the mean values and correlations with burnout of the conflict between home and work in seven different samples.

Table IX presents the mean values and correlations with burnout for a variety of home and work features in two samples, one involving 205 professionals, the other 724 human service professionals.

Table X presents mean values and correlations with burnout of home and work features for 205 professional men and women.

Table XI, the last table, presents mean values of frequency and success in the use of various coping strategies for 220 professional men and women.

**TABLE VIII**

Means and Correlations with Burnout of Home-work Conflict

|  | Mean | Correlation |
|---|---|---|
| 205 professional men and women | 4.2 | .36* |
| 277 professional women | 3.6 | .22* |
| 724 human service professionals | 3.6 | .33* |
| 294 undergraduate students | 4.1 | .26* |
| 118 Canadian human service workers | 4.1 | .38* |
| 55 Israeli male managers | 3.7 | .28* |
| 21 Israeli men and women managers | 4.0 | .24* |

*p < .05.

## TABLE IX
### Means and Correlations with Burnout of Home and Work Features

| | 205 Professional Men & Women | | | | 724 Human Service Men & Women | | | |
| | Home | | Work | | Home | | Work | |
| | Mean | r | Mean | r | Mean | r | Mean | r |
|---|---|---|---|---|---|---|---|---|
| Variety | 5.2 | −.23* | 5.0 | −.21* | 5.2 | −.22* | 4.8 | −.20* |
| Complexity | 4.9 | −.11 | 5.1 | −.20* | 4.9 | −.09* | 5.2 | −.03 |
| Autonomy | 5.7 | −.15* | 5.0 | −.28* | 5.8 | −.19* | 4.7 | −.19* |
| Overextension | 4.1 | .22* | 4.2 | .23* | 3.8 | .23* | 4.4 | −.31* |
| Overload | 3.8 | .13 | 4.0 | .13 | 3.9 | .27* | 4.5 | .35* |
| Underload | 3.2 | .29* | 3.3 | .15* | 3.3 | .22* | 3.5 | .20* |
| Decision load | 3.4 | .21* | 3.9 | .19* | 3.2 | .18* | 4.1 | .30* |
| Innovation load | 4.7 | −.15* | 4.7 | −.17* | 4.9 | −.12* | 5.0 | −.08* |
| Significance | 5.2 | −.22* | 5.3 | −.21* | 5.7 | −.18* | 5.9 | −.15* |
| Feedback | 4.9 | −.23* | 4.7 | −.15* | 5.0 | −.21* | 4.4 | −.15* |
| Success | 5.2 | −.48* | 5.2 | −.24* | 5.4 | −.28* | 5.2 | −.17* |
| Negative consequences | 4.3 | −.07 | 5.0 | −.19* | 4.6 | .00 | 5.3 | .04 |
| Self-expression | 5.6 | −.31* | 4.9 | −.22* | 5.7 | −.15* | 4.9 | −.20* |
| Self-actualization | 5.5 | −.28* | 4.7 | −.22* | 5.4 | −.24* | 4.7 | −.20* |
| Self-worth demand | 3.6 | .11 | 4.2 | .00 | 3.8 | .08* | 4.6 | .17* |
| Guilt | 3.2 | .51* | 3.1 | .29* | 3.3 | .41* | 3.6 | .42* |
| Physical danger | 2.0 | −.03 | 1.9 | −.06 | 2.2 | .10* | 2.9 | .12* |
| Environmental pressures | 2.5 | .26* | 2.8 | .27* | 2.4 | .19* | 3.3 | .21* |
| Comfortable environment | 5.6 | −.35* | 4.6 | −.29* | 5.5 | −.20* | 4.4 | −.24* |
| Bureaucratic pressures | 3.0 | .20* | 4.2 | .11 | 2.7 | .10* | 4.6 | .24* |
| Administrative hassles | 2.8 | .20* | 4.5 | .06 | 2.5 | .10* | 5.1 | .26* |
| Policy influence | 5.2 | −.24* | 4.0 | −.15* | 5.5 | −.16* | 4.1 | −.18* |
| Rewards | 5.0 | −.41* | 4.4 | −.33* | 4.9 | −.17* | 4.0 | −.17* |
| Opportunity to take off | 4.4 | −.18* | 4.2 | −.11 | 4.5 | −.16* | 4.3 | −.09* |
| Social overextension | 4.4 | .28* | 4.2 | .16* | 3.7 | −.33* | 3.9 | .38* |
| Support | 5.0 | −.29* | 4.5 | −.27* | 5.1 | −.12* | 4.6 | −.17* |
| Personal relations | 5.7 | −.32* | 5.5 | −.27* | 5.9 | −.26* | 5.6 | −.25* |
| Sharing | 4.7 | .28* | 4.4 | .13 | 5.1 | −.20* | 4.9 | .23* |
| Conflicting demands | 3.8 | .38* | 3.9 | .27* | 3.5 | −.30* | 4.0 | .31* |

## TABLE IX (continued)

| | Home | | Work | | Home | | Work | |
|---|---|---|---|---|---|---|---|---|
| | Mean | r | Mean | r | Mean | r | Mean | r |
| Appreciation | 5.0 | −.31* | 4.6 | −.32* | 5.1 | −.13* | 4.3 | −.16* |
| Responsibility | 4.4 | −.12 | 4.1 | −.06 | 4.3 | −.01 | 4.3 | −.07* |
| Emotional reciprocity | 5.2 | −.29* | 4.5 | −.18* | 5.2 | −.22* | 4.2 | −.18* |

*$p < .05$.

## TABLE X
**Means and Correlations with Burnout of Home and Work Features**

### for 205 Professional Men and Women

| | Men | | Women | | Men/Women |
|---|---|---|---|---|---|
| | Mean | r | Mean | r | Mean Comparison t |
| Variety | Life 5.4 | −.17 | 5.0 | −.22* | 1.98* |
| | Work 5.3 | −.19 | 4.8 | −.20* | 2.10* |
| Complexity | Life 5.1 | −.04 | 4.9 | −.11 | .035 |
| | Work 5.4 | −.02 | 4.9 | −.30* | 2.52* |
| Autonomy | Life 5.8 | −.02 | 5.7 | −.18 | .040 |
| | Work 5.4 | −.20* | 4.7 | −.30* | 2.99* |
| Underload | Life 3.1 | .19 | 3.2 | .32* | −0.63 |
| | Work 3.1 | .03 | 3.5 | .21* | −1.75 |
| Overload | Life 3.9 | .17 | 3.9 | .12 | 0.25 |
| | Work 4.3 | .21* | 3.9 | .10 | 1.57 |
| Decision load | Life 3.5 | .14 | 3.3 | .30* | 1.44 |
| | Work 4.1 | .22* | 3.8 | .17 | 1.20 |
| Overextension | Life 4.1 | .20* | 4.2 | .27* | −.0.41 |
| | Work 4.4 | .20* | 4.1 | .25* | 1.56 |
| Self-worth demand | Life 3.7 | −.05 | 3.7 | .19 | 0.06 |
| | Work 4.5 | −.07 | 3.9 | −.03 | 2.44* |
| Innovation load | Life 4.7 | −.14 | 4.7 | −.12 | 0.04 |
| | Work 5.2 | −.02 | 4.4 | −.25* | 2.97* |
| Significance | Life 5.1 | −.22* | 5.3 | −.21* | −.1.20 |
| | Work 5.3 | −.24* | 5.3 | −.22* | 0.15 |
| Success | Life 5.3 | −.41* | 5.2 | −.48* | 0.48 |
| | Work 5.3 | −.22* | 5.1 | −.23* | 0.76 |

TABLE X (continued)

| | Men | | Women | | Men/Women |
|---|---|---|---|---|---|
| | Mean | r | Mean | r | Mean Comparison t |
| Feedback | Life 4.7 | −.29* | 5.0 | −.17 | −1.34 |
| | Work 4.8 | −.17 | 4.6 | −.11 | 0.75 |
| Self-expression | Life 5.5 | −.09 | 5.6 | −.42* | −0.51 |
| | Work 5.2 | −.09 | 4.6 | −.28* | 2.62* |
| Self-actualization | Life 5.5 | −.18 | 5.5 | −.29* | 0.27 |
| | Work 5.1 | −.15 | 4.5 | −.24* | 2.49* |
| Guilt | Life 3.0 | .43* | 3.5 | .57* | −2.28* |
| | Work 3.0 | .30* | 3.2 | .25* | −0.64 |
| Environment | Life 2.3 | .15 | 2.6 | .33* | −1.60 |
| pressures | Work 2.6 | .11 | 3.0 | .37* | −.2.04* |
| Bureaucratic | Life 3.0 | .22* | 3.1 | .18 | −0.27 |
| pressures | Work 4.2 | .08 | 4.3 | .13 | −0.23 |
| Administrative | Life 2.9 | .20* | 2.8 | .18 | 0.44 |
| hassles | Work 4.7 | .06 | 4.5 | .03 | 0.50 |
| Comfortable | Life 5.7 | −.42* | 5.5 | −.30* | −1.28 |
| environment | Work 4.9 | −.25* | 4.2 | −.31* | 2.97* |
| Responsibility | Life 4.3 | .05 | 4.3 | .16 | −0.34 |
| | Work 4.1 | −.19 | 4.2 | .00 | −0.44 |
| Policy influence | Life 5.2 | −.22* | 5.3 | −.28* | −0.61 |
| | Work 4.5 | −.13 | 3.7 | −.12 | 3.16* |
| Rewards | Life 5.1 | −.34* | 5.0 | −.44* | 0.18 |
| | Work 4.7 | −.24* | 4.2 | −.36* | 1.96* |
| Opportunity to | Life 4.5 | −.14 | 4.3 | −.21* | 0.78 |
| take off | Work 4.5 | −.09 | 3.8 | −.05 | 3.08* |
| Support | Life 4.8 | −.31* | 5.2 | −.31* | −2.13* |
| | Work 4.4 | −.28* | 4.6 | −.27* | −0.93 |
| Appreciation | Life 5.0 | −.34* | 5.1 | −.27* | −0.47 |
| | Work 4.8 | −.25* | 4.4 | −.33* | 1.56 |
| Emotional | Life 5.1 | −.31* | 5.4 | −.30* | −1.74 |
| reciprocity | Work 4.4 | −.20* | 4.5 | −.13 | −0.43 |
| Sharing | Life 4.6 | −.27* | 4.9 | −.30* | −1.05 |
| | Work 4.1 | −.20* | 4.6 | −.11 | −2.19* |

**TABLE X** (continued)

| | | Men | | Women | | Men/Women |
|---|---|---|---|---|---|---|
| | | Mean | r | Mean | r | Mean Comparison t |
| Personal | Life | 5.6 | −.21* | 5.9 | −.42* | −1.96* |
| relations | Work | 5.4 | −.24* | 5.6 | −.30* | −1.10 |
| Social | Life | 4.0 | .16 | 4.7 | .34* | −2.76* |
| overextension | Work | 3.9 | .04 | 4.6 | .21* | −2.16* |
| Conflicting | Life | 3.7 | .30* | 3.9 | .44* | −1.38 |
| demands | Work | 4.0 | .29* | 3.8 | .25* | 1.05 |

*$p < .05$.

**TABLE XI**

**Means of Frequency and Success of Coping Strategies**

*(N=220 professional men and women)*

| | Frequency | | Success | |
|---|---|---|---|---|
| | Men | Women | Men | Women |
| *Direct-Active* | | | | |
| Changing the source | 3.5 | 3.4 | 3.5 | 3.3 |
| Confronting the source | 4.3 | 4.1 | 4.5 | 4.4 |
| Finding positive aspects in the situation | 4.5 | 4.5 | 4.4 | 4.1 |
| *Direct-Inactive* | | | | |
| Ignoring the source | 3.7 | 3.1 | 3.2 | 2.6 |
| Avoiding the source | 3.4 | 3.6 | 3.2 | 3.1 |
| Leaving the source | 3.5 | 3.3 | 4.2 | 3.7 |
| *Indirect-Active* | | | | |
| Talking about the source | 4.7 | 5.3 | 4.8 | 5.3 |
| Changing self | 3.8 | 3.6 | 3.9 | 3.5 |
| Getting involved in other activities | 4.4 | 4.6 | 4.6 | 4.9 |
| *Indirect-Inactive* | | | | |
| Drinking or using drugs | 2.5 | 2.6 | 3.0 | 3.0 |
| Getting ill | 1.8 | 2.8 | 2.5 | 2.4 |
| Collapsing | 1.5 | 2.3 | 2.3 | 2.5 |

# References

Alberoni, F. *Falling in Love.* New York: Random House, 1983.

Aronson, E. "Attraction: Why Do People Like Each Other?" In *The Social Animal,* ch. 7. San Francisco: Freeman, 1973.

Barbach, L. *For Yourself: The Fulfillment of Female Sexuality.* New York: Doubleday, 1976.

Baron, R. A., and D. Byrne. *Social Psychology: Understanding Human Interaction.* Boston: Allyn and Bacon, 1984, pp. 88–97.

Basow, S. A. *Sex-Role Stereotypes: Traditions and Alternatives.* Monterey, Calif.: Brooks/Cole, 1980.

Becker, E. *The Denial of Death.* New York: Free Press, 1973.

Bellah, R. N., et al. *Habits of the Heart: Individualism and Commitment in American Life.* Berkeley: University of California Press, 1985.

Bengis, I. *Combat in the Erogenous Zone.* New York: Knopf, 1972.

Bernard, J. *The Future of Marriage.* New York: Bantam Books, 1983.

Berscheid, E., and E. H. Walster. *Interpersonal Attraction.* Menlo Park, Calif.: Addison-Wesley, 1969.

Block, J. D. *Friendship.* New York: Macmillan, 1980.

———. *The Magic of Lasting Love.* New York: Cornerstone Library, 1982.

Blumstein, P., and P. Schwartz. *American Couples.* New York: William Morrow, 1983.

Bossard, J. H. S. "Residential Propinquity as a Factor in Mate Selection." *American Journal of Sociology* 38 (1932): 219–24.

Branden, N. *The Psychology of Romantic Love.* New York: Bantam Books, 1983, pp. 5–6.

Bridges, W. *The Seasons of Our Lives.* San Francisco: The Wayfarer Press, 1977.

Bryson, R., et al. "The Professional Pair: Husband and Wife Psychologists." *American Psychologist* 31 (1976): 10–16.

Burgess, E. W., and P. Wallin. *Engagement and Marriage.* Philadelphia: Lippincott, 1953.

Burney, C. *Solitary Confinement.* New York: Coward-McCann, 1952.

Cantril, A. H., and C. W. Roll, Jr. *Hopes and Fears of the American People.* New York: Universe Books, 1971.

Chodorow, N. *The Reproduction of Mothering: Psychoanalysis and the Sociology of Gender.* Berkeley: University of California Press, 1978.

Cobb, S. "Social Support as a Moderator of Life Stress." *Psychosomatic Medicine* 5, no. 38 (   ): 300–14.

Cooperman Nadelson, C. "Marital Therapy from a Psychoanalytic Perspective." In *Marriage and Marital Therapy: Psychoanalytic, Behavioral and Systems Therapy Perspectives,* edited by T. J. Paolino and B. S. McCrady. New York: Brunner/Mazel, 1978.

de Rougemont, D. *Love in the Western World.* New York: Pantheon Books, 1956.

de Tocqueville, A. *Democracy in America.* New York: Doubleday, 1969. Published originally in two parts in 1835 and 1840.

Dinnerstein, D. *The Mermaid and the Minotaur: Sexual Arrangements and Human Malaise.* New York: Harper and Row, 1976.

Donelson, E. "Social Influences on the Development of Sex-Typed Behavior." In *Women: A Psychological Perspective,* edited by E. Donelson and J. Gullahorn, pp. 140–53. New York: Wiley, 1977.

Dyer, D. Everett. *Courtship, Marriage, and Family American Style.* Homewood, Ill.: The Dorsey Press, 1983.

Duffy, E. *Activation and Behavior.* New York: Wiley, 1962.

Ehrenreich, B. *The Hearts of Men: American Dreams and the Flight from Commitment.* Garden City, N.Y.: Anchor Press, 1983.

Ephron, N. *Heartburn.* New York: Pocket Books, 1983.

Epstein, C. F. "Law Partners and Marital Partners: Strains and Solutions in the Dual Career Family Enterprise." *Human Relations* 24 (1971): 549–63.

Etzion, D. "Burning Out in Management: A Comparison of Women and Men in Matched Organizational Positions." Paper presented at the

Second International Interdisciplinary Congress on Women, Groningen, Holland, April 17–19, 1984.

Etzion, D., A. Pines, and D. Kafry. "Coping Strategies and the Experience of Tedium: A Cross-cultural Comparison between Israelis and Americans." *Journal of Psychology and Judaism,* 1983.

Farrel, W. *Why Men Are the Way They Are.*

Framo, J. "The Integration of Marital Therapy with Sessions with Family of Origin." In *Handbook of Family Therapy,* pp. 131–58. New York: Brunner/Mazel, 1981.

Frankl, V. E. *Man's Search for Meaning: An Introduction to Logotherapy.* New York: Washington Square Press, 1966.

French, M. *The Women's Room.* New York: JOVE/HBJ, 1977, p. 558.

Fromm, E. *The Art of Loving: An Enquiry into the Nature of Love.* New York: Harper and Row, 1956.

Glick, P. "A Demographer Looks at American Families." *Journal of Marriage and the Family* 37 (1975): 15–26.

Goffman, E. "On Cooling the Mark Out: Some Aspects of Adaptation to Failure." *Psychiatry* 15 (1952): 451–63.

Gove, W. R. "The Relationship between Sex Roles, Marital Status, and Mental Illness." *Social Forces* 51, no. 1 (1972): 34–44.

Haley, J. *Problem Solving Therapy: New Strategies for Effective Family Therapy.* San Francisco: Jossey-Bass, 1977.

Henning, M., and A. Jardim. *The Managerial Woman.* New York: Doubleday, 1976.

Johnson, R. *We: Understanding the Psychology of Romantic Love.* New York: Harper and Row, 1983.

Kafry, D., and A. Pines. "The Experience of Tedium in Life and Work." *Human Relations* 33, no. 7 (1980): 477–503.

Kasl, S. V., and S. Cobb. "Blood Pressure Changes in Men Undergoing Job Loss." *Psychosomatic Medicine* 6 (1970): 95–106.

Keleman, S. *Emotional Anatomy.* Berkeley: Center Press, 1985.

Kerkoff, A., and K. Davis. "Value Consensus and Need Complementarity in Mate Selection." *American Sociological Review* 17 (1962): 295–303.

Kessel, N. "Self Poisoning." *British Medical Journal* 2 (1965): 1265–340.

**Kierkegaard, Søren.** *The Concept of Dread.* Translated by Walter Lowrie. Princeton, N.J.: Princeton University Press, 1957. Originally published 1844.

**Kobasa, C., and S. Maddi.** "Personality and Constitution as Mediators in the Stress-Illness Relationship." *Journal of Health and Social Behavior* 22 (1981): 368–78.

**Lasswell, M., and N. Lobsenz.** *Styles of Loving: Why You Love the Way You Do.* New York: Ballantine Books, 1980.

**Lauer, J., and R. Lauer.** "Marriages Made to Last." *Psychology Today* 19, no. 6 (June 1985): 22–26.

**Lazarus, R. S.** *Psychological Stress and the Coping Process.* New York: McGraw-Hill, 1966.

**Lazarus, R. S., and S. Foldman.** *Stress, Appraisal, and Coping.* New York: Springer, 1984.

**Lederer, W., and D. Jackson.** *The Mirages of Marriage.* New York: Norton, 1968.

**Martin, T. W., K. J. Berry, and R. B. Jacobsen.** "The Impact of Dual-career Marriages on Female Professional Careers." Paper presented at the annual meeting of the National Council on Family Relations, Salt Lake City, Utah, August 1975.

**Maslow, A.** *Toward a Psychology of Being.* New York: Van Nostrand, 1962.

**May, R.** *Love and Will.* New York: Dell, 1969.

**Meissner, W. W.** "The Conceptualization of Marriage and Family Dynamics from a Psychoanalytic Perspective." In *Marriage and Marital Therapy: Psychoanalytic, Behavioral and Systems Therapy Perspectives,* edited by T. J. Paolino and B. S. McCrady. New York: Brunner/Mazel, 1978.

**Minuchin, S.** *Families and Family Therapy.* Cambridge: Harvard University Press, 1974.

**Moles, O. C., and G. Levinger, eds.** "Divorce and Separation." *Journal of Social Issues* 32 (1976): 1–4.

**Murstein, B. I.** *Who Will Marry Whom?* New York: Springer, 1976.

**Nadelson, C. C., and T. Nadelson.** "Dual-Career Marriages: Benefits and Costs." In *Dual-career Couples,* edited by F. Pepitone-Rockwell, pp. 91–109. Beverly Hills: Sage, 1980.

**Nicholson, J.** *Men and Women: How Different Are They?* Oxford: Oxford University Press, 1984.

Norton, A. J., and P. C. Glick. "Marital Instability Past and Future." In *Journal of Social Issues* 32 (1976): 1–4.

Nye, F. I., and L. W. Hoffman, eds. *The Employed Mother in America.* Chicago: Rand McNally, 1963.

Oakley, A. *The Sociology of Housework.* New York: Pantheon, 1935.

Oates, W. E. *Confessions of a Workaholic.* Nashville: Abingdon Press, 1971.

O'Leary, D. K., and H. Turkewitz. "Marital Therapy from a Behavioral Perspective." In *Marriage and Marital Therapy: Psychoanalytic, Behavioral and Systems Therapy Perspectives,* edited by T. J. Paolino and B. S. McCrady. New York: Brunner/Mazel, 1978.

Ovid. *The Art of Love.* Translated by R. Humphries. Bloomington: Indiana University Press, 1957.

Paolino, T. J., and B. S. McCrady, eds. *Marriage and Marital Therapy: Psychoanalytic, Behavioral and Systems Therapy Perspectives.* New York: Brunner/Mazel, 1978.

Paul, J., and M. Paul. *Do I Have to Give Up Being Me to Be Loved by You?* Minn.: Compcare, 1983.

Peck, S. M. *The Road Less Traveled.* New York: Simon and Schuster, 1978.

Pepitone-Rockwell, F., ed. *Dual-career Couples.* Beverly Hills: Sage, 1980.

Pines, A., "Changing Organizations: Is a Work Environment without Burnout an Impossible Goal?" In *Job Stress and Burnout,* edited by W. S. Paine. Beverly Hills: Sage, 1982.

———. "Helper's Motivation and the Burnout Syndrome." In *Basic Processes in Helping Relationships,* edited by T. A. Wills, pp. 453–75. New York: Academic Press, 1982.

———. "The Influence of Goals on People's Perceptions of a Competent Woman." *Sex Roles* 5, no. 1 (1979): 71–76.

———. "On Burnout and the Buffering Effects of Social Support." In *Stress and Burnout in the Human Service Professions,* ed. B. Farber. New York: Pergamon, 1982.

———. "Sexual Jealousy as a Cause of Violence." Paper presented at the annual convention of the American Psychological Association, Anaheim, Calif., 1983.

———. "Who Is to Blame for a Helper's Burnout?" In *Self Care for Health-Care Providers,* edited by C. Scott. New York: William Morrow, 1985.

Pines, A., and E. Aronson. "The Antecedents, Correlates, and Consequences of Sexual Jealousy." *Journal of Personality,* March 1983.

———. *Burnout: From Tedium to Personal Growth.* New York: Free Press, 1981.

———. "Polifidelity: An Alternative Lifestyle without Jealousy?" *Alternative Lifestyles* 4, no. 3 (August 1981): 373–92.

———. "Coping with Burnout." In *Burnout in the Helping Professions,* edited by J. Jones. Park Ridge, Ill.: London House, 1981.

Pines, A., and D. Kafry. "Tedium in the Life and Work of Professional Women as Compared with Men." *Sex Roles* 7, no. 10 (1981): 963–77.

Pines, A., D. Kafry, and D. Etzion. "Job Stress from a Cross Cultural Perspective." In *Burnout in the Helping Professions,* edited by K. Reid. Kalamazoo: Western Michigan University Press, 1980.

Prochaska, J., and J. Prochaska. "Twentieth-Century Trends in Marriage and Marital Therapy." In *Marriage and Marital Therapy: Psychoanalytic, Behavioral and Systems Therapy Perspectives,* edited by T. J. Paolino and B. S. McCrady, p. 3. New York: Brunner/Mazel, 1978.

Rank, O. *Will Therapy and Truth and Reality.* New York: Knopf, 1945.

Rapoport, R., and R. Rapoport. "The Dual Career Family." *Human Relations* 22 (1969): 3–30.

Reik, T. *The Need to Be Loved.* New York: Bantam, 1964.

Rogers, C. R. *On Becoming a Person.* Boston: Houghton Mifflin, 1961.

Rubin, L. B. *Intimate Strangers: Men and Women Together.* New York: Harper and Row, 1983.

Scarf, M. "The More Sorrowful Sex." *Psychology Today* 12, no. 11 (1979): 44–52.

Sluzki, C. E. "Marital Therapy from a Systems Theory Perspective." In *Marriage and Marital Therapy: Psychoanalytic, Behavioral and Systems Therapy Perspectives,* edited by T. J. Paolino and B. S. McCrady, p. 3. New York: Brunner/Mazel, 1978.

Snyder, M., E. D. Tanke, and E. Berscheid. "Social Perception and Interpersonal Behavior: On the Self Fulfilling Nature of Social Stereotypes." *Journal of Personality and Social Psychology* 35 (1977): 656–66.

Stuart, R. B. *Helping Couples Change: A Social Learning Approach to Marital Therapy.* New York: The Guilford Press, 1980.

———. "Operant-interpersonal Treatment for Marital Discord." *Journal of Consulting and Clinical Psychology* 33 (1969): 675–82.

Suyin, H. *A Many Splendoured Thing.* New York: Penguin, 1960.

**Taylor Segraves, R.** *Marital Therapy: A Combined Psychodynamic-Behavioral Approach.* New York: Plenum Medical Book Company, 1982.

**Walster, E. H., and E. Berscheid.** "Adrenalin Makes the Heart Grow Fonder." *Psychology Today,* June 1971, pp. 47–62.

**Walster, E. H., and W. G. Walster.** *A New Look at Love.* Reading, Mass.: Addison Wesley, 1978, p. 9.

**Watts, A.** *Nature, Man and Woman.* New York: Pantheon, 1958.

**Welwood, J.** *Challenge of the Heart.* Boston: Shambhala, 1985.

**Whitaker, C., and D. V. Keith.** "Counseling the Dissolving Marriage." In *Klemer's Counseling—Marital and Sexual Problems,* edited by R. F. Stahmann and W. J. Hiebert. Baltimore: William and Wilkins, 1977.

**Winch, R.** *Mate Selection: A Study of Complementary Needs.* New York: Harper, 1958.

**Wolman, B. B.** *Dictionary of Behavioral Science.* New York: Van Nostrand, 1973.

**Yalom, I. D.** *Existential Psychotherapy.* New York: Basic Books, 1980.

**Zilbergeld, B.** *Male Sexuality.* Little Brown, 1978.

# Related References
by the Author

Pines, A., and E. Aronson. *Career Burnout; Causes and Cures,* 2nd ed. New York: Free Press, 1988.

Pines, A. and E. Aronson, *Burnout: From Tedium to Personal Growth.* New York: Free Press, 1981. French and German editions of the book published in 1983.

Pines, A. *Emotional Attrition.* Tel Aviv: Tcherikover, 1984.

Pines, A. "Marriage Burnout from Women's Perspective." In *Everywoman's Emotional Well-being,* edited by C. Tavris. New York: Doubleday Books, 1986.

Pines, A. "Who's to Blame for Helper's Burnout?" In *Heal Thy Self: The Health of Health Professionals,* edited by C. D. Scott. New York: Bruner-Mazel, 1986.

Pines, A. "The Burnout Measure." In *Police Burnout,* edited by J. Jones. Park Ridge, Ill.: London House Press, 1985.

Pines, A. and M. Silbert. "Police Officer's Burnout." In *Police Burnout,* edited by J. Jones. Park Ridge, Ill.: London House Press, 1985.

Maslach, C., and A. Pines. "Burnout: The Loss of Human Caring." In *Experiencing Social Psychology,* edited by A. Pines and C. Maslach. New York: Random House, 1979, 1984.

Pines, A. "On Burnout and the Buffering Effects of Social Support." In *Stress and Burnout in the Human Service Professions,* edited by B. Farber. New York: Pergammon, 1983.

Pines, A., and D. Kafry. "Occupational Tedium in the Social Services." In *Introduction to Applied Psychology,* edited by M. A. Williamson. Richmond, B.C.: Open Learning Institute. 1983.

Pines, A. "Changing Organizations: Is a Work Environment without Burnout an Impossible Goal?" In *Job Stress and Burnout,* edited by W. S. Paine. Beverly Hills, Calif.: Sage, 1982.

Pines, A., and A. Kanner, "Nurses' Burnout: Lack of Positive Conditions and Presence of Negative Conditions as Two Independent Sources of Stress." In *Burnout in the Nursing Profession,* edited by E. A. McConnell. St. Louis: C. V. Mosby, 1982.

Pines, A. and C. Maslach. "Characteristics of Staff Burnout in Mental Health Settings." In *Crossroads: A Reader for Psychosocial Therapy,* edited by A. Briggs and A. Agrin. Rockville, Md.: The American Occupational Therapy Association, 1982.

Pines, A. "Helper's Motivation and the Burnout Syndrome." In *Basic Processes in Helping Relationships,* edited by T. A. Wills. New York: Academic Press, 1981.

Pines, A., and D. Kafry. "Coping with Burnout." In *The Burnout Syndrome,* edited by J. Jones. Park Ridge, Ill.: London House Press, 1981, pp. 139–150.

Pines, A., D. Kafry, and D. Etzion. "Job Stress from a Cross Cultural Perspective." In *Burnout and the Helping Professions,* edited by K. Reid. Kalamazoo, Mich.: Michigan University, 1980.

Pines, A. "Sex Differences in Marriage Burnout." *Israel Social Science Research: A Multidisciplinary Journal,* 1988. In press.

Pines, A. "Marriage Burnout: A New Conceptual Framework for Working with Couples." *Psychotherapy in Private Practice* 5, no. 2 (1987): 31–44.

Etzion, D., and A. Pines. "Sex and Culture in Burnout and Coping among Human Service Professionals: A Social Psychological Perspective." *Journal of Cross Cultural Psychology,* 17, no. 2 (1986): 191–209.

Pines, A. "Marriage Burnout: A New Conceptual Framework." *Marriage and Divorce Today,* 11, no. 7 (September 1985).

Etzion, D., A. Pines, and D. Kafry. "Coping Strategies and the Experience of Tedium: A Cross-cultural Comparison between Israelies and Americans." *Journal of Psychology and Judaism* 8, no. 11 (1983): 41–51.

Pines, A., and E. Aronson. "The Antecedents, Correlates and Consequences of Sexual Jealousy." *Journal of Personality* 51, no. 1 (1983): 108–36.

Pines, A., and E. Aronson. "Combatting Burnout." Children and Youth Services Review (1983): 263–75.

Pines, A., and A. Kanner. "Nurses' Burnout: Lack of Positive Conditions and Presence of Negative Conditions as Two Independent Sources of Stress." *Journal of Psychosocial Nursing* 8, no. 20 (1982): 30–35.

Etzion, D., D. Kafry, and A. Pines. "Tedium among Managers: A Cross Cultural American-Israeli Comparison." *Journal of Psychology and Judaism* 1, no. 7 (1982): 30–41.

Pines, A. "Burnout: A Current Problem in Pediatrics." *Current Problems in Pediatrics,* May 1981.

Pines, A., and E. Aronson. "Polyfidelity: An Alternative Lifestyle without Sexual Jealousy?" In special issue, "Jealousy," edited by G. Clanton. *Alternative Lifestyles,* August 1981, pp. 373–392.

Pines, A., and D. Kafry. "Tedium in the Life and Work of Professional Women as Compared with Men." *Sex Roles* 7, no. 10 (1981): 963–77.

Pines, A., and D. Kafry. "The Experience of Life Tedium in Three Generations of Professional Women." *Sex Roles* 7, no. 2 (1981): 117–34.

Kafry, D., and A. Pines. "Life and Work Tedium." *Human Relations* 33, no. 7 (1980): 477–503.

Pines, A., and D. Kafry. "Tedium in College." *College Student Personnel Abstracts,* 1980.

Pines, A., and C. Maslach. "Combatting Staff Burnout in a Child Care Center: A Case Study." *Child Care Quarterly* 9, no. 1 (1980): 5–16.

Pines, A. "Tedium in the Work of Infection Control Practitioners." *Asepsis* 1, no. 5 (1980).

Pines, A. "The Influence of Goals on People's Perceptions of a Competent Woman." *Sex Roles* 5, no. 1 (1979): 71–76.

Pines, A., D. Kafry, and D. Etzion. "Burnout: An Occupational Danger." *Shurot* (Hebrew), April 1979, pp. 12–15.

Pines, A., and T. Solomon. "The Social Psychological Double Bind of the Competent Woman." *Research in Education,* February 1979.

Kanner, A., D. Kafry, and A. Pines. "Conspicuous in Its Absence: The Lack of Positive Conditions as a Source of Stress." *Journal of Human Stress* 4, no. 4 (1978): 33–39.

Pines, A., and D. Kafry. "Occupational Tedium in Social Service Professionals." *Social Work* 23, no. 6 (November 1978): 499–507.

Pines, A., and C. Maslach. "Characteristics of Staff Burnout in Mental Health Settings." *Hospital and Community Psychiatry* 29, no. 4 (1978): 233–37.

Maslach, C., and A. Pines. "The 'Burnout' Syndrome in Day Care Settings." *Child Care Quarterly* 6, no. 2 (1977): 100–13.

Pines, A., and C. Maslach. "Burnout in Mental Health Professionals." Child Abuse and Neglect: *Issues on Innovation and Implementation* 2 (1977): 239–45.

Pines, A., and T. Solomon. "Perception of Self as Mediator of the Dehumanization Process." *Personality and Social Psychology Bulletin* 3, no. 2 (1977): 219–23.

Stapp, J., and A. Pines. "Who Likes Competent Women?" Human Behavior 5, no. 11 (1976): 59–60. Job Burnout and Marriage Burnout: Two Responses to Failure in the Existential Quest for Meaning." American Psychological Association, New York, August 1987.

Pines, A. "Marital Burnout: Love Gone Wrong." American Psychological Association, New York, August 1987.

Pines, A. "Marriage Burnout: A Theoretical Model and Some Research Findings." The International Congress of Applied Psychology, Jerusalem, Israel, July 1986.

Pines, A. "A New Integrated Approach for Work with Couples." International Congress of Family Therapy, Jerusalem, Israel, June 1986.

Pines, A. "Marriage Burnout from Women's Perspective." The Association for Women in Psychology, Oakland, Calif., March 1986.

Pines, A. "Sex Differences in Marriage Burnout." American Psychological Association, Los Angeles, Calif., August 1985.

Pines, A. "Marriage Burnout: A New Conceptual Framework for Working with Couples." American Psychological Association, Los Angeles, Calif., August 1985.

Pines, A. On Men, Women, and Marriage Burnout." Association for Humanistic Psychology Twenty-fifth Anniversary Conference, San Francisco, Calif., March 1985.

Pines, A. "Burnout in Marriage and Other Long-Term Relationships." American Psychological Association, Anaheim, Calif., August 1983.

Pines, A. "Burnout in Marriage." Fourth International Congress of Family Therapy, Tel-Aviv, Israel, July 1983.

Pines, A. "The Organizational Implications of Defining Burnout as a Social Problem." American Psychological Association, Washington, D.C., August 1982.

Pines, A., and D. Etzion. "Burnout and Coping with Its Antecedents: A Cross Cultural/Sexual Comparison." International Interdisciplinary Congress on Women, Haifa, Israel, December 1981.

Pines, A. "The Burnout Measure." First National Conference on Burnout, Philadelphia, Pa., November 1981.

Pines, A., and E. Aronson. "Polyfidelity: A Lifestyle without Jealousy?" American Psychological Association, Los Angeles, Calif., August 1981.

Pines, A., and E. Aronson. "Burnout: From Tedium to Personal Growth." American Psychological Association, Montreal, Canada, September 1980.

Aronson, E., and A. Pines. "Sexual Jealousy." Western Psychological Association, Honolulu, Hawaii, May 1980.

Pines, A., and D. Kafry. "Tedium in College." Western Psychological Association, Honolulu, Hawaii, May 1980.

Kanner, A., D. Kafry, and A. Pines. "Stress Results from the Absence of Positive Experience as Well." Western Psychological Association, Honolulu, Hawaii, May 1980.

Pines, A., D. Kafry, and D. Etzion. "A Cross Cultural Comparison between Israelis and Americans in the Experience of Tedium and Ways of Coping with It." Western Psychological Association, San Diego, Calif., April 1979.

Kafry, D., and A. Pines. "Coping Strategies and the Experience of Tedium." American Psychological Association, Toronto, Canada, August 1978.

Pines, A. "Characteristics of Burnout in Human Service Workers." Twenty-first Annual Clinical Conference, Asilomar, Calif., June 1978.

Pines, A., and T. Solomon. "The Double-Bind of Professional Women." Western Psychological Association, San Francisco, Calif., April 1978.

Pines, A. "How to Develop 'Detached Concern' and Prevent Burnout." American Association of Mental Deficiency, San Antonio, Tex., October 1977.

Pines, A. "Burnout and Life Tedium in Three Generations of Professional Women." American Psychological Association, San Francisco, Calif., August 1977.

Pines, A. "Emotional Involvement of Helping Persons—Where Do You Draw the Line?" Annual Convention on Child Abuse and Neglect, Houston, Tex., April 1977.

Pines, A., and T. Solomon. "Perception of Self as Mediator of the Dehumanization Process." American Psychological Association, Washington, D.C., September 1976.

Stapp, J., and A. Pines. "Career or Family? The Influence of Goals on Liking for a Competent Woman." Western Psychological Association, Los Angeles, Calif., April 1976.

*Burnout.* MTI Teleprograms, a division of Simon & Schuster. Accompanying Manual, *Burnout,* by A. Pines and E. Aronson.